POLITICS

THE BASICS

Now in its fifth edition, *Politics: The Basics* explores the systems, movements and issues at the cutting edge of modern politics. A highly successful introduction to the world of politics, it offers clear and concise coverage of a range of issues and addresses fundamental questions such as:

- Why does politics matter?
- Why obey the state?
- What are the key approaches to power?
- How are political decisions made?
- What are the current issues affecting governments worldwide?

Accessible in style and topical in content, the fifth edition has been fully restructured to reflect core issues, systems and movements that are at the centre of modern politics and international relations. Assuming no prior knowledge in politics, it is ideal reading for anyone approaching the study of politics for the first time.

Nigel A. Jackson has worked as a parliamentary agent for a UK political party, for an MP and as a parliamentary lobbyist. Teaching at the University of Plymouth, his research interests are in political communication and political marketing, especially online.

Stephen D. Tansey has taught Politics at the universities of Ife, Nigeria, Bournemouth, Exeter, and the Open University, UK, as well as for the WEA. He is the author of *Business, Information Technology and Society* (2002). He currently leads a Philosophy Workshop for University of the Third Age, Poole, UK.

THE BASICS

LAW
GARY SLAPPER AND DAVID KELLY

LITERARY THEORY (THIRD EDITION)
HANS BERTENS

LOGIC
J.C. BEALL

MANAGEMENT
MORGEN WITZEL

MARKETING (SECOND EDITION)
KARL MOORE AND NIKETH PAREEK

MEDIA STUDIES
JULIAN MCDOUGALL

METAPHYSICS
MICHAEL REA

THE OLYMPICS
ANDY MIAH AND BEATRIZ GARCIA

PHILOSOPHY (FIFTH EDITION)
NIGEL WARBURTON

PHYSICAL GEOGRAPHY
JOSEPH HOLDEN

POETRY (SECOND EDITION)
JEFFREY WAINWRIGHT

PUBLIC RELATIONS
RON SMITH

THE QUR'AN
MASSIMO CAMPANINI

RACE AND ETHNICITY
PETER KIVISTO AND PAUL R. CROLL

RELIGION (SECOND EDITION)
MALORY NYE

RELIGION AND SCIENCE
PHILIP CLAYTON

RESEARCH METHODS
NICHOLAS WALLIMAN

ROMAN CATHOLICISM
MICHAEL WALSH

SEMIOTICS (SECOND EDITION)
DANIEL CHANDLER

SHAKESPEARE (THIRD EDITION)
SEAN MCEVOY

SOCIAL WORK
MARK DOEL

SOCIOLOGY
KEN PLUMMER

SPECIAL EDUCATIONAL NEEDS
JANICE WEARMOUTH

STANISLAVSKI
ROSE WHYMAN

SUBCULTURES
ROSS HAENFLER

TELEVISION STUDIES
TOBY MILLER

TERRORISM
JAMES LUTZ AND BRENDA LUTZ

THEATRE STUDIES (SECOND EDITION)
ROBERT LEACH

WOMEN'S STUDIES
BONNIE SMITH

WORLD HISTORY
PETER N. STEARNS

POLITICS

THE BASICS

5TH EDITION

Nigel A. Jackson and Stephen D. Tansey

Routledge
Taylor & Francis Group

LONDON AND NEW YORK

Fifth edition published 2015
by Routledge
2 Park Square, Milton Park, Abingdon, Oxon OX14 4RN

and by Routledge
711 Third Avenue, New York, NY 10017

Routledge is an imprint of the Taylor & Francis Group, an informa business

First edition published 1995
Fourth edition published 2008

British Library Cataloguing in Publication Data
A catalogue record for this book is available from the British Library

Library of Congress Cataloging in Publication Data
A catalog record for this title has been requested

ISBN: 978-0-415-84141-2 (hbk)
ISBN: 978-0-415-84142-9 (pbk)
ISBN: 978-1-315-75473-4 (ebk)

Typeset in Bembo
by Taylor & Francis Books

To the next generation – especially Eliot, Toby, Jon, Sam, Mike, Emma, Freya and Jake.

CONTENTS

ILLUSTRATIONS

BOXES

FIGURES

TABLES

PREFACE

WHO THE BOOK IS FOR – AND WHAT IT IS ABOUT

This book is designed as a basic introduction to twenty-first-century politics. We do not claim to be able to predict with certainty the political shape of the new century. However, it is already clear that many of the old perspectives of superpower rivalry and ideological warfare which dominated the Cold War seem to be of reduced relevance. Issues such as ecology, new technology, Islam, terrorism and the role of the what used to be described as the Third World (referred to as 'the South' in this book) are likely to move to centre stage. An introduction to politics that takes a parochial single-country approach no longer seems sensible in an era of increased international interdependence.

The readers we have in mind are without a systematic knowledge of, or rigid attitudes towards, politics. This book is intended to both enable such readers to make up their minds about politics and understand more about the academic discipline of political science. In particular, pre-university students, whether or not they have studied politics at school, have found this book a useful indication of the ground covered by university courses. The book has also been found useful for undergraduates beginning courses in politics. It has also formed the basis of short subsidiary courses in politics at undergraduate, postgraduate and extra-mural level. However, we hope that open-minded and intelligent older and younger readers will also find much of interest in this approach. Nor would we have any objection to the occasional practising politician quarrying something useful from the work!

We have not taken the view that a 'social scientific' approach requires the assumption of an attitude of detachment from the politics of the day. But neither have we tried to sell a short-term political programme. The approach here is to search for long-term principles that can help guide political actions. 'Politics' has been taken to mean the essential human activity of deciding how to live together in communities. This activity has been put in a long-term and wide geographical context. The focus is on the relatively prosperous industrialised countries of the 'West', but this cannot be detached from those of the rest of the world. Previous editions of the book have sold all over the world and been published in Polish, Arabic and Chinese. We hope that this edition too will be of interest to readers worldwide. In considering such an ambitious agenda we have drawn extensively on the work of many academics, whose ideas have in many cases already been borrowed (often in caricatured form) by politicians.

In a book designed to help readers make up their own minds about politics, no attempt has been made to hide the authors' liberal and socially progressive point of view. This has inevitably been reflected in such matters as the choice of topics for discussion. But it is hoped that it gives a fair representation of all other major points of view and an indication of where the reader can find accessible versions of alternative perspectives at first hand.

HOW THE BOOK IS ORGANISED

The book begins with a discussion of the nature of politics and the variety of academic approaches to its understanding. The next two chapters illustrate how and why politics is exercised; the following two chapters then survey competing ideas about the aims of that political activity.

The next four chapters consider in more detail what and how political decisions are reached. Chapter 5 reviews the variety of different states and Chapter 6 views politics beyond domestic confines and considers international politics. Chapter 7 considers the detail of how decisions are made, with Chapter 8 addressing more specifically some particular areas of public policy making, the limitations of public policy-making processes and the role of individuals in politics. The last chapter looks ahead to the key issues and problems which liberal democracies face.

To assist users of the previous editions of the book, it may be helpful to point out the major innovations in the fifth edition:

- We have restructured the chapters so that there are now nine instead of eight. Power, global perspectives and challenges to democracy each have a whole chapter.
- Each chapter now begins with clear learning outcomes and hopefully explains why the chapter is important. We have updated the material in the further reading section at the end of each chapter.
- There is more explicit consideration of whether politics matters, and the idea of anti-politics is assessed in Chapter 1.
- Chapter 1 also introduces the debates within American political science concerning the so-called 'perestroika' movement.
- A new chapter, 2, addresses what power is and how it is exercised and changes over time.
- In Chapter 3 we have sought to compare in more depth the similarities and differences between different political systems.
- Chapter 3 also introduces the concept of deterritorialisation and the idea of politics beyond territory.
- Chapter 4 has updated the literature and examples relating to many of the ideologies. In addition we have addressed the Tea Party movement in the US, which has arisen since our last edition.
- In Chapter 5 we provide more recent research on the trend towards democracy and how the idea of totalitarianism is evolving.
- Throughout, we have sought to offer more international examples reflecting the greater influence of international relations within the study of politics. In addition, we have a chapter, Global, designed to solely address relations beyond states.
- In Chapter 6 we look at specific international organisations in more depth. We have also considered the creation or otherwise of a non-Western study of politics.

- We have introduced a whole new chapter, Mechanisms, to consider how government is operated. As a result we have more on pressure groups, political parties and the media. Moreover, since our last edition technology has played a greater role in politics, so there is more on online politics.
- In Chapter 8 we have added more on the policy-making process, such as the application of policy communities and networks. We have also added a section on non-Western policy making.
- Our new last chapter, Challenges, seeks to look at the problems which liberal democracies currently face.
- In Chapter 9 we consider the implications on democracy of new technologies.

This new edition, in addition to obvious changes following such developments as the first coalition government in the UK for over 70 years and the two-time election of Barack Obama in the US, has been further amended to strengthen its international references both for the benefit of its many international readers (including readers of editions in Polish and Chinese) and to counter the parochialism of many introductory courses and books in Britain.

HOW TO USE THIS BOOK

There are many ways to attempt to introduce students to a discipline, and in this book we have chosen to concentrate on introducing some of the major arguments within politics and the concepts associated with them. Logically we have begun with the methodology and boundaries of the discipline. Complete novices to the subject may find this introductory chapter of limited interest at first and can be forgiven for skipping through the second half of the chapter at first reading.

Students already started on a politics course should find that this broader perspective on their studies stimulates more thought than many more detailed and limited textbooks. It should prove useful especially at the beginning of such courses and by way of revision at the end. It is also intended to help those contemplating such courses to decide whether or not politics is the appropriate subject for them. By encouraging an evaluation of the reader's own political position and analysing many basic political concepts as part of a sustained argument, we hope to encourage a critical and individual approach which is more valuable than a more 'factual' approach both in the examination room and in practice.

A feature of the book which readers should find particularly useful is the definition of key concepts found in boxes at intervals in the text. Students will quickly find that any work they submit which does not clearly define its terms will obtain an unfriendly reception, and, conversely, such definitions contribute greatly to clear analysis and communication.

ACKNOWLEDGEMENTS

Finally, a word of thanks to students on various politics and public sector management and public relations courses at Plymouth and Bournemouth universities – with especial mention of Rory Shand for his thoughts on power – and the WEA and U3A, for their comments and suggestions on this material.

In addition to the help from colleagues and friends acknowledged in earlier editions, this latest edition has also benefited from useful comments and suggestions by a number of readers and the work of our editor at Routledge, Siobhán Poole, and her colleagues has been much appreciated. The amendments to the fifth edition are primarily the work of Nigel Jackson. The blame for infelicities and errors remains, of course, with us.

ACKNOWLEDGEMENTS

POLITICS

THIS CHAPTER ...

discusses what politics is and the ways in which scholars have attempted to understand it. The first serious professional teachers (Greeks such as Plato (427–347 BC) and Aristotle (384–322 BC)) made politics the centre of the curriculum. In the twenty-first century, academics are still seeking to explain politics 'scientifically'. This chapter discusses the meaning, importance and problems of such an enterprise.

Much of our understanding of politics is what we may refer to as formal politics, such as debates, meetings and elections, which are indeed part of politics. However, this chapter, in seeking to provide a clearer understanding of what is politics, addresses both its formal and informal components. The concept, and practical application, of politics also includes a host of constraints and opportunities which shape our everyday lives, even if we are not overtly aware of them. Politics is ubiquitous.

By the end of the chapter students will be able to:

- understand why politics is important at both a systemic and individual level;
- assess the meaning of politics;

- identify how politics can be studied;
- evaluate the different approaches to the study of politics.

DOES POLITICS MATTER?

This book, and the vast majority of political science literature, is based on the assumption that politics does matter, but not everyone automatically agrees. Weldon (1953) notes that while for some politics is a 'hurrah' word, for others it is a 'boo' word. This implies that politics can be interpreted essentially as a dirty expression. More recently, Tansey (2010) has noted that while the orthodox view is that politics is either a desirable or neutral activity, this is not true for all. We can suggest that any hostility towards politics can be referred to as an undercurrent of anti-politics, and Tansey cites the first poem by Carol Ann Duffy as British Poet Laureate, *Politics* (2009), as an example of this. Expressions of anti-politics feeling such as Duffy's can possibly be explained by the context of extensive media coverage given to scandals involving UK politicians.

An alternative view to anti-politics is what can be termed de-politicisation. This is not so much an antagonistic view of politics as an observation of where politics does not, or an author feels should not, exist. For some this is an unintended outcome of aid to the developing world. Thus Ferguson (1990: xv) suggested that the impact of development aid to Lesotho was 'everywhere whisking political realities out of sight', with issues discussed in purely technical rather than political or policy terms. Issues that Ferguson believed should have been based on overt political discourse became an implicitly technological process. A different, and normative, approach to de-politicisation emphasises that politics has no role to play in some human activities. For example, Jayasuriya (2002) talks of a post-Washington Consensus that seeks to take the destabilising effects of politician-based bargaining out of the market. This approach suggests that politics has no role to play in the global economic system. De-politicisation is a critique of the boundaries of politics, but unlike anti-politics is not a critique of politics *per se*.

Bernard Crick in his essay *In Defence of Politics* (2000) set out to justify politics by saying what it is, and suggested that the negotiating processes of politics are the only practical alternative to government by coercion. This implies that while the practice of politics may often be imperfect, it is the main bulwark against anarchy. A more functional reason for why politics matters is its impact on policy choices and societally important acts (Castles and McKinlay, 1979; Schmidt, 1989). The outcome of discourse, and the political process, may explain why some countries prosper and the different access people have to services such as education and health. The shape of government and decisions on policy, resource allocation and individual rights and responsibilities will dramatically differentiate the daily life expectations and opportunities of a person living in Buenos Aires (Argentina) from those of a person in Abuja (Nigeria).

It is not just big policy issues, standards of living or freedom of choice that politics affects. Many of your friends might say, *'I am not interested in politics'*, without realising the impact it has on them every day.

Suppose you are a 17-year-old living in the United Kingdom, working at a McDonald's, and hoping for a university place in the autumn. Waking up you realise that Parliament has legislated to convert what was a local time of 6:30 to 7:30. Turning on the local radio station, whose franchise was granted by a QUANGO (quasi autonomous non-governmental organisation), you may hear the weather forecast from the government-financed Meteorological Office. After hearing a few music tracks (legislation outlines the royalties that must be paid to authors and performers by the radio station), you drag yourself out of bed (legally mattress materials must be non-flammable), down to your breakfast cereal (ingredients listed on packet in due form by another law). If you unwisely reach for a cigarette, the government/ European Union has insisted on a health warning on the packet and levies a tax on it. Once you pass through your front door, the impact of government continues via, for instance, air-quality controls, traffic regulations and spending on local government.

The bigger issues that might affect you are shaped by government policy. How is higher education funded? Does the state provide or do you have to pay your way – and if the latter, can you afford it? Is university attendance for an elite, or is much wider participation encouraged? If you are looking for employment your prospects may depend on how the economy has been managed. Your continued employment with McDonald's could be influenced by government policy towards foreign companies and the extent and effectiveness of health education campaigns.

So far we have only considered you and the government. Suppose on reaching the kitchen your father snaps at you: 'Can't you clear up the pizza cartons you and your friends littered the place with last night?' Arguably this is a political situation too. Within the family, fathers are sometimes thought to have 'authority' – some sort of legitimate power over children. As a 17-year-old, you might react negatively on the grounds that you are no longer a child to be given orders. This situation can be seen as a clash of wills in which only one can prevail. And wider politics might complicate the matter: in some countries your father is your legal guardian until you are 18.

Similarly, when you arrive at McDonald's it may well be you discover that the assistant manager is busy establishing in the eyes of the area manager that she can do a better job than her boss. Here we have a struggle for power in which people within the organisation may take sides (form factions, as political scientists might say) – in short, we have organisational politics.

It soon becomes clear that 'politics' is used in at least two senses. In the narrowest conventional (dictionary) usage – what governments do – politics affects us intimately every day. In the wider sense – people exercising power over others – it is part of social relationships, be they kinship, occupational, religious or cultural. Like it or not, you are, as Aristotle suggests, an inherently political animal.

WHAT IS POLITICS?

The word has its origins in ancient Greece and comes from the Greek word *politikos*, which means pertaining to citizens. Aristotle is responsible for our association with the *polis* or city state. From the outset, therefore, the concept of politics linked people with government. However, as noted by Sartori (1973), the term 'politics' virtually disappeared from common usage for nearly two millennia. Rather, terms such as ethics, power, rights, law and justice – which may be components of politics – were employed, and it was not until the early seventeenth century, as Sartori identifies, that the term politics was used again.

If we try to define 'politics' more formally and precisely, we run into the sort of problems which will be found to recur again and again in this book. One of these is associated with whether we are talking about politics as a human activity or politics as an academic activity – or, in American terminology, politics or political science. The search for truth about how human beings exercise power might be thought to be completely separate from actually seeking to exercise that power. In practice, political ideas are some of the most important weapons in the politician's armoury. Attempts to ignore this are either naïve or a deliberate attempt to present a controversial political ideology as a political fact.

We shall deal with the exercise of power in more depth in the next chapter, but here we will consider critically the meaning and implications of some of the standard academic definitions of politics (Box 1.1).

BOX 1.1   DEFINITIONS OF 'POLITICS'

The science and art of government; the science dealing with the form, organisation and administration of a state or a part of one, and with the regulation of its relations with other states.

(Shorter Oxford English Dictionary)

a way of ruling divided societies by a process of free discussion and without undue violence.

(Bernard Crick, 2000)

who gets what, when, how.

(H. Lasswell, 1936)

man moving man.

(Bertrand de Jouvenal, 1963)

... the authoritative allocation of value.

(David Easton, 1979)

responding to conflict with dialogue.

(Charles Blattberg, 2009)

Money is power. Money is politics.

(Kirshner, 2003)

The definitions in Box 1.1 show considerable differences. Most political scientists' definitions of politics are much broader in scope than the first, dictionary, definition which focuses on the state (although admittedly 'part of a state' could be interpreted widely). In effect, they largely endorse the view suggested above: that politics is about the social exercise of power, rather than just the state. However, this may reflect the natural 'imperialism' of academics on behalf of their own discipline. Sociologists might argue that 'man moving man' would be more appropriate as a definition of their concerns.

Consider also, though, the unit of analysis, in terms of which these definitions are couched. Lasswell and de Jouvenal appear to be thinking primarily in terms of individuals exercising power, Crick focuses upon whole societies, the *Shorter Oxford English Dictionary* talks about governments. Blattberg focuses on the alternative to violence for solving public conflicts. Easton links the concept of formal authority to the exercise of power. Contrary to the de-politicisation approach we noted above, Kirshner makes an overt connection between politics and the management of money. This reflects a split between individualistic and collectivist theories.

There is a growing sense that politics in the established Western democracies is struggling. This unease has been referred to as a democratic deficit, political alienation or civic disillusionment. The possible explanations for such changes are examined by Gerry Stoker (2006), but the argument is that citizens have been increasingly 'turned off' by traditional political behaviour, such as voting in elections. This has manifested itself in a decline in partisanship or a lessening sense of identifying with key political actors and structures. It has been suggested that, increasingly, politically active citizens have ignored the coalitions and compromises offered by the existing political elite and have instead turned to single-issue pressure-group activity. However, this apparent decline in traditional partisan electoral politics in some countries does not automatically indicate a decline in the importance of politics; it may just presage a change in the nature of politics.

Another aspect of the democratic deficit has been identified by Lax and Phillips (2012), who looked at state-level support of 39 policies. They found that only in half of them was policy congruent with the majority will and there was thus a deficit with half the policies. In these examples political professionalisation, ideology and party policy was of more importance than public or interest-group opinion. However, we should not necessarily assume this is a major criticism of democracy: it would be unrealistic to expect all decisions to reflect policy-specific opinion.

We shall address power in Chapter 2, but we note here its impact on the meaning of politics. Maurice Duverger (1972: 19) argued that 'The two-faced god, Janus, is the true image of power'. In other words, both conflict and consensus are essential elements in the creation of a political situation. The imposition of the interests of one person (or group) on others by force, without any element of consent, seems far from what most people understand by 'politics', as Crick (2000) argues. On the other hand, a situation (perhaps unlikely) in which a group in total agreement (as to goals and methods) proceed to achieve more and more of their objectives does not sound like a political process either.

Thus, 'politics' encompasses a broad range of situations, in which people's objectives vary but where they work together to achieve the aims they have in common as well as competing when aims conflict. Both co-operation and competition may involve argument, negotiation and coercion. Politics may often be more an art than a science, and the art of politics may often be to seek out the potential of alliances rather than stress antagonisms between differing groups.

APPROACHES TO THE STUDY OF POLITICS

One of the joys, and frustrations, of the study of politics is the variety of approaches to the subject adopted by academic writers. This is a joy in that you will be introduced to a rich spectrum of writing, ranging from classic philosophers like Plato and Aristotle, through radical sociologists such as C. Wright Mills (1956) and Pareto (1976), to modern social scientists wielding statistical tests of significance to analyse huge volumes of computerised data. For example, Grimmer and Stewart (2013) explain how they use computer-automated analysis of weblogs, press releases and congressional speeches. It is frustrating in that the conclusions of such writers cannot be simply accumulated to form a certain body of knowledge representing the political scientist's view of politics. Students of politics must sift through varied sources and accept what seems to them to be relevant and valid.

The remainder of this chapter attempts to provide tools to help the student do this 'sifting' and explain why writers on politics differ so radically. We shall be outlining the boundaries of political study and also highlighting some of the schisms within the discipline. We shall look at three main approaches to the study of politics and, within these, various schools of thought. This can only be a sort of preliminary crude map of the terrain to be covered, not a rigorous analysis of what kinds of writing on politics is possible or series of watertight divisions. However, two writers within a 'school' generally have more in common, and are more likely to agree on what has already been established and perhaps refer to each other, than two writers in different schools.

The three main contemporary academic approaches to the study of politics can be described as 'traditional scholarship', 'social science' and 'radical criticism'. With an element of exaggeration they might also be thought of as the British, American and French approaches.

'Traditional scholars' often approach matters on a rather piecemeal basis, looking at one specific country, political institution, theoretical concept or writer in depth, often with the tools and preconceptions of another academic discipline – especially history or philosophy. Thus, the core of the politics curriculum in Britain, at least until recently, has been the study of individual political institutions in their historical context; the great political philosophers; and what was misleadingly titled 'comparative government'. The latter was, in practice, largely the separate study of American, French and Soviet government and politics. In continental Europe, politics has often been a subsidiary part of departments or faculties of law, sociology or history.

'Social scientists' would denounce the traditional approach as 'idiographic' (a word derived from 'ideogram' – a personal mark or signature), espousing instead a 'nomothetic' or generalising approach in which the endeavour of scholars of politics must ultimately be to derive general theories or laws about the nature of political behaviour. Thus a typical American-style curriculum presents political science as one of a group of related social science disciplines, including sociology and economics, all using modern computer-orientated methods of 'analysing data' scientifically.

'Radical critics', while not denying the need to produce useful generalisations from the study of politics, have denounced the conservative bias of US-dominated political science. Their primary allegiance has appeared to be to a general doctrine calling for the radical change of existing (Western) societies. Most frequently this has been a variety of Marxism, but similar criticism can be produced from an ecological, theological or feminist perspective.

The basis of the distinction being drawn is mainly in terms of what writers see their task to be, the methods they employ, the level and type of their analysis, and the values they espouse, rather than the details of specific theories advanced. Where writers from different approaches and schools deal with what is apparently the same topic (e.g. 'democracy', 'elections', 'society'), their concerns and assumptions are often so different that no real dialogue can be said to have occurred. Table 1.1 offers an overview of these major approaches and schools.

Table 1.1 Major contemporary approaches to politics

	Traditional	*Social science*	*Radical*
Task	Piecemeal explanation	Science of politics	Radical social change
Methods	Descriptive, historical, philosophical analysis	Quantitative or theorising illustrated	Ideological criticism
Values	Liberal Democratic	Pro-US democracy and 'development'	Anti-establishment
Levels of analysis	Political, philosophical and psychological	Political and social	Multi-level
Scope	Individual institutions or countries	US or area studies	Global and historical
Content	Constitutional consensus disturbed by cataclysmic events	Pluralism	Class/Gender/Species conflict
Schools	(a) Liberal–institutional (b) Historical (c) Philosophical	(a) Functionalist (b) Economic (c) Systems	(a) Marxist (b) Feminist (c) Ecologist (d) Religious Fundamentalist (e) Post-modernist
Typical concepts	Constitutional Convention Great Man	Political culture Market Feedback	Contradiction Patriarchy Jihad

Source: Adapted from Tansey (1973)

Before we explore each of these three approaches in more depth we offer a health warning: each of them reflects a primarily Western culture – there is not yet a distinctive African, Asian and South American approach to politics. We shall explore this point in more depth in Chapter 6, but it is worth noting here that if you are studying politics beyond the North American and European heartland of the discipline, you need to take into account differing context, culture and historical practices.

TRADITIONAL SCHOLARSHIP

The first academic writers on politics – Plato and Aristotle, whose works are still studied in detail in most British universities – were unaccustomed to the modern practice of compartmentalising knowledge into separate disciplines. They combined insights from history and current affairs with discussions of big moral issues such as 'What is the best form of government?' This somewhat 'eclectic' approach (combining insights from various different sources) was also adopted by some of the more readable classic writers in the nineteenth century such as John Stuart Mill (1806–1873), Bryce (1838–1922) and de Tocqueville (1805–1859). These writers saw the rise of democracy as the major political development of their time and sought to analyse not only the idea but also its emerging reality in different countries.

Commentators on 'political theory' have tended to divide into two main camps. One group comprises the philosophers who see their main task as the elucidation of political concepts (such as justice and democracy), with at least an eye to their relevance to contemporary concerns. A second group consists of the historians of ideas who are concerned with tracing the evolution of writings on politics, the intent of the writers of these texts and their influence on events.

Those who have written on 'political institutions' have often been less explicit in their theoretical intent, but writers such as Ridley (1991), Rhodes (1997) and Liu (2011) have articulated the rationale and assumptions of much of this writing. In established and relatively stable democracies like Britain and the United States, much of what we call politics centres around important governmental institutions like assemblies, elections, government departments and local government. The study of how these institutions have evolved and the rules and practices surrounding them and consideration of how they may be improved is clearly of the utmost importance.

However, the sceptical and the ambitious may combine to throw doubt upon the academic credentials of such activities. Is the result really 'knowledge' which can be legitimately examined in universities or merely pragmatic common sense which can be used by those who agree with its (conservative and liberal) assumptions? To meet such objections there has been the development of more methodologically aware 'new institutionalism', of which Peters (1999) discerns no less than seven varieties. The sceptical will continue to argue that the operations of representative institutions are merely a deceptive mask for the real politics of exploitation (see 'radical criticism' below), while the ambitious see scientifically established theories as the only acceptable basis of knowledge.

We note one trend which is challenging this approach, namely the growth of international relations courses. This reflects increasing global economic, political, technological and social developments which mean that single countries cannot solve all the issues facing them on their own. This is inherently placing the study of politics within a broader perspective. Such courses, while not overly called politics, are essentially about politics between and beyond the state. The study of politics does not remain static.

SOCIAL SCIENCE AND POLITICS

The proposition that our knowledge of politics should be scientifically derived seems, at first sight, undeniable. The application of scientific method in many other spheres (e.g. physics, biochemistry and astronomy) has yielded not only a broad consensus regarding the truth of various scientific 'laws' but also practical results in the shape of space travel and 'miracle' drugs. If the application of systematic observation, computerised analysis of data, the testing of hypotheses through experiment and the painstaking building of small bricks of fact into enormous edifices of knowledge can work in one sphere, why not in another?

The problems of creating a valid science of politics seem, however, to be so enormous that they place the whole project in some doubt. They include problems of value conflict, of complexity, of method and of philosophy. Not all political science can be objective: some is clearly normative, positing a particular view, often reflecting the nature of the political society that the author is writing in or what they want their society to become. For example, it is no surprise that the work of Professor John Makumbe (1949–2013), an activist in the opposition MDC-T looked at political events in Zimbabwe (Makumbe, 2003) from a different perspective to that of the ruling ZANU PF government. Such normative analyses provided by Makumbe are not always neutral; rather they are part of the political process. So what he said and wrote about the Zimbabwean political system could have an impact on it by shaping the opinions of other political practitioners and citizens.

It is tempting to dismiss conflicts of value as irrelevant to scientific investigation. The conventional argument is that science is morally neutral ('value-free') but can be used for good or evil. Thus, the structure of the atom is the same everywhere, whether our knowledge of this structure is used to destroy civilisations, fuel them, or merely understand their most basic constituents.

It is easier to apply knowledge of biochemistry to creating individual health than it is to use knowledge of politics to create a healthy society. This is because there is more agreement on what an ill person looks like than on what an ill society is. As a result, in social analysis it is impractical to create a 'value-free' vocabulary acceptable alike to social democrats, neo-liberals, Marxists and feminists. For example, creators of the Internet such as Tim Berners-Lee wanted information freely available online, but this idea is now challenged by the different values of those who want to control access to such information for political or economic reasons. A social democrat might observe a form of e-representation in operation (Jackson and Lilleker, 2012). A neo-liberal may see only a series of businesses asserting their commercial interests (McLaughlin and Pickard, 2005). A Marxist may identify how the Internet helps capitalism by encouraging commodification (Fuchs and Dyer-Witheford, 2012). Meanwhile a feminist might suggest that the dominant culture of the Internet ignores the politics of gender inequalities (Adam, 2005). The same 'fact' could be interpreted in a variety of different ideological or normative ways.

Typically, science is seen as characterised by the testing of hypotheses, through experiment. The experimental method is largely closed to political scientists since they do not possess the power to dictate to whole human societies how they should behave. In any case, experiments require identical control groups for comparison which, it is arguable, cannot be created. Although there has been an attempt to use 'natural experiments' as a means of assessing political participation, elections and political psychology, Sekhon and Titiunik (2012) note that the treatment and control groups may not be comparable. It is possible to control what information the treatment sample have access to, say knowledge of a political event, but it is much more problematic to ensure the knowledge the control group might have of it. Some small-scale laboratory simulations of human power situations have been attempted with interesting results (e.g. Milgram, 1965), but the applicability of the results of these to whole societies is disputable.

Statistical manipulation of existing sets of data about human societies may be a partial substitute for experimental techniques, but it could be argued that few convincing data sets exist. Attempts at marshalling these include those of the *World Handbook of Political and Social Indicators* (Taylor and Jodice, 1983) and the Country Indicators for Foreign Policy Project at Carleton University, Canada (www.carleton.ca/cifp). One very basic problem for international data sets is that many countries do not have reliable population figures; for example, Nigerian census figures have been politically contested because of their influence on the ethnic balance of power. It is also difficult to compare financial values in different currencies because of artificial exchange rates and differences in purchasing power.

Scholars committed to a scientific approach to politics have sought to overcome this problem by collecting quantitative data about political behaviour. Classically this has been done through social surveys which may be carried out on a large scale by market research firms or on a smaller scale by researchers themselves. For example, Jansen *et al.* (2013) created a quantitative data set from the questionnaires of 188 national studies to assess the impact of party ideology on the strength of class voting.

Modern statistical analysis enables the researcher to make judgements regarding the existence, or not, of significant associations between variables. There is a logical gap between a statistical association and a causal relationship, which is what such researchers generally aspire to establishing (see Johns, 2002). On a philosophical level it has been argued that the sort of causal explanation that would be perfectly satisfactory in physical science would be unsatisfactory in explaining social phenomena – social explanations need to explain the motives of the persons involved, not just predict successfully what will happen (Runciman, 1969). Additionally, if we accept that human knowledge and motivation are an important part of each political system, every advance in political knowledge is potentially available to the members of the systems we study. The knowledge we produce by analysing political systems becomes potentially a part of those systems and may, of course, upset any predictions we make about them (Popper, 1960).

Such considerations often lead to an emphasis on more qualitative methods of investigation, such as participant observation, in-depth interviews, case studies, textual deconstruction and focus groups. The stress in such investigations is often on contextualising and understanding the meaning of events to participants (see Devine, 2002). Such methods are more frequently applied by traditional or radical scholars – especially postmodernists.

One recent interesting trend has been an attempt to combine natural science research with political science. For example, Frienda *et al.* (2013) tested over 5,000 respondents on false memories, the respondents being asked about their memories of three true and one fabricated political event. The fabricated event was accompanied by a photographic image purportedly depicting that event. Approximately half the participants remembered that the false event happened, with 27 per cent suggesting that they saw the event happen on the news. This however is more an example of psychology within the political sphere than political science *per se*. Another example of this hybrid between science and political science research has involved behavioural genetics, the so-called 'genopolitics', which explores the influence on political behaviour of a person's genes. One of the best-known pieces of research in this field was by Alford *et al.* (2005), who suggested that genes more than environment shape whether a person views themselves as a liberal or conservative. Fowler and Dawes (2008) suggested that a gene, MAO-A, existed which had an effect on the likelihood of someone voting or not. However, in assessing the work on 'genopolitics' Charney and English (2012) suggest that the analysis has been too simplistic, that it is unlikely that single genes alone are the key to understanding voting behaviour, ideology and policy views.

SCHOOLS OF POLITICAL SCIENCE

Perhaps the most influential group of 'political scientists' are those stemming from Gabriel Almond and the deliberations of the Committee on Comparative Politics of the American Political Science Association in the 1960s. Although much criticised on theoretical grounds, the terminology and approach adopted by these 'functionalist' writers is still widely prevalent in empirical studies of American, British and comparative politics.

In a vastly influential early work, Almond and Coleman (1960) argued that we should speak of:

'Political System' instead of 'State'
'Functions' instead of 'Powers'
'Roles' instead of 'Offices'
'Structures' instead of 'Institutions'
'Political Culture' instead of 'Public Opinion'
'Political Socialization' instead of 'Citizenship Structure'.

Their argument was that by studying the processes necessary to maintain any political system in a variety of environments, rather than focusing on conventional liberal democratic institutions, they were creating a conceptual vocabulary that was the basis for a 'probabilistic science of politics'.

This attempt has been highly successful in that thousands of writers have employed the vocabulary suggested. Unfortunately, there is little evidence that the vocabulary is used any more precisely than its 'old-fashioned' predecessors (Sartori, 1970) or that the assumptions implicit in the approach are any less arguable than (or, indeed, very different from) the liberal institutional approach. For instance, there has been no substantial agreement on what functions are necessary to maintain a political system (Dowse, 1972) or on the desirability of understanding politics in terms of the maintenance of the stability of existing sovereign states. Luard (1990) argues for a global perspective.

A good illustration of some of the problems of employing this newer vocabulary is to consider the concept of 'political system'. This is used rather loosely by most of the functionalists to indicate that politics is not merely limited to traditional constitutional institutions but encompasses the influence on them of social and economic conditions within a country. As Nettl (1966) has pointed out, this usage often assumes that the system is an entity that exists and carries out some defined role – such as 'the allocation of value'. Alternatively, the idea of system may be used more as a conscious analogy with engineering systems, as with Deutsch (1963), who sees the political system as a steering mechanism for society – a flow of information through decision-making mechanisms which can be improved. This idea has been updated by Buechler (2000), who takes into account a more global approach to present a world-systems theory, one which reflects the growing importance of transnational social movements and the corresponding loss of hegemony by nation states.

Systematic sociological thinkers such as Talcott Parsons (1957) see that 'functions' are highly theoretical processes analytically distinguished from a messy empirical reality. The difficulty then becomes seeing what predictions such a theory is making. The 'emptiness' of system theory is perhaps most clearly seen if the writings of David Easton (1979) are considered. Easton states that 'political system' is a purely analytical concept which can be applied to any collection of entities the theorist finds convenient. He then suggests the possibility of the system responding to 'input' from the outside 'environment' by 'outputs' which in turn may affect the environment so as to stabilise it. In such a case a stable 'homeostatic' system has been achieved. However, such an outcome is by no means inevitable – the problem then is to know when such an analysis is appropriate, and when a breakdown of the system might occur. Thus, many writers now claim to be adopting a 'system' approach, but it is often unclear whether they believe that political systems are observable entities, analytical frameworks, useful analogies or a problem-solving device.

By way of contrast, let us consider a more recent and perhaps trendier group of political scientists – the 'rational choice' theorists. They have adopted an alternative approach which, instead of starting with the behaviour of whole societies, focuses on the behaviour of individual political 'actors'. Mainstream economists have analysed markets starting with the behaviour of individual consumers and entrepreneurs who are assumed to rationally pursue their own interests (maximise utility or profit). The behaviour of individual voters, bureaucrats or legislators can be considered in the same way (Downs, 1957; Tullock, 1965; Himmelweit et al., 1985). For example, Aldrich (1993) suggests that rational choice by looking at costs and benefits can explain in which situations citizens are more or less likely to vote. Stokman and Zeggelink (1996) extended the basic principle of rational choice at individual level to apply a mathematical approach to understand the development of policy within policy networks. As with economics, it is not asserted that all actors are rational. The assumption is only that the system functions on the basis that most actors will be rational and that irrational actors will cancel each other out.

BOUNDARIES AND SCHISMS IN POLITICAL SCIENCE

Marsh and Savigny (2004) estimate that 75 per cent of the world's political scientists work in US universities; therefore, it is there that we need to identify and assess any conflict between different approaches.

Over a 150-year period, Dryzek (2006) suggests, there has been at least four phases in the history of political science in the US. In the first, statism – from the mid-nineteenth century through to the early twentieth century – the focus was on the state as the central player in politics. However, US society was not as static as this approach implied, and from the early twentieth century pluralists such as Harold Laski suggested that different and competing power centres existed. From the 1950s pluralism was challenged by those who, like Dahl, took a behavioural approach, which was scientific in nature. The last distinct phase which Dryzek identifies is the New Political Science, in which writers such as Bachrach focused on the social problems and political crises of the time. Clearly, this implies that there exist tensions within the study of political science.

This friction is especially to be found in considerations of the correct methodological means of conducting political science research. The orthodox view in US universities is judged to be a rational choice approach, which encourages the collection of empirical data through primarily quantitative methods. The rationale behind this methodology is to create a more scientific approach aiming at universal understanding. This orthodoxy is to be found not only within US universities but also in the American Political Studies Association (APSA), the body representing political scientists. This perceived scientific hegemony was challenged in October 2000 when an anonymous Mr Perestroika sent out an email critiquing both APSA and the teaching of political science in the US. This email soon gained some support, and a loosely formed perestroika movement evolved; indeed, it became successful enough to gain positions on the decision-making bodies of APSA. The perestroikans support a pluralist approach, applying a range of methodologies, both qualitative and quantitative, and maintaining that political science should focus more on providing contextual knowledge within specific situations (Schram, 2003; Jacobsen, 2005). The debate was not just about how to conduct research but also a suggestion that those who followed a scientific approach actively recruited and promoted those who saw the world through the same prism. So that as Marsh and Savigny (2004) argue, the supporters of the dominant positivist paradigm are the gatekeepers of the profession, who have control through key appointments and the type of articles accepted in academic journals.

Anecdotally, one of the authors has witnessed an interesting example of this debate in the UK. At a political science conference addressing a general election, the vast majority of paper presenters had used a quantitative methodology based upon the statistical interpretation of questionnaires. There was an almost audible gasp when one presenter got up and discussed voting behaviour based on a series of detailed interviews with less than ten voters. At the time this qualitative approach to psephology (the study of elections) was extremely unusual. Interestingly, by the end of the presentation the feedback was effusive and enthusiastic, and the speaker was told how refreshing their paper was.

This whole debate about whether political science requires the collection of mass data analysed by computer software programs or can be smaller case studies assessed by the researcher in itself demonstrates some of the political discussions we have addressed earlier. One approach appeared to be dominant and able to exercise power by appointing like-minded researchers and influencing the agenda through favourable journal output, but was challenged by another. Amusingly, this suggests that the study of political science is an example of pluralism in practice.

It would be too rigid to suggest an unbreakable divide; there have clearly been shifts on both sides. Indeed, Roger Smith (2002), although preferring political science to address issues of interest, does recognise the value of scientific contributors. More overtly, Keating (2009) suggests that there exists a third way, where it is possible to work across disciplinary boundaries and so encourage the cross-fertilisation of ideas. The future of political science should allow for a range of methodologies, which would reduce the current schism.

One other boundary question exists, and it is a normative one: namely, what is the relationship between the study of political science and the practice of politics? The answer appears to be that political science supports a democratic approach. The history of democracy is tied up with the health of the study of political science. Huntington (1988) believes that political science, by looking at issues such as justice, order, liberty and responsible government, helps democracy by generating understanding of political processes. If he is correct this does raise the issue of whether political science can be of value to non-democratic countries, though as we shall see later the definition of democracy can be broad.

THEORIES, MODELS AND PARADIGMS

Faced with a thicket of rival approaches and theories, readers may be tempted to demand who is right and who is wrong. However, no simple, omniscient answer is available, so what may help clarify matters is to try to separate out a number of activities that are frequently confused in the effort to generate a science of politics. To do so, we need to consider how scientists normally work.

Popper (1960) has convincingly argued that scientific laws are useful general predictive propositions, which have been extensively tested and not disproved. Few of the propositions advanced by political scientists seem to meet this test, especially applying theoretical propositions to the real world of politics. However, some more limited propositions might be regarded as testable hypotheses, the production of which constitutes a preliminary to the creation of usable theories.

It used to be thought that scientists derived their hypotheses for testing from the observation of as many 'facts' as possible (the 'positivist' view of science). More recently it has been suggested that most innovative hypotheses come from a combination of acute observation and the application of 'models' of reality often derived from another area of science. A 'model' is a simplification of reality that enables us to suggest relationships between the things we observe.

In politics, numerous different models have been, and still are, applied. For instance, medieval thinkers tended to prefer an organic model of the state – e.g. seeing the parts of a state as being like the parts of the human anatomy. Easton/Deutsch's application of a cybernetic (information system) model in the age of the computer thus becomes unsurprising in the 'postmodern' age.

Clearly, as Deutsch (1963) points out, models are not in themselves right or wrong, merely helpful or unhelpful. Choice of models will depend on their relevance, economy and predictive power – the latter encompassing ideas of rigour (do theories based upon it give unique answers?); combinatorial richness (the number of patterns that can be generated from it) and organising power (can a model be applied in many different circumstances?).

Really successful models can be at the heart of what Kuhn (1970) terms a scientific paradigm. Thus, the Newtonian model of matter as a series of particles whose relationships could be described in terms of a series of simple mathematical equations dominated physics for several centuries. Evolutionary development proposed by Darwin continues as the dominant paradigm in modern biology. Despite the positivist view of scientific development referred to above, Kuhn argues that most scientific endeavour ('normal science') consists of the further application of existing models to new areas or the explanation of apparent deviations from the dominant model in terms derived from it. Nor should this be despised: a great deal of modern technological and scientific progress has rested on this process of 'pygmies standing on the shoulders of giants' – ordinary knowledge workers amassing detailed information within the dominant paradigm.

In these terms, political studies can be seen as an academic discipline in the pre-scientific stage, in which no dominant paradigm has yet emerged. What are described here as 'schools' can be seen as aspirant paradigms. The main question that has to be asked is how useful a source these are of models applicable to new situations, of testable hypotheses, and of concepts for helpfully describing and analysing events? Absolute truths cannot be found.

RADICAL AND POSTMODERNIST CRITICISM

One characteristic of a scientific theory is that it should be value-free – there is no left-wing physics and right-wing physics, just good physics and bad physics. Yet consideration of many approaches put forward by political scientists reveals that the models upon which they are based, the concepts they employ and the theories they espouse frequently imply a clear set of values which others might well wish to dispute. As we noted earlier, they are subjective and normative, not objective, observations. For example, Almond's functionalist model seems to view politics as a matter of maintaining political stability by enabling political interests in a system to be conciliated ('interest articulation and aggregation'). This is done by a state that functions through a traditional liberal pattern of legal rules ('rule making, rule enforcement and rule adjudication'). The model thus stresses values of 'pluralism' and consensus which may be uncontroversial in the United States but less acceptable in sub-Saharan Africa. Moreover, it creates a set of interesting challenges for China's political elite. Similarly, a glance at the individualistic model put forward by the 'economists' reminds one of Margaret Thatcher's famous remark that 'there is no such thing as society – only individuals'. Such theories clearly imply a fashionable suspicion of big government and stress the 'profit motive'. Political models and political science cannot be divorced from the culture and values of the authors that subscribe to them.

The obvious alternative approach to political analysis stressing individualism and consensus is the collectivist and conflict-orientated view of politics put forward by Marxists. At this stage we shall generalise, and the basic model, stemming back to Marx and Engels's *Communist Manifesto* (1848), is of a society divided into large collectivities (classes) whose interests are in basic conflict. The only long-term resolution of such conflicts, which stem from the basic relationship of exploitation between the capitalist bourgeoisie (the owners of the 'means of production') and the proletariat ('wage-slaves'), is through a socialist revolution. This analytical approach may seem perfectly acceptable in some countries but totally alien to others because of different norms and values.

A number of writers (Miliband, 1969; Gramsci, 1969) have approached the analysis of modern politics through a variety of Marxist models with, in some cases, enlightening results. Conventional assumptions have been questioned and further economic and political dimensions to problems exposed. In the Western world, for instance, the cultural and media influence of capitalism has been emphasised, while in the 'third' world the Marxist emphasis on the international economic environmental influences (Williams, 1976) seems much more realistic than analysis of political parties who are liable to disappear overnight in a military coup (Sklar, 1963).

Two other approaches which have developed since the 1970s and provide different frameworks are the green movement and feminism. They are normally considered radical, often with links to Marxism, though they can be critiques to both left and right ideologies and have developed their own unique approaches. From a green perspective politics is seen in a very particular light: as Torgerson (1999) notes, nature is placed at the centre of its attention. He suggests that the political focus goes beyond human concerns to consider non-human interests such as individual species and the planet as a whole. This means that a central tenet of this approach has been to challenge the view that industrialisation is good. So where both a Marxist and a liberal democrat would be interested in achieving growth, though of different natures, the likely green approach is to ask why should we have economic growth at all since it will further harm the earth. This is a very different outlook on politics, cogently expressed by Schumacher (1973) in *Small is Beautiful*, where he suggests that modern economies based on growth are unsustainable because of finite natural resources. A large part of green politics is therefore based on a green economics, but as noted by Cato (2012) there is also an ethical approach that emphasises equality. However, as with the other approaches there is not one single agreed view. Barry (1999) has identified at least two different interpretations, a green ideological view which is utopian in nature and a more pragmatic approach. The latter is more likely to make compromises on the issue of economic growth. Jamison (2001) has referred to this potential divide within green politics as a bifurcation – between the green politics of the industrialised north which views science as the answer and a cultural critique of science from Asian green politics. With the latter the concern is with the effect on individual societies of environmental issues caused by two centuries of Western industrialisation. With the former there is a belief that a synthesis is possible between capitalism and sustainability: green growth. Certainly, we see some Western governments viewing the development of green technologies as the solution to the problem of slowing economic growth and unemployment.

Radical feminists have questioned the assumptions implicit in conventional political analysis (for a good introduction see Bryson, 2003). They too have seen society primarily in terms of an exploitative relationship ('patriarchy') between collectivities (adult heterosexual males versus the rest). (It should be emphasised that this is a discussion of radical feminist writers – many feminists adopt a more liberal and moderate stance.) Like later Marxists they have stressed cultural and media aspects of political relationships, but also the political aspects of personal relationships. Whereas conventional analysis has looked at explicit political conflicts reflected in conventional party divisions, these writers have seen potential (seismic) splits repressed by conventional politics.

Lest the idea of repressed political divisions is dismissed out of hand it is worth considering the case of Afro-Americans in the United States. As recently as the 1950s in many parts of the US they were deprived of basic human rights and discriminated against. Although they lived in a 'democracy' and resented their condition, sometimes even as the majority in their local community, Afro-American concerns still did not even feature on the political agenda. Starting from this situation, Bachrach and Baratz (1970) put forward an interesting model of political activity, combining insights from both the pluralist and Marxist models. They suggest that an apparently free play of political interests in a 'democratic' system may coexist with suppressed conflicts in which the interests of certain groups often fail to reach the political agenda. Policies favouring suppressed groups, even if nominally adopted by governments, will not be fully implemented by the machinery of government. In short, what Schattschneider (1960: 71) calls a 'mobilization of bias' is built into the system against them. While Bachrach and Baratz are mainly concerned with racial biases, clearly these biases can equally well be those of gender, ethnicity or religion.

The radical writers discussed do not necessarily dismiss the enterprise of a science of politics – old-style Marxists frequently claimed that 'scientific' socialism gave them a superior insight into contemporary economy and society. They merely question the assumptions on which contemporary analysts base their work. However, postmodernist critics, influenced by philosophers such as Wittgenstein and Foucault, throw doubt upon the possibility of an impartial analysis of political behaviour. They stress that the very language used to describe political events is the product of struggles between different users of language and is 'internally complex, open, appraisive and fought over' (Gibbins and Reiner, 1999: 7). A good illustration of this is the contemporary concept of 'a war on terrorism'. Traditionally political science uses a vocabulary that assumes the primacy of the nation state, and political conflicts based upon producer interests. Postmodernist critics often stress the impact of globalisation and consumerism in undermining these assumptions (Gibbins and Reiner, 1999). A postmodern approach would abandon the idea of a unitary study with a consensus on methods, and encourage greater use of writing by a global network of excluded and non-professional groups (Gibbins and Reiner, 1999).

CONCLUSION

This chapter suggests that it is relatively easy to understand why politics matters, be it at a society level, the impact on the wider economy or just how our everyday lives are influenced by it. However, we have seen that there is no one single agreed definition of what politics actually means. It could include the formal mechanisms of government, but also the informal relationships between individuals and groups. This divide between the governmental and society levels of politics is something we shall explore further in the next chapter. It is not a surprise that there is no one agreed approach to the study of politics, but, as Box 1.2 outlines, the key differences concern the methodologies for understanding politics. What we can say as students of politics is that the important question is whether their methodology is appropriate, consistently applied and helpful.

BOX 1.2   ASSESSING THE USE OF METHODOLOGY
IN POLITICS

Is the approach employed appropriate to the problem in hand?
Are theories, concepts and models clearly defined and consistently
  applied?
Are theoretical assumptions distinguished from empirically established
  conclusions?
Is *all* the evidence on the issues examined?

There is good work published by writers of all persuasions.
Conversely, some authors seem only to look for evidence sup-
portive of their theoretical assumptions. In the present state of
knowledge, it will often be found that a combination of insights
derived from different approaches often throws the most light on
an issue.

What we shall see in later chapters is that politics does not exist
in a vacuum: context is important to understanding it. Politics is a
fluid concept which is based on behaviours and institutions set in
different environments, subject to a variety of stimuli and motivations.

FURTHER READING

Flinders, M. and John, P. (2013) 'The future of political science',
Political Studies Review, 11 (2): 222–227.

Hall, P. and Taylor, R. (1996) 'Political science and the three new
institutionalisms', *Political Studies*, 44(5): 936–957.

Hay, C. (2002) *Political Analysis*, London: Palgrave.

Heywood, A. (2013) *Politics*, Basingstoke: Palgrave Macmillan.

Hindmoor, A. (2011) 'Major combat operations have ended?
Arguing about rational choice', *British Journal of Political Science*,
41 (1): 191–210.

Leftwich, A. (1983) *Redefining Politics*, London, Methuen.

McLean, I. (2009) *Concise Oxford Dictionary of Politics*, Oxford:
Oxford University Press.

Quinn, T. (2012) 'Spin doctors and political news management: a rational choice exchange analysis', *British Politics*, 7 (3):
272–300.

Wanna, J. (2002) 'Commentary, APSA presidential address 2002, politics as a new vocation: the future of political science', *Australian Journal of Political Science*, 38 (1): 141–148.

Zuckerman, A. (1991) *Doing Political Science: An Introduction to Political Analysis*, Oxford: Westview Press.

WEBSITES

www.HaveYourSayOnline.net
UK political system for citizenship education.

www.apsanet.org
American Political Science Association; includes an explanation of what is political science.

http://ejw.i8.com/polsciweb.htm
List of political science websites.

http://legacy.c-span.org/politics/default.aspx –
Cable channel offers articles and videos on US politics.

www.psr.keele.ac.uk
Richard Kimber's excellent political science resources web page.

www.psa.ac.uk
Political Studies Association (UK); includes latest information and blog postings.

http://ipsaportal.unina.it
International Political Science Association portal gives access to, describes and assesses for accessibility and usefulness 'the top 300' international sources on politics.

www.rockthevote.org/
Intersects popular culture with politics.

2

POWER

THIS CHAPTER ...

discusses how and why politics is exercised and the ways in which it can be understood. Power – its meaning and how it is exercised – is one of the core concepts political scientists seek to explain. The previous chapter identified the tension between whether the study of politics can be viewed as a science or not; this schism can also be applied to debates about power. Possibly the most famous and influential single piece of practical work on power was written by Niccolò Machiavelli in 1517. Machiavelli's *The Prince* created a blueprint for how to gain and then exercise power, which we could interpret as a positivist, scientific approach. His attitude to power was to suggest that individual rulers could apply theory to the craft of exercising power.

At a simple level politics centres on the exercise of power, who has it, who wants it and what the influences are. The actual exercise of power is an ever-shifting proposition, but to understand power we need to look at it from more than one angle. In addition, we need to recognise that it is affected by the environment – for instance, social and economic – in which it exists. Journalists may focus more on the personalities, who is exercising power or trying to seize it, but for political scientists this can be a distraction. It is important to understand how power is being exercised, and indeed why one source of power is more successful than another at any given time. If we do not have this conceptual context, political science is little more than the historical study of individual regimes.

By the end of this chapter students will be able to:

- understand the meaning of power;
- assess different interpretations of power;
- identify the components of power;
- assess how the exercise of power changes over time;
- evaluate how power is exercised, and the limitations to power.

WHAT IS POWER?

There are hundreds of different definitions of power, and it is no surprise that there is no single agreed explanation. As a consequence we shall identify the tensions between the different approaches that prescribe one or another meaning for power. Before we address these key approaches, which are normally based on the application of power in real life, it is interesting to note that there is a conceptualisation of power within fiction. Phalen *et al.* (2012) looked at how Hollywood producers presented fictional US presidents in their films, and found that power was associated with acting decisively during a crisis. Thus, in this cinematic world power was about being a strong individual, with the very characteristics Machiavelli approved of five hundred years ago. However, as we shall see, power is rarely the preserve of one person alone, and what the movies consider strong leadership may not always be appropriate.

The first issue that we face is determining the exact boundary and scope of power. One of the most dominant thinkers on power was Max Weber (1864–1920), who viewed power as a social concept. Weber suggested that power is the result of social stratification and he broke down society to a number of levels, implying that social status is important. He noted that it was possible for a group such as the East Elbian Junkers, weak economically but with high social status, to have disproportionate political influence. Although challenging the top-down Weberian approach, more recently Roscigno (2011) has restated a core Weberian interpretation by suggesting that power is a feature of social life and is thus linked to background, status, position and relational exchanges. At the time of writing, David Cameron's government in the UK can be put forward as an example of power as a social construct. A number of the senior advisers and politicians attended the same school as the prime minister, Eton: the Weberian approach suggests that the dominance of Old Etonians is based on personal relationships and status. Power is therefore a social construct.

An alternative to the Weberian social approach is to view power as a more precise concept, namely as being about political power and its exercise. Such an approach focuses more on government structures, who controls them and how those in control exercise power. For example, Dahl (1961) views political power as the overt decisions made by political elites who hold the key posts in governing bodies. In different countries, political systems and cultures there will be a range of people who hold political power, but what we have to identify is who controls the reins of government. C. Wright Mills suggested that political power is visible in terms of the activities of 'powerful people'. So we need to identify what are the means by which power is exercised, which could involve formal bodies such as legislatures as well as informal networks: Vander Broek (2009) notes that nearly a third of US presidents attended one of the eight Ivy League universities. Thus, in many Western societies we are likely to see the political elite characterised by a shared education, possibly professional background and similar levels of economic wealth. In non-Western countries other factors such as geography, tribe and military experience may be relevant, but what links both is that we need to know who in formal and informal ways is running a country or part of a country.

The key people in a country may be elected politicians, religious leaders, trade unionists or the military. However, looking at the US, Wright Mills implied that it might be difficult to identify who the powerful people are, referring in that context to a military industrial complex. This suggested a shadowy, non-transparent arrangement, in which the armed forces, defence industry and politicians combined to work together, making part of the power source transparent (the politicians) but the rest not so easy to identify. Commentators may use clues to indirectly assess who is holding power in less than transparent political systems. For example, in the days of Soviet Russia, many Kremlinologists tried to extrapolate from where senior military, party and government officials were standing at major events. Those closest to the leading political figure had more influence, and the key relationships, and consequently where they stood, changed regularly. The case of North Korea is currently taxing the commentators who are trying to identify who is exercising power. The leader, or first secretary, of the Workers Party of Korea is currently Kim Jong-un, who is clearly the figurehead that the official North Korean media focus on. However, given that he is the third generation of his family to hold this post, which he assumed on the death of his father in 2011, there has been speculation on whether it is the 'supreme leader' who alone exercises power or whether he needs the support of the military and key trusted relatives. Indeed, one interpretation is that Kim Jong-un has little or no power and is primarily a public figurehead, while others exercise power.

Rose and Miller (2010) have developed Wright Mills's basic idea and suggest that the exercise of political power reflects a number of shifting coalitions and alliances, which come together, collaborate and then break up. This would suggest that in our example above, Kim Jong-un might rely on the military early on in his reign, but as he develops his experience and personal networks and takes on more official posts he may seek other avenues of support.

Power as a social construct is to be found everywhere and is socialised, whereas from the political power viewpoint it is to be found within structures and agencies.

In the later 1970s and early 1980s Michel Foucault (1982) developed a third viewpoint, but one that is closer to the idea of social power. He used the idea of 'governability', which applied to both the macro-level of state politics and the micro-level of everyday social life. The latter was based on knowledge – he looked, for example, at how doctors use their knowledge to maintain power. Foucault rejected the belief that power was held only in the hands of specific agencies; rather, he viewed power as all-pervasive, using the phrase 'power is everywhere'. He suggested that power does not move down from one body to the next below 'like a chain' but is circulated throughout by everyone in what is akin to a 'net' (Foucault, 1980).

Another contrast in these definitions is that between what has been described as 'zero-sum' and 'non-zero-sum' theories of politics. This terminology is derived from the mathematical theory of games. A zero-sum game is the usual sort of game, such as chess, in which a win by one player is, by definition, a loss for the opposing player or players. There is a fixed amount of 'winnings', which means that the gains of one side are, by definition, losses to the other. Obviously, many politicians – and political scientists – see politics this way. Thus Weber (1978: 53) views power as 'the probability that one actor within a social relationship will be in a position to carry out his own will despite resistance regardless of the basis on which the probability arises.' This appears to suggest that the political success of one individual may well be at the expense of those who oppose them. It is also a feature of Marxist theories; for example, Poulantzas (1973) views power as the ability of one social class to realise its objectives, seeing the interests of classes as opposed and only gained at the other's expense. This competitive approach views power as exercised by one agent over another and hence, as Simon (1953) suggests, power is asymmetrical.

However, not all games are of this sort. In others, there is no fixed amount of 'winnings' and through co-operation both sides can achieve more. For example, Talcott Parsons (1957) explicitly argues that through co-operation different groups can each obtain greater benefits than would be the case if they competed. Similarly, Hannah Arendt (1959) suggested power is not about domination; rather, it is based on consent. This non-zero-sum view seems to fit well with the practice in many parts of the contemporary Western world of mainstream politicians seeking to build coalitions through compromise. For example, the 'third way' proposed by Bill Clinton as president of the United States implied a synthesis of economic policies from the political right and social policies from the political left. Aitken-Turff and Jackson (2006) looked at nine lobbying campaigns and found evidence of co-operative game strategies where organisations did not have diametrically opposed views or interests.

Thus, different theories place radically different emphases on conflict and consensus in the exercise of power. These differences were categorised by Parsons (1963) as either power over or power to. The former focuses on how a person, group or institution has power over others; it is thus based on hierarchy and, possibly, force. The latter is the ability to 'get things done' and thus make changes to society. For Parsons this is an either – or situation – that is, power will be exercised either one way or the other – whereas Agnew (1999) suggests that the two approaches are not exclusive and are both applied in international state relations. He suggests that this takes two forms: first, an attempt by a country to control other states by making them do its will, and second, a co-operative strategy to encourage mediation and consent. A state can pursue both at the same time, and Agnew views the former as negative power and the latter as positive power.

Traditionally, international power has been viewed as between states and their government structures. However, Held (1991) argues that globalisation has challenged this simplistic Weberian viewpoint. He argues that the US-led 'war on terror' following 9/11 signals the decline of Western state power because of the growth of a multipolar global landscape (Held, 2011). He points out that while the US is still clearly a global state power, it is not able to pacify relatively weak states such as Afghanistan. At the same time he notes that the West is facing a challenge from a growing power bloc based in the east. Thus, the growth of non-state powers such as Al Qaeda and new state power sources is leading to the decline of the West.

This international aspect raises an additional issue, namely geography. Slowe (1990) argues that physical geography is at the heart of the exercise of political power. Thus, power sources such as physical resources and nationhood shape decision-making. The contrary view is put by Castells (2009), who suggests that power is a relational process based on networks and so is not constrained by geography. Castells particularly points to the impact of those networks encouraged, created and enhanced by IT such as the Internet. We shall return to this schism in Chapter 9 when we look at how communication technology may be shaping the concept of democracy.

The dominant theorists such as Weber, Foucault, Arendt and Parsons appear to view power as a single concept that is widely pertinent, whereas more recent work has suggested that power is culturally divergent and not universally applicable. Torelli and Shavitt (2010) suggest that there are different cultural attitudes to power, be they individualistic or collectivistic. They use America as an example of an individualistic culture, in which political leaders gain position by promoting their self-interest, whereas in Latin America, they argue, political leaders can take a more collectivistic approach and are sometimes perceived by voters as community benefactors. Similarly, considering who has power in Israel, Ben-Eliezer (1993) argues that in this collectivistic society people participate but do not have power and this is accepted, whereas in an individualistic society it would not be.

We can see, therefore, that the concept of power can be assessed through the prism of a range of tensions, including:

- social power versus political power;
- conflict versus co-operation;
- state versus non-state power sources;
- geographic versus non-geographic;
- individualistic versus collectivistic.

ELITES, POLITICAL PLURALISM AND CLASSES

Typically, most political science degree programmes will introduce three mainstream approaches to understanding power: elitism; pluralism; and Marxism. Each of these approaches has a different focus, with the elitist looking for where power is concentrated, the pluralist focusing on where it is distributed, and the Marxist concerned with where economic power is located.

The elitist approach argues that power is concentrated in the hands of a few. These could be individuals or groups made up of those who go to certain universities, owners of certain industries, landowners, senior members of certain religions, or another applicable category. As Pareto (1976) puts it, for every desirable unevenly distributed social quality, there exists an 'elite' who possess that quality in abundance – whether it be economic, political, social, sporting, or even 'sex appeal' – and a usually more numerous 'mass' which suffers from a relative lack of that quality.

It is striking that writers supporting different models tend to discuss different types of evidence. Thus, elite theorists such as Pareto (1976), Mosca (1939), Michels (1915) and Mills (1956) focus on who rules. They often lay great stress on alleged universal traits of human nature (e.g. the desire for power, status and wealth) and their consequences for politics. They then demonstrate the existence of hierarchies of power, wealth and status in many societies. The strategies which individuals adopt to achieve such positions are often considered with realism (even cynicism). It is shown that ruling elites tend to share a privileged lifestyle. (Michel's famous observation that two deputies, one a socialist and the other not, have more in common than two socialists, one a deputy and the other not, is fairly typical). Mills is interested in seeking to demonstrate in some detail the social, economic and educational inter-relationships and common lifestyle of a number of 'separate' US elites – the businessmen, the military and top federal government appointees. Similarly, in Britain a whole literature exists analysing such interrelationships within a British 'Establishment' whose members tend to have attended the same schools, universities and clubs (Sampson, 2004).

Bachrach and Baratz (1970) refined the elitist approach to add the idea of non-decision making – that is, the way elites are able to keep issues off the political agenda if they might negatively affect their interests. Thus, if an elite has commercial links it is likely that tax increases that could adversely affect them would not be publicly debated, let alone implemented.

Pluralist writers have tended to concentrate on how political decisions are made. In particular, they reject the view of a single hegemonic power; rather, they identify competing power sources. Power is therefore diffuse. Analysts such as Dahl (1961) and most mainstream writers on British and American politics have stressed that any group of citizens is free to influence politicians in competitive party systems, and that the latter must listen to groups outside the elite if they are to remain in office. Numerous case studies have found that a narrow group of professional politicians does not make all the decisions; rather, in different policy fields different interests have a say. For example, doctors' professional associations strongly influence decisions on health policy, neighbourhood action groups can influence planning decisions, and so on.

Moloney (2006) notes that pluralism encourages different sections within society to have their voice heard. Thus, as new interests (these could be, for example, cultural, commercial or geographic) come together they have the opportunity to have their voice heard, influence wider public opinion and eventually change policies. The obvious example is the growth in Western countries since the 1950s of pressure groups which have put forward different points of view and often led to legislative change. The inherent logic of pluralism is that the locus of power is not static, it is ever-evolving, so what was a major power source fifty years ago may no longer have that influence. For pluralists, power is dynamic.

Marxist evidence has often been concentrated on the question of in whose interest decisions are taken. Thus, on the basis that the proof of the pudding is in the eating, the distribution of income and wealth in capitalist societies is shown to be still grossly uneven, despite decades of 'progressive' taxation and the welfare state activity. Similarly, the educational and health opportunities of the working classes can be demonstrated to be far fewer than those of the upper classes. The argument is that the apparent opportunities for political participation by workers in a democracy are negated by continued bourgeois control of social structures such as the educational system, the mass media and the state apparatus, as well as the economy. Indeed, Lenin suggested that there would only be true democracy once there was no longer any private ownership.

For most Marxists, power is indivisible from the concept of class. For example, a slightly more sophisticated explanation of political power is provided by Gramsci, who spoke of a hegemony in which one class dominated another. This meant that the world view of one class is accepted by all others. Building on the idea of hegemony, Poulantzas argues that the state's role is not solely the oppression of class but must also involve gaining the consent of other classes. This idea of 'relative autonomy' was developed by Ralph Miliband (1983). He suggested that if class domination is the primary purpose of political power, two secondary purposes exist in the exercise of power – namely, upholding the self-interest of key politicians and national self-interest. Class power is used to maintain class position.

Marxists have therefore sought to explain why a socialist revolution has not come about – in other words, how capitalists have retained their power at the expense of the working class. One typical explanation was provided by the Frankfurt School, which, writing in the 1930s, sought to rationalise the rise of fascism by concluding that the state uses the media to persuade the working class that it is operating in their interest. Thus, entertainment, diversion and commodification are the means by which power is retained by the bourgeoisie. The ruling class uses its power to provide the means for distracting the working class.

To some extent, therefore, it can be argued that the findings of these different groups of writers are actually complementary rather than – as they often claim or imply – conflicting. Consider all the propositions in Box 2.1. Are they in fact inconsistent? More sophisticated versions of each model do often concede many of these points. For instance, a neo–pluralist school of thought can be identified (Moloney, 2006). This approach refines the traditional pluralist position by suggesting that (a) not all groupings are equal, with businesses having disproportionate power and influence, and (b) that new sources of power such as pressure groups representing social movements have increased in influence since the 1960s. More recently, technological developments has created new power sources aligned to the use of the Internet. This is sometimes described as 'accelerated pluralism'.

BOX 2.1   PROPOSITIONS FROM PLURALIST, ELITIST AND MARXIST MODELS OF POWER

1   People in different elite groups have a great deal of interaction and a substantially common lifestyle.
2   Politicians are often unscrupulous in search of their personal objectives.
3   Political change in democracy does not necessarily result in social and economic equality.
4   Power is conditioned by cultural and ideological assumptions that reflect those of existing dominant minorities.
5   Competitive party systems enable groups of like-minded people to influence the policy process, though they do not ensure it.

Yet important differences of perspective do remain. In the end, readers will need to make a personal judgement about the relative importance of the issues discussed and the strength of the empirical findings. Are the similarities between members of the 'power elite' so great that the ideological and policy differences they profess pale into insignificance? Does the welfare state represent a triumph for popular mass influence, or is it merely a device to cloak the continuing injustice of the capitalist economic system? Does the machinery of pressure groups and elections have a real effect on the policy process? These are issues on which both one's own value judgements and enhanced knowledge of how actual political systems work must have an influence.

An alternative analysis is provided by Steven Lukes, outlined originally in 1974 and then significantly revised and expanded in 2005. Lukes identifies three 'dimensions' to power. His first dimension is that of the pluralists, especially Robert Dahl, which focuses on the behaviour of individuals. Lukes's second dimension is that of the elitists, in particular Bachrach and Baratz, who assess the importance of shaping the agenda. So far this covers how we have looked at power here, but then Lukes suggests his own third dimension. This involves looking at where people are dominated and acquiesce to that domination. These three dimensions suggest different aspects of power: the first dimension focuses on how decisions are made, the second on the importance of not making decisions and the third the means, often ideological, by which individuals agree to something that might not appear to be in their interests.

THE COMPONENTS OF POWER

We need to clarify the concept of authority by distinguishing it from power. The definitions of power quoted earlier all included the idea of achieving results by a variety of means. Authority can be seen as a particular kind of power relationship in which the legitimacy (literally 'lawfulness') of the exercise of power is accepted, to some degree, by the other actors in the situation. Some power relationships may be based on force, persuasion or manipulation rather than the acceptance of authority. Theodore Roosevelt (US president 1901–1909) used the realpolitik phrase 'speak softly and carry a big stick'. This meant that an international statesman would discuss and negotiate, but if necessary use force to get their country's way.

In most political situations legitimacy implies an appeal to an established system of law, but it may take on the broader meaning of 'in accord with moral law'. Weber (Gerth and Mills, 1948: Ch. 10) distinguishes between 'traditional authority' and 'rational legal authority'. Both of these will normally refer to an appeal to an established system of law. Thus, in a tribal society the customary law gives authority to chiefs, while in a modern liberal democracy a rationally organised system of statute law gives authority to political and bureaucratic office holders. Both of these arrangements will be reinforced by moral doctrines – e.g. that the gods/ancestors have bequeathed their way of life to the tribe, or the sanctity of majority votes. In stable societies, ideally, there is no conflict between moral and political obligations.

On occasion, however, rival claims to authority may conflict, particularly in societies in transition or crisis. Thus, in South Africa before its changeover to full democracy, the traditional authority of the king of the Zulus on occasion conflicted with the rational-legal authority of President Botha (head of the apartheid regime). In the end both had to defer to the authority of the leader of the largest popular movement – Nelson Mandela. Weber suggests the description 'charismatic' for the authority of leaders such as Mandela who are followed because of their personal qualities rather than any legal position they may hold. Literally, this term derives from its Greek root, 'a favour specially vouchsafed by God – especially a gift or talent' (*Shorter Oxford English Dictionary*) and emphasises the exceptional qualities of those exercising such authority. But, as Weber points out, such divine gifts are not always recognised; it is only in moments of crisis, when normal claims to leadership are losing their authority, that charismatic authority is likely to appeal. Equally, such leaders usually claim to represent potential new sources of moral authority – be they God (Mohammed), the Nation (Hitler) or the People (Mandela). These examples suggest that such authority may be exercised for good or for evil. These categories of authority were intended by Weber to be morally neutral.

Modern psychology offers an explanation of how charisma works and influences the idea of authority. The basic concept is that we like the charismatic, we warm to people with charisma: it is elusive, valuable and can often be interpreted in ways that are specific to the receiver. Credible communicators influence attributes not through compliance, but through internalisation – citizens accept their recommendations because they are congruent with their own values. Perloff (2008) suggests that charisma is made up of three components:

1 Authority
2 Credibility
3 Social attractiveness.

Authority can sometimes be explained by a belief in 'the men in white coats', i.e. belief in experts. Stanley Milgram conducted a series of experiments in and around Yale University 1960–1963. Volunteers ended up giving what they thought were electric shocks to others. They were not in reality, but the explanation of their acceptance of this apparently violent requirement is that social influence has a powerful effect on our behaviour, indicating why we might conform to instructions from those in authority.

James Madison, often referred to as the 'Father of the American Constitution', saw the people as the ultimate source of authority, and argued that safeguards to liberty required balances of power between different government institutions (Madison, 1788). One modern interpretation is provided by Morgan (1981), who argues that Madison identified two sources of authority: public opinion and the perceived motives of office holders. Madison, writing in the eighteenth century, noted that the larger the country the more difficult it is to gauge public opinion. This would suggest that in complex modern societies the balance of authority has moved towards public officials and away from public opinion. Schier (2011) suggests that over the past 70 years the US presidency has lost political authority because the changeable nature of public opinion means that presidents have been less able to maintain support. Regarding Morgan's second point, Edmundson (2010), writing from a legal perspective, refers to this as political authority based on the moral power invested in the state. Put another way, political authority is legitimate if individuals believe that public officials have a right to exercise power and citizens have given them this right.

Therefore, we might argue that in liberal democracies, serving public opinion is the basis of political authority, but this basic idea may also apply to systems that would not claim to be liberal democracies. For example, Saeidi (2001) notes that Ayatollah Khoemeini's political legitimacy in Iran was based on charisma and his economic policies were based on gaining popular approval.

Some religions have a particular perspective on the meaning, legitimacy and exercise of political authority. Von Brück (2010), looking at Christianity, notes that the papacy's political authority was invested by Christ, which as a result sometimes brought the Church into conflict with kings. However, he also notes that following the Reformation and the Enlightenment of the seventeenth century, divine intervention played a decreasing role and political authority was based more on the nature of the king or other key government officials. Lai (2010) identified a Buddhist approach to political authority which would traditionally have supported a monarchy. However, given that monarchies are now rare as governing systems, the Buddhist would now view political authority more from a minimalist or decentralised state perspective.

Skogstad (2003) identifies at least three models of political authority:

1 Popular authority
2 Expert authority
3 Market-based authority.

The first of these may occur when an individual politician is especially popular. The second is where a politician is seen to have a specific expertise in a field, be it economic, military, education or whatever. This is often based on their previous political or non-political experience. The UK politician Vince Cable is widely considered to have been one of the first to correctly predict the economic downturn, and it is suggested that this is the basis of his authority within the British cabinet with a business portfolio. In short, he proved in the past he was right, and this gives authority to his subsequent opinions. The third implies some ability to shape the economy or encourage employment. The authors suggest, however, that authority should be limited to legal authority provided by democratic mechanisms.

Shaoul (2011) suggests that the growing use of public–private partnerships (PPPs) in the UK has meant a ceding of political authority by the state to finance in the shaping of economic policy. He argues that this is an example of a global trend, in which the financial sector is playing a greater role in decision-making.

Political authority does not always just reside within government organisations. Sabetti (1984) notes that in Sicily the Mafia gained political authority by acting as a broker between peasants, their absent landlords and public authorities.

An interesting case with regard to identifying where power and political authority lies is the government of Zimbabwe 2008–2013. In the first presidential election of 2008 the incumbent Robert Mugabe with 43 per cent of the vote appeared to have lost to the challenger, Morgan Tsvangirai, who secured 48 per cent. A second run-off election was required, but violence during the campaign led to the challenger withdrawing. After this the president of South Africa, Thabo Mbeki, acted as a negotiator to facilitate negotiations between the two protagonists and their respective parties. The resultant compromise, a Global Political Agreement (GPA), made clear where power and authority actually lay. Robert Mugabe's party Zanu-PF realised that the hyper-inflation affecting the country required foreign intervention, which would only happen with the involvement of Tsvangirai's MDC-T. There appeared to be, on the face of it, a fairly equitable numerical divide of government ministries, and Tsvangirai was made prime minister, while Mugabe remained as president. However, Zanu-PF maintained control of the departments relating to key state powers, including security, the military and the media (the Home Office was shared but the MDC-T minister was sidelined by the actions of officials who largely ignored him). Moreover, management of the executive, the Cabinet, lay in the hands of the president. Tsvangirai and the MDC-T may have gained an apparent cloak of authority, but in reality political authority and power remained with Zanu-PF.

There is unlikely to be a single basis of authority, and Figure 2.1 sums up the various possible sources. We can see that there is likely to be some conflict, with the formal versus the informal and those based on mass support opposed to those residing with an elite. Authority, like power, is competed for.

Formal	Informal
Institutions of government	*Personal relationships*
Political mechanisms (such as elections)	*Charismatic individuals*
Mass	**Elite**
The people	*Businesses*
God	*Office holders*

Figure 2.1 Sources of authority

POLITICAL CHANGE

An examination of past history suggests only the inevitability of
political change and the likelihood that the twenty-first century will
not be much like the twentieth. This in itself is worth stressing
since it is all too easy to assume that the future will represent a
continuation of the present. Many readers of this book will have
lived in a relatively stable, prosperous and peaceful liberal democratic nation state. Yet it is only necessary to imagine that, instead,
you had been born in the former Soviet bloc or in one of the
countries of North Africa to realise how rapidly the political
framework of your life can be transformed.

Political change is probably thought of most readily in terms of
violent and rapid transitions such as the English Civil War and the
French, American and Russian revolutions, while more recently we
have witnessed civil war in Libya and Syria. However, it is worth
bearing in mind that in the English and Russian instances at least,
such violent and rapid changes were largely reversed within two
generations without extensive violence. Conversely, a series of
piecemeal and evolutionary changes may result in a 'new' political
system based on fundamentally different principles.

Thus, Britain in the eighteenth century was fundamentally still an
oligarchic, if constitutional, country. It was controlled by a coalition
of aristocrats and country gentlemen with limited participation by
a few city businessmen. By the middle of the twentieth century, a
series of limited reforms of the franchise and to the powers of
the two houses of parliament (and a whole host of economic and

social changes) meant that Britain could claim to be a democratic country.

Much the same could be said of the United States of America – whose Founding Fathers were careful to defend their new constitution against the charge of democracy (Hamilton *et al.*, 1961). Yet that same constitution (with only a limited number of formal amendments) is now seen by many as the very model of a democratic constitution. A series of piecemeal changes helped the US transform its political system into a democratic one. These included the change from indirect election of the president by an electoral college to, effectively, direct election through national political parties. The introduction of the direct popular election of senators was accompanied by the progressive extension of the vote to all male whites, all women and finally to blacks. This was done largely through state legislation, or even changes in political practice outside of the law (Amendments 15, 17 and 19 broadened the franchise, but 15 was ineffective and 17 and 19 mainly codified previous practice at state level) (Morison and Commager, 1962).

Returning to the three models of social and political power we introduced earlier, we can relate these to ideas about political change. Most elite theorists have been unimpressed with the likelihood of real political change, since they see elites as holding all the best cards in the political game. Political stability is achieved by elites through ideological dominance (Mosca's political 'myths') and the superior organisation of a smaller group with greater economic resources and social prestige. However, both Pareto and Mosca see the possibility of cycles of apparent change which may result in an adjustment in the personnel of government but not in the fundamental fact of elite dominance. Thus, Pareto describes cycles in which 'Lions' who rule largely by force are succeeded by 'Foxes' who attempt to rule by guile and deception. Mosca describes the possibility of popular leaders taking power in the name of democracy – but sees this process as a deception, since the new leadership will inevitably rule in its own interest.

Classic Marxist writers (including Marx, Engels and Lenin) saw key political changes as occurring through violent revolutions, in which discrepancies between the political system and the underlying social and economic class system were resolved. These discrepancies were the result of longer-term gradual changes in the relations of production brought about by changes in technology and trading patterns: in other words, the proletariat will take over from the bourgeoisie.

Pluralist writers have tended to emphasise the possibility of gradual change in response to a host of factors, allowing the continuance of stable government through negotiated compromises between groups. This has especially been in evidence since the 1950s and 1960s, with the rise in many countries of single-interest groups promoting a cause. Thus Allardt and Littunen (1964) argue that the most stable political situation is where many social divisions overlap and different groups go into political coalitions for different purposes. All groups feel that they can influence the situation and thus remain committed to the system, forced to stress those aspects on which they agree in order to build co-operation with others. The premium on bargaining in such situations means that as new developments arise, piecemeal adjustments to them can be made and stability maintained.

THE TRANSFERENCE OF POWER

American poet Gil Scott Heron's most famous song is *The Revolution Will Not Be Televised*. His lyrics point out that a revolution is not a spectator sport, rather it is about people agitating for change. This implies a widespread systemic change, not just a shuffling of who is sitting at the 'top table' of government.

Our understanding of the meaning of revolution is probably shaped by a limited number of large events such as the American, Russian and Chinese revolutions. It should also be made clear that not every use of violence (or the threat to do so) in order to change the political system can sensibly be called a revolution. The term revolution (associated with the idea of a wheel turning and hence things being turned 'upside down') may be helpfully reserved for occasions when major changes in the nature of politics and society take place. Revolution implies not just a change in political leadership but the more fundamental replacement of one political (and very often economic) system by another. This includes replacing the structures and mechanisms of government and the parts of society that were dominant within them. An examination of the historical record suggests that such events are relatively rare, while the use of force (or its threat) to change the government is much more commonplace.

In the absence of an established tradition of election or inheritance of top offices within the state, violence has been the usual way to power. In the ancient world, the emperor of Rome was frequently the most successful general of his day, his bodyguard – the Praetorian Guard – effectively controlling succession. In much of Africa, Asia and Latin America, in the twentieth century, a similar state of affairs has been found, with the army constituting perhaps the most effective route to political power (Huntington, 1957; Finer, 1976).

In contrast, full revolutions can be seen as rarer, more fundamental changes to the political system, in which new social groups achieve power and the state carries out new tasks in a different way, perhaps with a different claim to legitimacy. Writers such as Crane Brinton (1965) and Lyford Edwards (1927) have perceptively analysed major revolutionary episodes such as the English Civil War and the French and Russian revolutions and suggested that they tend to go through a series of distinctive phases.

Paradoxically the old regime often collapses in a relatively bloodless triumph of popular forces following a loss of legitimacy and a manifest failure to cope with the economic, political or military demands put upon it. This is followed, after a honeymoon period, by confusion and conflict amongst the revolutionary forces. In face of real or imaginary counter-revolutionary reaction, extremist forces then often take control, launching a reign of terror, not only against declared counter-revolutionaries, but also against moderate reformers. Such a situation may then be resolved by power being taken by a tyrant (Cromwell, Napoleon, Lenin/Stalin) who leads a post-revolutionary regime which may draw upon the pre-revolutionary tradition, as well as claiming descent from the revolution itself.

Revolution is not just associated with ideology or the suppression of a particular group or particular groups within a society, it can also reflect national aspirations. For example, the Portuguese colonial war of the 1960s in Angola, Mozambique and Portuguese Guinea reflected a fight for independence. In parts of sub-Saharan Africa much of the legitimacy of the political elite is based on their 'revolutionary credentials', with those who had not fought colonial masters unable to gain power. It could take twenty, thirty or more years for the leaders of the 'revolution' to be replaced by others. In Zimbabwe the political symbolism of 'the revolution' still has resonance in everyday politics. After the 2008 general election the senior military and law-enforcement leaders associated with ZANU-PF who had fought in the war of independence with Britain in the 1970s refused to accept the legitimacy of the MDC-T led by people who had not fought in the war or were too young to be revolutionaries. Here the terms revolutionary and freedom fighter were interlinked.

One might add that, in the still longer term, further compromises with the pre-revolutionary tradition are likely. This is not to deny, however, that revolutions can transform societies – they are often accompanied by a major transformation in the role and power of the state and massive changes in property ownership and in the type of legitimacy claimed by the state.

While a revolution leads to radical change, with the creation of completely new political structures for the exercise of power, a coup d'état or putsch leads to a change in who runs those structures, but the structures remain in place. They can occur within the existing ruling elite, the so-called 'palace coup', so, for example, Saddam Hussein, who became a member of al-Bakr's government in 1968 and then from within the regime forced him to resign in 1979. Alternatively a coup might be the result of one elite, typically the military, seeking to replace another.

If revolutions are fairly rare, coups are comparatively common; Dilly (1991) estimated that there were 586 worldwide between 1945 and 1986.

While most commentators would view revolutions and coups as different means of changing political power, Acemoglu and Robinson (2001) have identified a possible link between them in some countries. Looking at political transition in Latin America they found that non-democratic societies were controlled by the rich, but the rich were forced to 'democratise' in response to revolutionary threats from those with no political or economic power. However, they argue that redistributing power led to others in the elite mounting a coup to maintain their position. In essence, the threat of revolution from one part of society led ultimately to a coup in another.

Assessing the so-called 'coloured revolutions' of Serbia (2000), Georgia (2003) and Ukraine (2004, Lane (2009) has synthesised the idea of revolution and coup to suggest a 'revolutionary coup d'état'. This concept he believes encompasses both elite participation and high mass involvement.

Most political change comes from forces primarily resident within the country, but occasionally it is the result of external forces – so-called regime change. Aidt and Albornoz (2011) suggest that foreign governments with economic interests may either induce regime change or consolidate a regime depending on what suits their interests.

EXERCISING POWER

While the focus on power in the public eye is often on charismatic politicians or the case put by visible interests and groups, the actual implementation of policies and ideas is often quietly exercised behind the scenes. To fully understand power we need to assess how it is applied and what limitations there may be to how it is exerted.

Weber (Gerth and Mills, 1948: Ch. 8) convincingly described some of the key characteristics of bureaucracy (literally, government by offices), which he said 'compares with other organisations exactly as does the machine with non-mechanical means of production':

BOX 2.2   WEBER'S CHARACTERISTICS OF BUREAUCRACY

(a) Fixed and Official Jurisdictional Areas – official 'duties', stable rules, methodically carried out (specialisation)
(b) Official Hierarchy – pyramid of officials each reporting up to level above (integration)
(c) Use of Files – to create an 'organisational memory'
(d) Official Activity as Full-time Work – no conflict between private and public interests (dedication)
(e) Expert Training of Officials – technical competence and *esprit de corps*
(f) Corpus of Rules – leading to predictability of behaviour

(Weber in Gerth and Mills, 1948)

Bureaucracy originated in the need of empires for the efficient administration of huge territories. For example, Holland (2005) notes the central role that an effective administration played in the growth of Xerxes's Persian Empire in the fifth century BC. Similarly, from at least the seventh century Chinese rulers relied on a skilled civil service selected by merit (mandarins). In modern industrial societies with large populations and complex interactions between governments and citizens, especially democracies, bureaucracies have flourished. Weber suggests that such organisations are characteristic of a modern 'rational-legal' social order. They appear to be suited to making rational decisions on behalf of society. For example, Lindblom (1959) (Box 2.3) suggests an ideal-type model of policy-making that considers how decision-makers would proceed if they did so in a completely logical and rational manner. This then serves as a benchmark or standard of comparison against which to compare actual processes of decision-making.

BOX 2.3   A RATIONAL-COMPREHENSIVE MODEL OF DECISION-MAKING

1 Define and rank values.
2 Specify objectives compatible with these.
3 Identify all relevant options or means of achieving these objectives.
4 Calculate all the consequences of these options and compare them.
5 Choose the option or combination of options which could maximise the highest ranked values.

(Lindblom, 1959)

If such an approach to decision-making is treated as the paradigm for making public policy, then it is clear that few actual policy decisions are made in accordance with it. For example, Flitcroft *et al.* (2011) looked at the Australian federal government's policy to implement a national bowel cancer screening programme. They found that it is difficult to get empirical evidence into policy. They suggested a deliberative framework was required to encourage consultation.

One practical tool sometimes applied to a systematic and rational method of policy decision-making is cost-benefit analysis (CBA). This is an attempt to put monetary figures on the costs and benefits accruing from an investment over time. However, for public policy decisions there are problems in both establishing an agreed ranking of values and measuring outcomes.

The problem of interpreting organisational behaviour as if it is the product of rational decision-making by its top managers is illustrated by Allison (1987). Allison identified three possible models for explaining decision-making. His first was the rational actor model, in which he suggests that decision-makers' policies are designed to meet clear objectives. However, he rightly concludes that the rational approach to decision-making is a long way from empirical reality. For instance, in the 1962 Cuban Missile Crisis US policy-makers produced a series of hypotheses about 'Russian' behaviour in installing IRBMs (intermediate-range ballistic missiles) in uncamouflaged soft silos – none of which were very convincing because they assumed the behaviour was part of a single co-ordinated and rational policy.

Allison's second decision-making model, 'organisational process', stresses that organisations normally operate without explicitly defining organisational objectives. Rather, departments in organisations go on dealing with standard situations in their usual set ways without relating these to overall organisational objectives. This implies that there are a range of parochial decisions, not a single organisational approach.

Allison stressed organisational preference for avoiding the disruptive effects of uncertainty and conflict by concentrating on short-term problems rather than long-term planning by using 'rule of thumb' decision rules. This encourages incremental (bit by bit) changes, which is what Simon (1959) calls satisficing rather than optimising behaviour. Usually a small modification of standard operating procedures is introduced, rather than a new solution from a blank sheet.

Authors react to this (largely shared) perception of organisational decision-making in different ways. Allison is mainly concerned with formulating a realistic descriptive model of decision-making, whereas Lindblom (1959) argues that in a pluralist society incremental decision-making may be not only inevitable but also desirable. A third view is posited by Simon (1977), who made sophisticated suggestions for improving the management of organisations in the light of these observations.

Allison put forward a third model, 'governmental politics', which stresses that social decisions may often be more appropriately seen as political resultants rather than either individual rational choices or even organisational outputs. Essentially policy-making is seen as the outcome of a game between players occupying positions, the result of bargaining between players and dependent on (among other things) their bargaining skill, resources and the rules of the game.

Allison stressed the importance of mutual (mis)perceptions, the variety of stakes held by the players and the number of different issues being considered. Because of the complexity of the game players' actions are constantly focused on deadlines which have to be met by decisions – frequently made on the basis of inadequate information. One important maxim Allison stresses is 'Where you stand depends on where you sit', meaning that issues look radically different to players from different organisations or from different levels within the same organisation. Each player, too, will have made prior commitments to others within or outside the game and prefer a distinctive style of play.

Although this model is formulated primarily with US foreign policy-making in mind, an increasingly strong trend in the literature on organisations is to stress similar issues. In particular, writers like Ian Mangham (1979) have stressed the extent to which people in organisations pursue their own political (such as career) objectives, whilst others (e.g. Karpik, 1978) have emphasised that every organisation has an environment composed primarily of other organisations. Thus by negotiating with representatives of other organisations a more stable organisational world can be created.

What Allison reminds us is that many policy decisions are not taken in a bureaucratic vacuum but involve other players such as legislators and pressure groups. Critiquing how South Africa introduces new vaccinations, Ngcobo and Cameron (2012) noted that the three main policy-making bodies, the National Advisory Group on Immunisation, the National Department of Health and the Ministry of Finance, acted independently and there needed to be more deliberations between them.

Power is rarely absolute; one person or political body seldom exercises all the state's power. One idea that suggests there is a growing limitation to political power is that of 'hollowing out'. Rhodes (1994) argued that power is being given away from the core of government, so the capacity of the centre to steer the system is reduced. He identified four interrelated trends:

1 Privatisation
2 The loss of functions through local government reform
3 Globalisation
4 European integration.

The 'Westminster model', therefore, has lost power upwards to global and European bodies and downwards to the private sector and semi-governmental agencies. For Rhodes the idea of hollowing out is part of a wider trend in the direction of a fragmentation and disaggregation of power.

Saward (1997) tested Rhodes's thesis by looking at five countries, and suggested that there was some evidence to support it in terms of international trends. However, with regard to internal country-specific developments he suggested that there was a redefinition of the state, not a hollowing out. Thus, there was evidence of an external hollowing out, with national governments becoming more like local governments. However, we should note that Holliday (2000) rejects both viewpoints and finds no evidence that the British state is losing its grip on other institutions.

CONCLUSION

One interesting question is whether power is a fixed quantity or whether it can expand and contract depending on circumstances. The former would suggest that power is like a cake, with only so many slices available and unchanging volume. The latter implies it is more like a gas that can expand or contract, so that at some points in history those who hold power have more of it than at other points in history.

This chapter suggests that power is a contested concept, perhaps not surprisingly given its importance. Rather than trying to agree a single definition we have addressed the main ways in which political scientists look at the concept. While there is some common ground, we note significant differences in approaches, much of which can be explained by the different assumptions, methodology, weighting and analysis of commentators. Much of our understanding of the exercise of power can be explained by the psychological interaction between individuals, groups and political elites. Power as a concept is not static and it is as important to understand how power changes as it is to understand the exercising of power. In recent years there has been much interest in how the political hotspots of the world change their systems of government – often not so much a matter of ideological change but rather the means employed both internally and externally for replacing political elites and structures. The last area we have addressed reflects the modern global world, which challenges the existing premise of power residing within the set boundaries of the modern state. Power is an intangible concept which has tangible effects on all citizens.

FURTHER READING

Anderson, C. (2003) 'Power, approach and inhibition', *Psychological Review*, 110 (2): 265–284.

Bendor, J. and Hammond, T. (1992) 'Rethinking Allison's models', *American Political Science Review*, 86 (2): 301–322.

Cater, D. (1965) *Power in Washington: A Critical Look at Today's Struggle to Govern in the USA*, London: Collins.

Journal of Political Power, available at www.tandfonline.com/action/aboutThisJournal?show=readership& journalCode=rpow20.

Nye, J. (2011) *The Future of Power*, London: Perseus.

Posner, N. and Young, D. (2002) 'The institutionalization of political power in Africa', *Journal of Democracy*, 18 (3): 126-140.

Ricouer, P. (2010) 'Power and Violence', *Theory, Culture and Society*, 27 (5): 18–36.

Russell, B. (1938) *Power: A New Analysis*, London: George Allen & Unwin.

Schubert, J. (2010) '"Democratisation" and the consolidation of political authority in post-war Angola', *Journal of Southern African Studies*, 36(3): 657–672.

Scott, J. (2001) *Power*, Cambridge: Polity.
Tanter, R. and Midlarsky, M. (1967) 'A theory of revolution', *Journal of Conflict Resolution,* 11(3): 264–280.

WEBSITES

www.institutions-africa.org/
The Africa Power and Politics Programme considers good governance in Africa.

3

SYSTEMS

THIS CHAPTER ...

elaborates upon a point raised in Chapter 1: that politics is not an activity confined to modern liberal democratic national governments. In Chapter 1 we argued that politics can also be seen in personal and organisational activity; this chapter analyses the politics of societies without formal governments and the systems of government in kingdoms and empires before considering the focus of modern politics: the nation state. Most political systems are based on territory, but we shall also consider developments which might constitute a threat to the dominance of geographically based systems. Political 'system' is being used here in a loose sense to denote complex interconnecting political activities in society or societies – it does not imply the adoption of any particular system model.

As implied in both Chapters 1 and 2, there is a tendency in political science to focus almost exclusively on the state as the primary political system, and while the latter part of this chapter will assess modern nation states, we will start by considering other forms of political system. For many parts of the world this is primarily a historical study, assessing what countries were like before the modern nation state evolved. However, not all areas of the world are at the same level of development, and some of the forms we outline are still relevant to some societies. No political system is isolated – it exists with, shapes and is shaped by legal, economic and social systems; indeed, there is often a clear overlap between these different systems. Nor should a political system be viewed on its own: there are interconnections by which systems affect each other. Thus, war, economic trends and natural disasters such as famine can often be shared phenomena and will affect, and in turn be affected by, different societies.

By the end of this chapter students will be able to:

- challenge the assumption that the state is the only legitimate form of political system;
- identify the historical political developments which shape much of our understanding of modern political systems;
- assess the concept of the sovereign nation state;
- evaluate politics beyond the state within deterritorialisation.

STATES AND SOCIETIES

Before we explore politics beyond the state we need to explain what a state is. Max Weber (Weber in Gerth and Mills, 1948: 78) provides a working definition of an organisation 'that (successfully) claims the monopoly of the legitimate use of physical force within a given territory'.

This probably reflects the way most people see the world today. The globe is seen as divided into a series of exclusive geographical areas (countries or nations), each of which has a government and a people who recognise the government's authority to maintain order amongst them, by force in the last resort if necessary. This government may, of course, be divided into central, regional and local levels and executive, legislative and judicial arms, but all these bodies are seen as a system for taking decisions on behalf of the nation (or society) and maintaining law and order. A system, therefore, is seen to be a holistic organisation.

We shall return to the concept of the state in Chapter 5, but for now it is worth observing that it is assumed this is a geographical concept with clearly defined boundaries, with decisions being made within formal structures that inherently implies some people/

organisations/structures have authority over others. As we shall see, these assumptions are not necessarily the only ones indicating how societies may be politically organised. Moreover, at the end of the chapter we will challenge the geographical assumption.

POLITICS WITHOUT THE STATE: TRIBAL SOCIETIES

This system might appear outdated to many of us; however, we note that within living memory 'tribal' groups have been 'discovered' in the forests of Papua New Guinea and Brazil living apparently undisturbed by the governments which purport to represent them at the United Nations. More recently Scott (2009), looking at parts of South East Asia, suggests that there are societies which deliberatively seek statelessness.

Social anthropologists often avoid the use of 'tribal' in such contexts because it implies a condescending view of the peoples concerned as primitive. This is not our intention – rather we use a term that has a certain wide recognition. Many of the groups concerned have sophisticated cultures, high levels of artistic achievement and admirable ways of life. 'Tribal' is used here as an easily intelligible synonym for what anthropologists frequently term 'simple societies' – those having common cultures (e.g. one religion and language), undifferentiated role structures (most people do a small range of similar jobs), and a strong emphasis on kinship and custom (Mitchell, 1959). Following Weber, the defining characteristic of such societies may be taken to be a claim to common ancestry.

One way in which these groups differ from the state model of government is in terms of territory. While many such groups do have what they regard as their own territory, some are so nomadic that they can make no such claim. For example, the Kalahari Bushmen range broadly over deserts or forests which may also be used by other groups. They think of government as a property of what sociologists describe as the kin group – all the people descended from a common ancestor or married to such persons.

We also note an absence in some of them of anything resembling a fixed governmental organisation. While the absence of a chief or council might not be regarded as so strange in tiny groups such as the !Kung bushmen of the Kalahari desert (Marshall, 1961), it seems almost incredible in groups numbering as many as a million plus such as the pre-colonial Tiv of Nigeria (Bohannan, 1965).

How can centralised political institutions be avoided in such societies? One explanation lies in the attitude to law found in most tribal societies. Western societies (following the nineteenth-century English jurist Austin) tend to see law as the creation of a sovereign representative legislature. Tribal societies see law as a part of the way of life inherited from their ancestors. Thus, living human beings only interpret and enforce the authority of the ancestors and no legislature is necessary. Such a view is clearly only tenable in relatively stable societies – although, as Gluckman (1965) points out, rebellion against those interpreting the law is perfectly possible in such a system. What is unthinkable is the revolutionary process of replacing existing laws with new ones, though they can be reinterpreted in new circumstances or quietly ignored as being no longer appropriate.

We might reasonably ask: but does not the enforcement of law and defence of the group require centralised government? The example of the Tiv suggests one way round this problem. They operated what the social anthropologists term a 'segmentary lineage system'. This means basically that every Tiv's place in society is governed by the lineage to which they belong – i.e. how they are descended from the ancestor of the group 'Tiv'. It is not that the more closely related you are to the founder of the tribe the more important you are – there is no royal family since all are held to descend from the same source. Every Tiv is equal and a fierce egalitarianism reigns. Instead, in any dispute people claiming descent in the same line are expected to take the same side. Naturally, should a non-Tiv attack a Tiv, all members of the group would be expected to assist if necessary. If fighting or quarrelling takes place between Tiv, however, support would be offered to people in 'your' lineage.

Such a system might encourage conflict and disorder. If everyone can rely on a host of supporters in a dispute with others, this might make disputes become the norm. This might especially be the case when there are no established permanent tribal chiefs or headmen. In fact, the system seems to have worked well. One reason was the existence of a considerable consensus regarding the customs (laws) to be applied. Disputes were not automatically the cause of violence

or warfare but settled through meetings (or 'moots') of those concerned in the broad, Tiv, sense. After a certain amount of more or
less violent posturing, the form was for all to have their say on
the rights and wrongs of the dispute, with relatives helping the
aggrieved sides present their case. Then a resolution of the dispute
was attempted by mediation between the two lineages. The two
groups would remain 'at daggers drawn' until a solution was found.

In this situation a premium was placed on bargaining and
reconciliation rather than law enforcement. Many (on both sides)
might not feel too deeply affronted by (say) an alleged case of
adultery, failure to pay up on a dowry payment, or words said in a
drunken brawl. But everyone would be severely inconvenienced if
another lineage in the village was not prepared to co-operate in the
next hunt or harvest. An additional subtlety was the consideration
that your opponents in this dispute might be needed in a larger
dispute with more distantly related Tiv at some time in the future.

The Tiv are only one example of numerous tribal societies that
have existed without centralised governmental institutions. Other
societies practised a division of functions on an 'age grade' basis in
which, for instance, the oldest men might collectively manage
relationships with the gods, another male age group constitute the
leaders of the hunt, the oldest women practise medicine, and so on.
In some groups important functions connected with warfare, law
and order or magic might be vested in secret or title societies,
membership of which had to be earned by giving feasts to existing
members, undergoing initiation ceremonies, and performing subordinate roles in a trainee grade. In such societies skill in magic or
warfare might be rewarded by promotion 'on merit', or promotion
might depend on seniority.

Authority in such societies might rest upon a variety of founda-
tions – a reputation for wisdom in settling disputes, knowledge of
traditional remedies for illness, ability as a war leader, or merely
being the grandparent of a very large family. Such authority figures
might well be known by a title which translates into English
as 'chief', but their powers were often far from the absolute
despotisms imagined by many early Western writers on this subject.

In these tribal 'stateless societies' there is law rather than anarchy
(in the everyday sense of no guarantees of law and order); equally,
collective decisions on self-defence and economic co-operation are

also made, but in a decentralised fashion. It is not surprising that, consequently, some modern thinkers – anarchists in the technical sense – have argued that the same is possible in a modern context.

FEUDALISM

One form of government which probably no longer exists but which has shaped the world many of us live in is feudalism. Put simply, feudalism is a form of government which places a king (or on very rare occasions a queen) at the top, but he or she cannot rule without the help of a select body of nobles, who in turn provide a military in the form of a larger body of knights; at the bottom peasants provide the bulk of the population. This largely agrarian society is socially rigid, movement between the sectors is rare and typically linked to service given during conflict. There is also typically some system of tax collection alongside the socio-political structure, though this is often in kind rather than monetary. Feudalism is very much an elite-based political system, with power held in the hands of a very few.

The feudal system is most often associated with Europe between the ninth and fourteenth centuries, though it was probably strongest in the eleventh and twelfth centuries. It has however been seen to apply to other parts of the world as well, for instance pre-modern Japan (Reischaur, 1956; Prawer and Eisenstadt, 1968), and although widely considered to have been replaced as a political system by the fifteenth century in Europe, it could be argued that it did not end in Russia until the 1861 Emancipation Manifesto or in America until the passing of the thirteenth amendment of the Constitution abolishing slavery in 1865.

European feudalism is of interest as being perhaps 'nearer to home' for contemporary European readers. It shows us that the state as we know it is a more recent innovation than some have imagined. It may also suggest some lessons for the future of Europe.

At first sight, feudal Europe was full of states and mini-states, rather than stateless. Familiar modern-day states such as England, France and Poland existed in this period, although admittedly there were extra 'players' on the international scene we would no longer recognise as states, such as Burgundy, Saxony and Venice. The appearance of kings, dukes and doges on the scene would seem to indicate the presence of strong centralised decision-making institutions for these territories. The presence of names with institutions and territories of later periods may well, however, be quite misleading. Outside of England and France it soon becomes clear that the idea of a number of territories each with its own legal jurisdiction is quite inappropriate.

This is clearest in the area around what is now Germany, misleadingly called the Holy Roman Empire (accurately described as neither 'Holy', 'Roman' nor an 'Empire' by Voltaire (1694–1778)), (1756: Ch. LXX). The 'Holy Roman Emperor' was the nominal supreme ruler of a hotchpotch of kingdoms, dukedoms, sovereign bishoprics, independent or federated cities and the like. His powers over each were different and ill-defined. The Catholic Church, in the shape of the Pope, claimed powers over the emperor and his 'vassals' (those who had sworn allegiance to him), which in later times were felt to be 'sovereign' prerogatives. Equally, the Church claimed exclusive jurisdiction over all the clergy and many matters of family law – as well as rights to censorship and the levying of separate clerical 'taxes'. In some cases incumbents of independent kingdoms such as France and Spain held territory within the Empire as nominal vassals of the emperor or some other 'ruler'. Similar confusions were to be seen in the relationship between the king of England in his capacity as duke of Normandy and the king of France.

Law enforcement and defence were subject to a patchwork of rights and privileges, the consequence of a pyramid of personal relationships between lords and vassals. Each vassal was, in turn, lord to an inferior group of aristocrats, until one descends to the level of the ordinary knight in his manor. At the aristocratic level the possession of land entailed not only something like the modern idea of ownership but also the notion of government. In principle, in the early feudal period, land could only be held by those prepared to administer and, most importantly, defend it. If, for instance, the king gave land to a duke, the only way the duke could hope to hold on to it was by sub-contracting the administration and defence of much of it to a group of earls or counts. Each earl or count, in turn, would obtain the allegiance of knights to hold particular manors or fortified villages.

One consequence of this was an overlapping of jurisdictions: in our example a single area might be under the control of a king, a duke, a count and a knight. In addition, the Church would undoubtedly claim jurisdiction in some cases. For that matter it was common for hard-up lords to grant jurisdiction in commercial matters to town councils through charters – the terms of which some councils in Britain still preserve and attempt to enforce.

In the feudal period, as in tribal stateless societies, conflicts over the allocation of resources could be resolved and communities could make decisions about their defence and economic welfare, but no effective centralised state machinery existed to carry this out.

It is interesting to note that vestiges of this feudal system remained long after the political system itself was replaced. Thus in June 2000 the Scottish parliament passed the Abolition of Feudal Tenure, etc. (Scotland) Act, which was designed to remove the feudal system of land tenure. Under this a vassal did not own the land outright but held it based on terms set by a feudal superior, ultimately the Crown. The 2000 act effectively removed this idea of superiority interests.

When the Scottish parliament was repealing a feudal law relating to economic land rights, there still existed in Europe a feudal political system. In 2008 the tiny Channel Island of Sark, a British Crown dependency and so not part of the UK, became the last state in Europe to end its feudal political system. Sark had been governed by the Chief Pleas, comprising 40 landowners and headed by the Seigneur who was responsible to the Crown. Replacing this system with an elected Chief Pleas was the result of a conflict between old and new political systems. In part the change reflected the view that the old system was in possible breach of human rights laws, but it probably owed more to a court case brought by the newspaper owners, the Barclay brothers, who owned the tiny island of Brecqhou which was subject to Sark's laws. We can, therefore, see some remnants of the agrarian feudal system in a modern industrial state system.

STATES WITHOUT NATIONS: KINGDOMS

At a later stage in European history, some individual feudal territories evolved over several centuries into something much more like the modern state. Kingdoms emerged with distinct boundaries within which central authorities claimed exclusive jurisdiction, sophisticated judicial systems with rights of appeal from local courts up to the top, a taxation system divorced from the rents payable to the owners of land, and, in some cases, representative legislative assemblies. Part of the attraction of the Protestant Reformation for princes was the opportunity to both assert legal control over matters such as family law which had previously been Church matters and reassign Church property holdings. Henry VIII's example in these matters was accompanied by similar phenomena in countries such as Sweden, while even Catholic monarchs such as Louis XIV began to assert control over religious orders and negotiate greater influence over the Church in their territory.

By definition, a kingdom can be regarded as an example of dynastic politics – government by families, not individuals. In the European examples this usually meant that the state was regarded as the possession of a single family, regardless of geographical sense or ethnic or national origins. Thus the modern United Kingdom includes Scotland, Wales and parts of Ireland, as well as the Channel Isles, because the kings of England inherited these areas from the Duchy of Normandy, succeeded to the separate throne of Scotland, or conquered adjacent lands. The kingdom was not united by linguistic, cultural or religious similarities. Similarly, Belgium and Holland were regarded as possessions of the Spanish royal family.

In African kingdoms such as Benin, Yorubaland and Hausaland, the family's role took very different shapes. Within the context of polygamy, there was more scope for disputes over succession. Such disputes took the most drastic form in Zululand, where it was usual for the king to execute any brothers who failed to go into hasty voluntary exile (Lemarchand, 1977). In the Yoruba kingdoms a version of the succession crisis involved 'king-makers' selecting the heir from the ranks of a number of princely families who each provided a king in turn.

These monarchical political systems shared a 'court' style of politics in which the administration of the royal household and its estates was inseparable from the business of the kingdom as a whole. Power in such systems might well reside with those who had the ear of the monarch regardless of official position. This might include the king's mistress, confessor or hairdresser. Rose (2011) notes that a series of advisors would seek to shape the character of the monarch in order to defend their interests. The king therefore might have absolute power, but he required counsellors to help him rule.

The politics of such a system emphasises individual advancement through patronage; a powerful patron rewards his supporters and followers with benefits derived from his control or influence over government that might well be regarded as corruption in a contemporary democracy.

The assumption may often be made that a monarchic state is a 'despotic' one in which the monarch's will is final. This seems far from the case in practice. First, the tradition that places the king in power frequently sets distinct limits on the exercise of it. The king may be seen as divinely sanctioned and protected, but this implies that he respects the religious feelings of his people. These may be expressed by religious authorities – archbishops, high priests or synods – which are regarded as legitimate within their spheres as the monarch is in his. There are examples of the sort of limitations that might apply in the important area of taxation. In the African kingdoms mentioned, Hausa kings were traditionally entitled to levy taxes, but the Yoruba kings could only rely on a traditional level of offerings on specified occasions.

The limits to the exercise of royal power also include the lack of any strongly developed administrative machinery, particularly at local level, so that the king might effectively have to persuade nobles/gentry and municipalities to co-operate. The political capacity of the occupant of the throne was also a vital consideration. When minors succeeded to the throne, such a system might, in effect, become government by a committee of prominent court members, while the chief minister of a foolish or lazy king might easily hold effective power. In the Japanese case, the shogun (or prime minister) became the effective power for centuries, turning it into a hereditary office.

The dominance for centuries of this type of political organisation in many parts of the world is a caution against assuming contemporary state forms are inevitable. Although kingdoms of the type described are now rare, they are not extinct and can be found in Kuwait, Nepal and Saudi Arabia. One example of a kingdom where there has recently been political tension is Bahrain, which has been ruled by the Al Khalifa family since 1783 (Katzman,

2013). It would however be wrong to assume that this tension can be viewed simply as anti-kingdom; much of the 2011 uprising was caused by how Shiite aspirations are met within a largely Sunni-dominated political system.

One trait characteristic of kingdoms which has been adopted and adapted by some modern political systems is the existence of political dynasties. Since India achieved independence in 1947 there have been three prime ministers from the same family, the Gandhis. Jawaharla Nehru was followed in this role by his daughter Indira Gandhi and her son Rajiv Gandhi. In the US, several members of the Kennedy family have played key political roles since the 1960s, and George Bush and his son George W. Bush have both been elected president. Indeed, some critics believe that George W.'s brother Jed as governor of Florida played a key role in helping him win the 2000 presidential election. Dal Bo *et al.* (2009) argue that political dynasties have long been present in democracies; they conducted empirical research of the US Congress and found political power is self-perpetuating: legislators who hold power for longer are more likely to have relatives who also enter Congress.

STATES WITHOUT NATIONS: EMPIRES

Perhaps still more remote from contemporary experience is the concept of empire. Yet this form of rule has dominated large parts of the globe for millennia. The most notable examples are the ancient empires of China and Rome. But similar structures were to be found in India (e.g. the Moghul Empire), in Africa (Egypt and Mali), and in Central and South America (e.g. the Aztecs). Nor should it be forgotten that, more recently, a number of European nations sought to create colonial empires in Africa, Asia and the Americas, while the US and the former USSR could both be accused of having colonial possessions by other names.

An empire, especially in the eyes of the title holder, if there is one, might be considered a step up in importance from a kingdom. This is especially the case if individual kings are required to recognise an emperor. Traditional empires are based on a central dominant kingdom, with smaller, supplicant kingdoms around it. Since the nineteenth century, however, direct geographical connections via shared borders have not always been the basis for empires: economic power enables more geographically dispersed empires.

It is tempting, and not totally misleading, to attribute the longevity of many empires to the military advantage of a large and powerful state surrounded by much smaller states or tribal territories. While empires may briefly be built on military advantage alone – as, perhaps, was that of Alexander the Great – the longer-lasting examples can be attributed not only to military size but also to the advantages of a 'civilized' culture. This, in the literal sense, means a society centred on relatively large urban centres containing specialised personnel who contribute technical and organisational advantages to the empire. The prestige and self-esteem associated with such systems may well help them to survive. Certainly the ruling groups of the Chinese, Roman and British empires were firmly convinced of the superiority of their cultural inheritance and successfully imparted this ideology to many of their subjects and neighbours. However, this conviction did not prevent such systems from adopting and adapting to useful features of surrounding societies.

The history of China is particularly noteworthy for the way in which the empire was militarily subdued on a number of occasions by warlike tribes from the periphery of the empire. However, the conquerors on each occasion came to be merely a new ruling group operating a very similar political system to the one they had defeated (Eberhard, 1977). The adaptability of the Romans is well illustrated by their reaction to Greek culture in the early period and the transformation of a classical empire based on Rome into a Byzantine Christian empire based on Constantinople. One vital feature of such systems is the way the rulers must be prepared to tolerate linguistic, cultural and religious diversity, providing subjects are prepared to make the necessary political compromises to meet the primary needs of the empire.

Such empires have generally been characterised by the development of an extensive cash economy, permitting complex economic exchanges over long distances. These same distances have required efficient means of communication among the 'civil servants' of the empire, who must also be capable of working together in a coordinated fashion. The empire can only survive militarily by deploying its military resources over long distances to optimum effect. Thus, a literate population and a bureaucracy as well as good roads (or a navy) and professional soldiers become a necessity.

The Chinese mandarinate is a good illustration of the importance of professional soldiers, a good transport system and literacy. China was unified by an administrative pyramid of mandarins, linking the court and the rural districts, who were required to pass examinations in a common core of knowledge. Good government was mainly seen in terms of political stability rather than social or economic progress. Despite this, some writers stress the role of the Chinese bureaucracy in regulating the drainage and waterway system of China just as the Egyptian priesthood served the pharaoh, made sacrifices to the gods, and controlled the waters of the Nile through an elaborate drainage system (Wittfogel, 1957). Whatever the usefulness of the services they performed, it is clear that the cohesion of the system was vastly assisted by the common origins, knowledge and attitudes of these administrators, who were amongst the first who could reasonably be described as 'bureaucrats'.

One final point is worth emphasising: the contrast between the ancient empires and the nineteenth- and twentieth-century European colonial empires in terms of their attitudes towards their subjects. Basically this may be encapsulated in one rather nasty word – racism. The European empires were increasingly based on a core metropolitan state that claimed to be a nation and often a democracy. The empire was a separate area of colonies whose dependence on the metropolitan area could only be easily justified by an allegation of the inhabitants' incapacity to rule themselves. Nineteenth-century anthropologists' findings were used and abused to justify a doctrine of the racial or cultural inferiority of 'coloured' people compared with the 'white' race. In theory, official attitudes might not quite go so far as to allege permanent inferiority on the part of the governed. British policy was based in principle on grooming colonies for self-governing 'dominion' status (like the white ex-colonies of Australia, New Zealand and Canada), while the French were much more prepared to accord equal right to 'natives' if they assimilated French culture and behaved like black Frenchmen. However, the Nazi view of the permanent inferiority of 'non-Aryan' races probably reflected the practice of European colonial residents more accurately for most of the nineteenth and early twentieth centuries. The near extermination of the aboriginal inhabitants of Tasmania and the South African colonists' doctrine of apartheid are extreme examples of these attitudes at work.

In contrast to this, the Chinese restricted their empire mainly to groups who could be assimilated into the Chinese way of life, while viewing groups outside the empire as racially and culturally inferior. The Romans extended Roman citizenship to a number of other urban centres and made no systematic discrimination between Italian, Greek or African subjects of the empire.

Hardt and Negri (2000) provide a postmodern alternative construct to the nation state, namely empire. The idea fits within a global world and the core components include international organisations such as NATO, the International Monetary Fund (IMF) and the G8, as well as multinational commercial corporations. Within this form of globalisation they suggest that the enemy is not ideological or national, rather it is some sort of criminal or terrorist.

We have looked at each of these historical systems and, as noted in Table 3.1, it is possible to identify some progression from one to the next, though they also have differences which suggest more

Table 3.1 Political system characteristics

System	Power sources	Power structures	Organisation	Central beliefs	Economy
Tribal	Kin	Decentralised	Non-territorial co-operation	Importance of ancestors	Hunter-gatherer Agrarian
Feudal	King and aristocracy	Hierarchical and stratified Localised	Basic tax collection system Territorial (but probably small)	Everyone has their place	Agrarian
Kingdom	The king Patronage	Dynasty – government by families Limits to king's power	Distinct boundaries More sophisticated bureaucracy	Importance of military strength Basic idea of nationhood	Agrarian (but with some industry)
Empire	The emperor Military strength	Vassal kingdoms	Sophisticated bureaucracy Good communications	Cultural superiority of the lead kingdom	Agrarian (but likely to have more industrial than kingdoms)

radical departures. We can see that what is unique to tribal political systems is the importance of kin/family, both the dead and the living. Feudalism marks a significant change in that it is a highly stratified, pre-determined society which does not encourage social change. A feudal society is probably geographically small, with a kingdom a step up in size and with an enhanced ability to collect taxes and implement policy. Perhaps more importantly, kingdoms introduced the idea of rule by the family in terms of both who holds the key political posts and the succession. Empires are a progression from kingdoms in terms of economy, military strength and bureaucracy, but they also add new characteristics. An empire implies that there is a ruler above individual kings, the emperor, the land mass involved is far greater and communications and transport have to be much more effective. Thus different political systems generally borrow traits from previous systems but add their own uniqueness.

THE NATION STATE AND SOVEREIGNTY

Although an infinitesimally small part of the earth's population may still live in stateless societies, there are some remains of feudalism and kingdoms and empires still exist, the vast majority of us live in a modern state.

Earlier we took the state to be, in Weber's words, an organisation 'that (successfully) claims the monopoly of the legitimate use of physical force within in a given territory'. We suggested that the model of a world dominated by sovereign 'nation states' is a relatively new and arguable one. Europe did not look much like this until about 1919, after the Treaty of Versailles. Africa only came near fitting the model from the 1960s. Countries like the United Kingdom and, until recently, the Soviet Union and Yugoslavia are (or were) clearly multinational. The Antarctic remains the subject of (frozen!) conflicting claims to jurisdiction.

Although nation states are difficult to come by in practice, the predominant view of the state today, as incorporated in the concept of the United Nations and in international law, is that of the 'sovereign state'. State legitimacy is based mainly on the idea that each nation has a right to self-determination. The people of a nation are thus seen to consent to the establishment of a government over them which support a system of law appropriate to their culture and traditions. This idea came clearly to the fore in human history only with the French and American revolutions at the end of the eighteenth century.

The model of government in which a nation makes decisions through the state machinery may be helpful in justifying the establishment of self-governing democratic systems in opposition to alien or autocratic rule. Arguably it becomes an obstacle to understanding the working of a modern, sophisticated liberal democratic state, which is usually divided into executive, legislative and judicial arms and central, local and regional levels of government. The outcome of the constitutional working of these specific institutions of government can be regarded as 'the nation's' decision. An oversimplification that is, however, often put forward is that some individual element in the constitutional structure is the body which incorporates the national will. In the French tradition there has been a tendency to see the National Assembly as that body. The Soviet tradition was to see the Communist Party in that position. In the liberal tradition, however, the distinction between the government of the day and the state – between opposition and treason – is a clear and vital one. Wittman (1991) argues that a number of contemporary (to him) international disputes, such as those of Northern Ireland, Eritrea and Hong Kong, were issues of sovereignty. To this we could add occasional disagreements between the UK and Spain over Gibraltar. Moreover, Wittman suggests that the consolidation or dissolution of nations can be explained by economic theory. In particular he draws an analogy from how firms acquire others, and suggests that countries should merge when their economic value is greater as a unified entity than as separate sovereign states. This argument is germane to the recent discussions led primarily by the Scottish National Party (SNP) as to whether Scotland should be independent from the rest of the UK.

The idea of sovereignty is central to understanding relations between states. One interesting idea explaining the link between the two is offered by Branch (2011). He suggests that advances in mapping techniques during early modern Europe gave sovereign statehood its territorially exclusive character. Improvements in cartography led to the modern state because it drove the need for centralisation and bureaucracy and encouraged territorial security to move from the town/city to control of a mapped linear space. This change, he argues, explains both conflict and co-operation between states.

POLITICS BETWEEN STATES

In Chapter 6 we shall consider inter-state politics in more depth, but for now we shall briefly address the idea of politics between states. If we conceive of the world in terms of the nation-state model, then international politics looks much more like the politics of stateless societies than the internal politics of states. That is, there is something called international law, but no final authority to enforce, interpret or change it. Although the United Nations can be seen as a potential world legislature/government, it is at present based on the theory that individual states possess 'sovereignty' and are the final arbiters of what goes on within their territories. All powers of international organisations, including the United Nations, are held to depend upon the agreement by states of treaties authorising such powers.

Thus, politics at an international level can be seen to depend on compromise and negotiation rather than on authoritative decision-making by representative organs. In legal theory, Monaco is as sovereign as the United States, and both are equally free to turn to force in the last resort to defend their national interests. In practice it is clear that smaller states, with fewer military and economic resources to back up their bargaining, are more dependent on perhaps insubstantial international respect for law and treaty obligations. In addition, smaller states may be heavily dependent on a single, larger neighbour for economic and other support and to the outsider may seem one and the same: examples might be Andorra and Spain, Monaco and France, and San Marino and Italy. From the point of view of the study of politics, international relations offers a particular challenge, since the processes of decision-making are often even more obscure than at national level and the consequences potentially more profound. Traditionally historians tended to describe international relations in terms of the decisions of individual statesmen pursuing, more or less intelligently, 'the national interest', which was often related to the 'balance of power' between nations. Thus international relations can be seen as a game played between more or less rational players, generally of what we previously termed the 'zero-sum' variety – more power for one nation being gained at the expense of less for another, with skilful players achieving goals by forming winning coalitions.

Seeing international relations as a competitive spectator sport neglects the importance of consensual, non-zero-sum goals in international relations. It is more important to ordinary citizens that everyone stays alive and continues in mutually beneficial economic and trading activities than that they belong to a state which is more powerful than the others.

This in turn relates to the question of the 'national interest'. We have seen the difficulty in defining a nation – e.g. can it be assumed that someone from Hong Kong has the same interests as someone from the Tibetan Highlands? Similarly, professional politicians may experience much more satisfaction from being part of a powerful state than a simple peasant might. Again if, say, in the nineteenth century, British investor rights in some Latin American country were safeguarded at the cost of a number of sailors' lives, does the safe-guarding of one group's (relatively large) income justify the loss of several poor men's lives? The 'national interest', then, may obscure domestic conflicts of interest by wrapping them in the national flag.

To describe national policy-making in terms of individuals making choices may be a vast over-simplification, as Allison's (1987) work makes clear. Looking at the 1962 Cuban missile crisis he argued that for a full picture of the foreign-policy process, decision-making must be seen as part of processes of organisational decision-making and political bargaining. More recently, similar arguments could be applied to the Bush administration's decision to invade Iraq in 2003 and when the Obama administration in 2011 enforced a no-fly zone in Libya.

POLITICS BEYOND TERRITORY

Thus far we have looked at politics inherently linked to some form of territory, which implies the importance of boundaries. However, the nascent discipline of geopolitics looks beyond such boundaries to consider the reality and implications of a deterritorialised politics. Here it is not automatically assumed that politics can only take place within a set geography; rather, alternative spaces exist. Such a concept is often associated with globalisation, which we shall return to in Chapter 6, but for now we will consider the possible impact of the resurgence of ethical and national identities, technological change, environmental concerns and migration patterns (for more detail see Newman, 1998).

The term deterritorisation is often associated with Gilles Deleuze and Félix Guattari in their 1972 book *Capitalism and Schizophrenia (Anti-Oedipus)*, in which a territory is seen as an ever-changing 'assemblage', which forms and then is replaced by something else, hence the deterritorisation. For example, this would explain the break-up of the Soviet Union and the territorial restructuring of Eastern Europe. Thus, what Deleuze and Guattari were considering is the replacement of one form of territorial politics by another – that is, reterritorisation replacing deterritorisation. However, what we are evaluating in terms of deterrorisation has a different meaning, and we are not considering reterritorialisation because this is essentially based on territory. For political scientists deterritorisation means replacing political practice that is based on physical space by one that is not. For some commentators deterritorisation may mean the end of nation state and map-based boundaries and their replacement by a borderless world. However, for the authors it simply means that some aspects of politics are not to be found only within the confines of a physical boundary. As Newman (1998) suggests, national boundaries are increasingly permeable.

The idea of deterritorisation has grown since the late 1990s because territory has begun to lose its meaning or salience for some social, economic and political problems. Toal (1998: 139) defines the term as 'the rearranging and restructuring of spatial relations as a consequence of technological, material and geopolitical transformations'. This suggests that with recent developments within an increasing global world space is not automatically the stable force it once was. In particular, the logic of this is that while the state may still be the solution to most problems, its appropriateness is being questioned for some challenges. Toal suggests that the Clinton Doctrine of the US presidency under Bill Clinton in the early 1990s was centred on deterritorisation. Here the solution to increasing globalisation, borderless worlds and the nascent information age was deemed to be 'market democracies'.

Technology, especially in the form of the Internet, is deemed to be one of the key drivers for deterritorisation. Although one could argue that there are some national 'boundaries' online in the form of URL addresses for websites, and the protocols in some countries such as North Korea prevent full access to the World Wide Web, the Internet can create transnational communities. Those with the same interests or political views, who may live anywhere in the world, can share their viewpoints, prejudices, experiences or whatever. The potential impact is to create semi-formal networks which may challenge the state, both within a country and internationally. Indeed, Gregg (2012) posits a normative viewpoint that the existence of the Internet can create a post-national identity, what he refers to as a 'human rights state'. He suggests that we could move from collective allegiance based on people, culture and language to one based instead on individual freedom, legal equality and human rights. This is probably a utopian view, but it does highlight the potential wider global political impact that the Internet might have.

One of the other main drivers behind deterrorisation is the global response to terrorism. The term terrorism is a highly emotive one, and we can be faced with the issue of one person's terrorist being another's freedom fighter. Typically this debate relates to an individual state and its citizens; however, we will not try to define what is or is not a terrorist, rather our focus is on terrorists that owe allegiance not to a state but a borderless ideal. Certainly, since 9/11 and the terrorist attack on mainland America many states have focused significant resources on this. It may be a contestable point for some, but it can be argued that terrorist groups such as Al Qaeda believe in a non-territorial ideal; certainly they are not located in a single state area. According to Behr (2008), this creates a paradox for nation states simply because they are not dealing with other states, as the threat does not come from a defined territory. In order to effectively combat transnational terrorism states have to evolve 'deterritorised strategies', which in turn promote some concept of deterritorisation. So collectively states may have to use an approach to deal with one threat that could weaken their overall position by creating new norms.

CONCLUSION

The more international relations are analysed, the less important the differences between international and domestic politics seem to be.

As we shall see in Chapter 6, it can be argued that explaining relationships between member states and the EU (European Union) is very like explaining relationships between the states and the Federal Government in the US. Equally, insights from domestic politics, or even the politics of stateless societies, can be of relevance to international politics.

To return to the theme introduced at the beginning of this chapter, the evidence presented suggests that politics in the broad sense as we defined it in Chapter 1 is a more or less universal aspect of life in human societies. Strictly speaking we have not established this, only produced evidence that politics is widespread in many human societies. But we have established that centralised national governments – although a dominating feature of modern western societies – are by no means inevitable.

There is a clear link across our different classifications of political system. The modern empire has had a major impact on several of the others. For much of the world the state had little or no meaning until the European empire grab by Germany, Britain, France, Belgium, Italy and Spain in the nineteenth century. Then, due to the creation of empires in vast swathes of Africa, South America and Asia, physical boundaries came to have a political importance and rigidity that they did not have before. Indeed, it is possible to argue that deterritorialisation led by the growth of globalisation may create some of the social and cultural conditions that were in place hundreds of years ago.

FURTHER READING

Anderson, B. (1991) *Imagined Communities: Reflections on the Origin and Spread of Nationalism*, London: Verso.

Easton, D. (1957) 'An approach to the analysis of political systems', *World Politics*, 9: 383–401.

Finer, S. E. (1997) *A History of Government*, Oxford: Oxford University Press.

Fortes, M. and Evans-Pritchard, E. (1961) *African Political Systems*, Oxford: Oxford University Press.

Hix, S. and Hoyland, B. (2011) *The Political System of the European Union*, Basingstoke: Palgrave Macmillan.

Leach, E. (2008) *Political Systems of Highland Burma: A Study of Kachin Social Structure*, ACLS Humanities E-Book Project.

WEBSITES

www.fordham.edu/halsall/sbook.html
Internet Medieval Sourcebook of Fordham University Center for Medieval Studies (for Feudalism).
www.fride.org/eng/Publications/publication.aspx?item=787
Factual information on the political systems and governments of specific Arab countries.
http://pdba.georgetown.edu
Political database of the Americas provides information on the political systems of the Caribbean, Latin and South America.

IDEOLOGIES

THIS CHAPTER ...

is about the 'isms' of politics: conservatism, liberalism, socialism, Marxism, fascism and so on. It considers not only the general nature of these broad currents of political thinking, but also gives some idea of the relationship these have had with political regimes, parties and individual politicians. It addresses some ideologies that have only recently come to prominence in the West – communitarianism, feminism, 'ecologism' and Islamic 'fundamentalism'. The chapter begins with the concept of 'ideology' itself and how useful it may be. It then considers how ideologies may be classified and looks at what might be broadly regarded as the right, continuing with the left and ending with the centre.

We have already noted that politics matters, that most aspects of our daily lives are affected by political decisions, and it is in this context that we need to understand ideology. The political systems, structures and policies which you see as the norm for your society need not be – a range of different solutions to problems are possible. This is where ideology comes in: what is the possible current and future direction that politics should take? This assumes that the political elite does not use power in the form of power over, rather power to. In other words, the purpose of political activity is to achieve some greater ideal beyond just self-interest. Ideology, therefore, acts as the compass that directs political activity. The absence of ideology leads either to popularism, where politicians deliver the short-term gratifications that they think the population wants with limited recourse to wider beliefs of what is right and wrong, or decisions made solely in the interest of the decision-maker. Ideology provides the basic principles upon which political elites claim to base their actions. By the end of this chapter readers will be able to:

- understand the meaning of ideology;
- assess the development of the key traditional isms;
- assess the meaning and relevance of most recent isms.

IDEOLOGY

'Ideology' is a widely used but difficult term to interpret. One school of thought led by Karl Popper (1962) interprets 'ideology' as a way of political thinking typical of totalitarian movements: an all-encompassing and closed system of thought. Not only does such a system have something to say about virtually all political, social and moral issues, but it is virtually impossible to disprove because there is always an explanation, within the terms of the ideology, for any apparent deviation from its predictions. Thus for some (perhaps crude) Marxists the revolution is always 'imminent' – and when it fails to come about it is because the revolution was betrayed by its leaders, objective social conditions were misinterpreted, or capitalism found new outlets for its surpluses.

For Popper, then, ideological thinking should be opposed to scientific theorising, which always produces falsifiable hypotheses. A scientific approach to social matters consists in developing piece-meal explanations about how things work and testing them out – not in having a grand theory that explains everything. To make political judgements, however, people must also employ judgements about values, which are specific to them and cannot be resolved by looking at evidence. Political innovation therefore depends upon building a consensus regarding values between the people concerned, as well as correctly interpreting cause and effect. Consequently,

rather than building some grand Utopia on the basis of first principles, social change should proceed by means of 'piece-meal social
engineering' (Popper, 1960: 64).

From this point of view the political doctrines of the centre,
democratic socialism, liberalism and conservatism are all non-
ideological since they accept the need to base social policy on as
scientific as possible a review of its effects and the value-judgements
of the members of the community affected.

However, ideology can be used in a looser way to mean
any set of cohesive political principles. In this sense, liberalism,
socialism and conservatism can also be described as 'ideologies', and
this is the sense in which we have used the term in this chapter.
Marxists tend to use the word to suggest the dominant ideas of a
society, which they see as reflecting its means of production and
therefore the exercise of power. Thus, from many points of view
liberalism may fairly be described as the ideology of the capitalist era.
As with many political terms no definitive use of the concept
can be prescribed – McClellan (1986) notes 27 different interpretations of the term. What we identify here has three main
interpretations:

1 Popper – an all-encompassing and closed system of thought.
2 Broad sense – a coherent set of political principles.
3 Marxist – the dominant ideas in society reflect the means of
   production.

'RIGHT' VERSUS 'LEFT'

It is conventional to classify political movements and thinkers as
right-wing or left-wing. This apparently derives from the first
French National Assembly, when the pro-monarchist conservatives
sat on the right and the revolutionary republicans sat on the left of a
semi-circular assembly hall. The European and modern French
parliaments adopt a similar seating pattern to this day. Such a
classification can be controversial – the European Parliament groups
have often asserted they are to the left of the position that others
see them in. Clearly, what is radical and left-wing in one context
(e.g. republicanism in British colonial North America) can become

conservatism in another time or place (e.g. republicanism in the modern United States).

Generally speaking, however, the right is seen as against political, economic and social change, the left in favour of it. The right tends to be monarchist and clerical and favours the interests of the established propertied classes, while the left is identified with republicanism, anti-clericalism and the interests of the masses (workers or peasants).

The 'left'/'right' distinction is a shaky one – it conflates three different distinctions in attitudes:

1 The degree of change to the 'status quo' – in favour of or against change to the present situation.
2 The direction of change – in favour of or against capitalism, clericalism or some other key political value.
3 The method of change – constitutional or revolutionary.

In terms of the conventional linear distinction as outlined in Figure 4.1, fascism and communism may be seen as occupying opposite extremes, with liberal democrats at the centre. An alternative to the traditional linear model is the circular model in Figure 4.2. Here the extremes of fascism and communism are not at opposite ends but actually next to one another in the circle, because they share similar totalitarian traits.

THE OLD RIGHT: MONARCHISM

Monarchism might be seen in a medieval European context as a centrist rather than a right-wing ideology. Certainly, conventional Catholic thought has been happy to acknowledge the legitimacy of princes. The normal situation in medieval Europe was of secular government by kings or emperors who were crowned by the Pope or by archbishops authorised by him.

This was formalised in the theological and political doctrine of the 'Two Swords' – secular and clerical authority supporting each other and respecting each other's spheres of influence. In effect there was a division of powers.

It was only after the development of the modern idea of state sovereignty (e.g. by Bodin in his *Republic* of 1576) and especially

CONVENTIONAL VIEW

Marxist	Anarchist	Socialist	Liberal	Conservative	Monarchist	Fascist

LEFT	Degree of Change	RIGHT
	Direction of Change	
	Method of Change	

LIBERAL VIEW

Liberal	Conservative	Socialist	Fascist/Marxist

CONSTITUTIONAL	REVOLUTIONARY
INDIVIDUALISM	COLLECTIVISM

ANARCHIST VIEW

Anarchist	Monarchist	Liberal	Conservative	Socialist	Fascist	Marxist

LEFT	(By Degree of State Use of Force)	RIGHT

Figure 4.1 Classifying ideologies

after the assumption of leadership over the Christian church in their countries by Protestant kings (starting with Henry VIII) that the more radical idea of the divine right of kings became established. As parliamentary forces in seventeenth-century England increasingly stressed the idea of popular sovereignty, the Stuart kings were increasingly attracted to the idea that countries could only have one

Figure 4.2 The circular model of ideology

sovereign and that sovereigns held authority from God not man. In countries like France where republics were founded, the restoration of the power of an executive, rather than figurehead, monarchy became increasingly the trade mark of anti-democratic and ultra-conservative forces.

In other countries that retained a monarchy, a pro-monarchist position might be combined with a more moderate stance (as in nineteenth-century Germany where Bismarck combined social reformism and nationalism in a politically powerful combination with monarchism). Paradoxically, in recent years in Spain the monarch has used his appeal to the right to help engineer a return to constitutional democracy. There are monarchist parties in a number of countries like France, Italy and Russia, but they are all on the margins of politics.

THE RADICAL RIGHT: NAZISM AND FASCISM

In contemporary circumstances the forces which are generally seen as furthest to the right are fascism or nazism.

Hitler's 'National Socialist' party was, in rhetoric at least, anti-capitalist – with capitalism seen as a Jewish conspiracy to rob the 'Volk' (people) of its birthright. The state was seen as the embodiment of the public good and clearly had the responsibility of organising the economy, the educational system and the whole of social and cultural life. There was major emphasis on the mobilisation of the German people through a single party using the modern technology of mass communication.

In practice nazism was dominated by the urge to power of its elite and their commitment to xenophobia, racism and nationalism. The desire to right the perceived wrong of the Versailles settlement of 1919 and strong nationalist feelings (shared by many Germans) were elaborated into a nightmare doctrine. The right of an 'Aryan' master race to 'living space' in the East and to cleanse itself of 'alien' elements such as gypsies and Jews was asserted. The attempt to implement a state based on these doctrines resulted in the deaths of millions across the whole planet (the Holocaust).

Hitler's views, articulated in *Mein Kampf* ('My Struggle'), in many ways built upon more orthodox conservative German political theorists and philosophers. Hegel (1770–1831), for instance, had stressed the importance of a strong state, its role in defining culture and the existence of a logic (or dialectic) of history which justified the waging of war by superior states on inferior ones. Schopenhauer (1788–1860) glorified will over reason. Nietzsche (1844–1900) believed in the creation of a race of superior individuals. Views like this were combined with carefully selected 'scientific' findings about natural selection and the nature of human racial divisions to create an ideology which had a powerful appeal in the politically volatile atmosphere of an economically depressed 1930s Germany.

Italian fascism, by contrast, although drawing upon many of the same causes of social and political discontent and using many of the same methods to achieve power – street warfare and mass rallies, for instance – placed much less emphasis on racism. As an alternative to democracy the appeal of the leader was combined with an attempt to create a corporatist structure of representation in which bodies such as the Church, the army and employers' associations and even workers' syndicates could be represented. Spanish and Argentinian fascists developed similar ideas and institutions.

It is interesting that the most recent large-scale use of near-nazi symbolism (admittedly using a three rather than a four-legged 'swastika') has been by the South African AWB movement seeking to defend apartheid in its dying days. The South African apartheid regime could be seen as the last contemporary fascist state with an ideology based on racialism and supported by an apparatus of torture and repression. The Milosovich Serbian regime in the former Yugoslavia might also be interpreted in a similar way, although here, too, the ideology is nominally one of nationalism rather than racialism.

MARXISM

At the opposite end of the left/right political spectrum are the followers of Karl Marx (1818–1883). Though it is clear Marxists vary enormously in their beliefs.

Marx and Engels adopted a collectivist and conflict-orientated view of politics which is both a theory of history and a programme of political action. As Marx says, 'The philosophers have only interpreted the world differently – the point is to change it' (11th Thesis on Fuerbach, in Marx and Engels, 1962, Vol. 2: 403). Marx and Engels wrote extensively on theoretical and practical matters.

Marx and Engels placed nineteenth-century capitalism in perspective as one of several stages of history which lead inevitably to higher stages. They believed that ideas (ideology) reflect the underlying material 'means of production'. Class warfare will only cease to be the dynamic of history with the abolition of class in the future communist society.

Much of their work was also seeking to build up a socialist movement (the International Working Men's Association) which shared their moral rejection of the exploitative nature of capitalism. As *The Communist Manifesto* (1848) shows, the theory can be impressively marshalled as rhetoric to buttress an appeal to political action. The feeling of being on the side of history, having a 'scientific' insight into social processes and being morally in the right is a heady brew which still appeals.

LENINISM AND STALINISM

In the twentieth century the obvious heirs to Marx have been the leaders of the former Soviet Union. The most ideologically creative and politically influential of these were Vladimir Illich Lenin (born V. I. Ulanov) (1870–1924) and Joseph Stalin (born Joseph

Vissarionovich Djugashvili) (1879–1953). They led this successor state to the Russian Empire in their capacities as secretaries of the Russian Social Democrat Party (Bolshevik – 'majority'– faction) and later the Communist Party of the Soviet Union.

Marx and Engels envisaged socialist revolution taking place in the most developed capitalist countries through mass action by trade unions and democratic socialist organisations. Lenin and Stalin adapted the theory to suit the needs of a conspiratorial revolutionary organisation fighting an autocratic empire in which the majority of the population were still peasants. In order to justify permanent control of a monopoly single party hierarchy over the Soviet Union, the doctrines of 'the dictatorship of the proletariat' and 'democratic centralism' were developed. The party leadership was seen as representing the emergent majority – the working class – that would be the majority as industrialisation proceeded. Lenin developed Marx's concept of the dictatorship of the proletariat to mean 'the organization of the advanced guard of the oppressed as the ruling class, for the purpose of crushing the oppressors' (Lenin, 1917: 225). True democracy could only be created by eliminating the exploitative bourgeois minority. Within the party the dominance of the leadership was defended by appealing to their greater knowledge of the 'scientific' doctrine and the prevalence of infiltrating 'counter-revolutionary' forces. 'Democratic centralism' was defined by the 1961 Communist Party constitution as including the election of all party organs, strict party discipline, subordination of minorities to majorities and lower organs to higher organs. In practice, unwelcome criticism from below was denounced as 'factionalism' and 'unbusinesslike' discussion if not downright treason (Schapiro, 1965: 63–65). Similarly, Russian dominance in the former empire was effectively protected by a doctrine of the existence of a new 'Soviet' nationality which superseded both 'Great Russian chauvinism' and 'bourgeois [i.e. non-Russian] nationalism'.

It is interesting to note that Maoism as expounded by Mao Zedong, leader of China from 1949 to 1976, was founded on Marxism-Leninism (McDonald, 2011), but differed in a crucial context. Mao believed that the agrarian population of China could be the basis for the revolution.

The apparent success of the Soviet regime in building a strong industrialised state capable of defeating nazi Germany from a previously under-developed peasant economy led to the imitation of the regime in numerous East European countries, the Far East and Cuba. In many cases the 'cult of personality' developed around Stalin in the Soviet Union was imitated in relation to indigenous leaders such as Mao Zedong, Ho Chi Minh, Hoxha and Castro. Most of these claimed, with varying degrees of justification, to have produced their own ideologically improved versions of Marxism.

OTHER MARXISMS

As George Orwell (1903–1950) observed, the language employed in the totalitarian Marxist-Leninist regimes became increasingly divorced from reality. Dictatorship was described as democracy (for example, the formal name of post-war East Germany was the German Democratic Republic (GDR)). Enormous differences in lifestyle were characterised as equality. The repression of national movements (as in Hungary in 1956) was described as maintaining peace and freedom and so on. Regimes which were nominally revolutionary were actually characterised by bureaucratic conservatism and were increasingly seen as inefficient as well as hypocritical.

In the inter-war period, and during the Second World War, many European socialists were inclined to identify with 'communism'. The positive role of the Leninists in opposing fascism, and the achievements of the Soviet Union in terms of apparent economic growth and positive welfare measures, impressed intellectuals. A degree of direct financial subsidy to sympathetic western European parties and unions was also influential. The major socialist movements in such countries as France and Italy remained aligned with Moscow and continued to describe themselves as communist even during the Cold War period.

However, increasingly, western Marxists began to move away from the stultifying orthodoxy of Marxist-Leninism, as well as distancing themselves from the Soviet regime. In particular, the idea of rigid economic determinism in history came in for re-evaluation. In Italy, Gramsci (1969) stressed the humanistic strands in Marx's early writings and the role of ideology in influencing the functioning of the modern state.

The British writer Ralph Miliband stressed the role of the state in exercising a semi-autonomous role in history (Miliband, 1969). He believed that the system of 'capitalist democracy' is one of competition between capital and labour, with a strong bias in favour of the former. Miliband was pessimistic about the potential of social democrats to empower ordinary people, while regarding orthodox communists as too authoritarian. He appears to anticipate the danger of a drift from capitalist democracy to 'capitalist authoritarianism' (Miliband, 1984: 154).

A radical break with Stalinism is represented by a number of minor Marxist groups who were influenced by the writings of Leon Trotsky (born Lev Davidovich Bronstein) (1879–1940). Trotsky had been acting as military chief of staff during the revolution, and actually espousing the possibility of an independent Russian revolution before the Bolshevik party in the pre-revolutionary era. After his expulsion by Stalin from the USSR and before his assassination on Stalin's orders in Mexico in 1940, Trotsky denounced the way in which Communist Party rule had created a new class of exploiters in the Soviet Union – the party 'apparatachiks' (Trotsky, 1945). This theme was elaborated by other critics such as Milovan Djilas (1966), who aligned himself with the revisionist Yugoslav regime. Under Tito the Yugoslavs attempted to develop a more humane and participative version of communism, in which workplace democracy and multinational participation played a greater role than in the USSR.

The events in Paris of 1968 are a vivid illustration of the diversity of the modern left (Seale and McConville, 1968). A student protest against the Gaullist government's somewhat inept attempts to ban politics from university campuses mushroomed into larger demands for university reform, the end of the Vietnam War and finally the replacement of the de Gaulle regime by a true 'participative' democracy. The occupation of factories by strikers, the erection of barricades in Paris and a general strike were felt to lay the ground for a revolution by the student-led Trotskyist and Maoist 'groupuscules' who led many of the protests. The orthodox Communist Party, however, was more concerned to preserve its control over the bulk of the trade union movement and its parliamentary electability than to identify itself with immediate and radical political and social change.

RADICALISM

Another slippery political term is 'radical'. The authors are happy to follow the *Shorter Oxford English Dictionary* on this. In adjectival use radical is said to mean going to the root, origin or foundation. Politically in English it refers to 'an advocate of "radical reform"; one who holds the most advanced views of political reform on democratic lines and thus belongs to the extreme section of the [English] liberal party (1802)'. In France, radicals are particularly identified with republicanism and anti-clericalism. More generally radicalism can be used to characterise a style of politics that frequently returns to one set of theoretical first principles in seeking solutions to all sorts of problems. This may be contrasted with 'pragmatism', which emphasises the practical consequences of a decision rather than its theoretical roots.

Radicals in politics were once extreme democrats; more recently the term has often been applied to far-left socialists, but increasingly it has been on other dimensions that radicalism can be measured. Islamic fundamentalists, radical feminists, Greenpeace, even Thatcherite Conservatives in Britain have been described as 'radicals'. But the principles to which these groups appeal are very different from each other and from earlier generations of political activists. The similarity that these theorists share is a tendency to solve all sorts of different problems from their own rather limited repertoire of concepts. Everything comes down to the Koran, patriarchal domination, ecological crisis or the market, as the case may be.

RADICAL THEISM – CATHOLIC, PROTESTANT AND ISLAMIC

John Ball, the priest who led the Peasants' Revolt in 1381, was one of many popular leaders who placed a more radical interpretation on the Bible than did official church leaders. The radical possibilities of the gospel message that the poor would inherit the earth, and the Protestant stress on the sovereignty of the individual conscience, have strongly influenced those on the left of the British political tradition. The Diggers and Levellers in the Civil War period threw doubt upon not only the position of the established church but also the existing basis of property and political representation (Greenleaf, 1983).

In the New World, in colonies such as seventeenth-century Massachusetts and Connecticut, membership of the dominant Christian sect was virtually the same as citizenship (Morison and Commager, 1962). Similarly, in such continental cities as Calvin's Geneva, the processes of government and the interpretation of God's word were virtually indistinguishable (Tawney, 1938: 132). At a later stage in American history (1847), the Mormon leader Brigham Young led his people out of the United States to found Salt Lake City.

Thus it is clear that Christian fundamentalism can be a considerable political force – as it remains to this day in the United States where the backing of the Evangelicals may have proved decisive in securing victories for both Reagan and George W. Bush. 'Fundamentalism' – a literal approach to the interpretation of the Bible – is, strictly speaking, a theological doctrine and not equivalent to a belief in the political supremacy of the Church. Some fundamentalists would endorse a strict separation of secular and religious matters, but where they are in a majority this distinction has often ceased to be of practical importance.

Nonetheless it is Islamic fundamentalism which appears in many ways the most dynamic political-religious movement of the early twenty-first century. Islamic 'fundamentalism' is something of a misnomer since virtually all Muslims take the same sort of literal approach to the status and interpretation of the Koran that Protestant evangelicals take to the Bible. Because of a historic legacy deriving from European conflict with Islam during the crusades and as a part of colonialism, there is a tendency in the West to identify Islamic 'fundamentalism' with intolerance, fanaticism, terrorism and the like (Said, 1987). Historically there is little evidence for such an identification, Islamic doctrine being explicitly a tolerant one – at least in relation to 'The People of the Book', Jews and Christians. As the body count in Bosnia suggests, intolerance between Muslims and Christians has often been the other way around.

What is clear is the attraction of Islam in some of the less developed parts of the world as a sophisticated and 'civilized' religion that permits polygamy and is not identified, as is Christianity, with the former colonial powers (Gbadamosi, 1978). Hence in areas such as southern Nigeria, where tribal religions formerly predominated, Islam has often grown much faster than Christianity, while in areas which have been historically Muslim, such as Egypt, the reassertion of Islamic identity is a part of the rejection of Western colonialism.

Islam has the great advantage of offering not only a religious doctrine but also a social and cultural tradition separate from, and equal or superior in many respects to, that of Christian Europe. Centuries of theological and artistic achievement can be drawn upon. Pilgrims making the journey to Mecca will be greeted by the spectacle of vast assemblies of the faithful from all over the world with whom to exchange experiences. The doctrine of Islam has always been one of not only common religious observance but also the assertion of a social and political unity of all the faithful – the Ummat (Islamic community). Consider the Qur'anic verse, 'this your nation is a single nation, and I am your Lord so worship me' (Surah 21: verse 92).

The political appeal of Islam can be seen in the way in which pragmatic politicians, like Saddam Hussein in Iraq, turned to it as a way of generating political support. The Ayatollah Khomenei, in Iran, was immensely effective in denouncing the Shah as an agent of the American 'Satan' in allowing alcohol, Coca-Cola and miniskirts and discouraging polygamy and hashish. Khomenei described Islamic government as the government of the 'oppressed upon earth' in a reference to the Qur'anic verse, 'And we wish to show favour to those who have been oppressed upon earth, and to make them leaders and inheritors' (Surah 28: verse 5).

The problems of applying Islam to contemporary political situations and structures are considerable. Perhaps the major difficulty is its strict incompatibility with ideas with which it is often, in practice, confused. Thus, in the Middle East, nationalism, pan-Arabism and Islam are often identified together – yet Syrian or Egyptian nationalism may conflict with a sense of Arab identity; while many Muslims are Iranian (Persian), African, Indian or Indonesian rather than Arab. The contemporary Western tendency to identify Islamic fundamentalism with terrorism owes much to the use of force by Palestinian nationalists and their sympathisers.

ECOLOGY AS POLITICAL RADICALISM

As early as the beginning of the nineteenth century, Wordsworth opposed the coming of the steam train to the Lake District as fatal to its character, and Blake denounced the 'dark satanic mills' of the industrial revolution. The conservation of the natural environment did not, however, become a major element in practical politics until relatively recently, when Green parties began to be represented in European legislatures and presented a comprehensive political programme. Before this, pressure groups pioneered environmental causes such as rural planning, national parks and smoke and noise abatement which have now become mainstream public policies.

The green movement is unusual in deriving an overall coherent philosophy from a scientific discipline. Ecology is the science that studies the relationship between organisms and their physical environment. As scientific study has proceeded, the multiple interdependencies between the different organic species on the planet, and the crucial impact of climatic and geological influences, have become clearer to us.

With the development of an industrial urban civilisation dependent upon the consumption of fossil fuels, and our own increasing knowledge, it has become clear that the environment is being moulded in potentially dangerous ways. The Rio Earth Summit of June 1992 found political leaders from all over the globe discussing seriously the depletion of world resources; the phenomenon of global warming; the dangers of pollution in the atmosphere and oceans; and the destruction of animal and plant species. Non-governmental groups at the same summit stressed the human population explosion and the unequal distribution of resources between North and South as contributors to a single problem resulting from uncontrolled industrial growth. In 2012 a 20-year follow-up, Rio+20, was held which sought to enhance political commitment to sustainable development.

Green campaigners usually suggest that both capitalist and communist ideologies are part of the problem. Resources are being used up at an exponential (ever-increasing) rate, while the healthy complexity of the ecology of the planet is being continually reduced by commercial agriculture and industrial pollution. However, divisions within the movement can be observed – particularly between what one might call the romantics and the scientists. On the 'romantic' side, the stress is on back-to-nature ideas such as homeopathy, vegetarianism, naturism and developing folk-music-playing rural communities. On the 'scientific' side the stress is on projections of economic and ecological disaster if present trends in industrialisation and consumption continue. A different division has also been observed between what is sometimes called the 'light anthropocentric' and the 'deep ecology' wings (Vincent, 1992: 217). The first group stress the practical problems for human beings and may concentrate pragmatically on individual problems. Deep ecologists call for a total change of attitude by humans to recognise the intrinsic value of all other species.

As a political doctrine for intellectuals, 'ecologism' has great advantages: it has something to say on almost every issue, is opposed to many contemporary orthodoxies (especially the desirability of economic growth), has a variety of esoteric insights to offer, and has appealing emotional undertones. In this sense, ecologism can be seen as a rather radical and oppositional doctrine. On the other hand, in asserting the rights of succeeding generations against the present, there are echoes of the conservative sentiments expressed by Edmund Burke. He wrote: 'I attest the retiring, I attest the advancing generations, between which, as a link in the great chain of eternal order we stand' (quoted Sabine, 1951: 519).

FEMINISM

Despite the achieving of universal suffrage in virtually all Western democracies, feminism remains a live political issue. The vote has not brought equality of pay, status or opportunity for women. Attitudes to this fact may be roughly summarised in Table 4.1.

'Radical' feminists have tended to see feminism as all-embracing, something that should determine attitudes to a wide variety of issues — including the nature of work, authority structures, education, taxation and personal relationships. Western society has been warped by aggressive and acquisitive elderly males dominating and exploiting the young and the female.

Possibly as a result of media overreaction and misrepresentation of the views of a minority of radical feminists, many people of moderate views would now hesitate to describe themselves as 'feminists'. However, moderates are now found endorsing what most people of the older generation of feminists would have regarded as a feminist stand. Thus they take for granted the desirability of equal

Table 4.1 Attitudes to gender differences

	Radical feminist	Moderate feminist	Conservative
Problem	**Patriarchy – government by men** Domination and exploitation of women by older men. Ideology dominates many women's thoughts as well as social institutions and socialisation.	**Under-representation of women; sexual discrimination**	**None** Apparent inequalities reflect *different* role women play in society: caring for others; beauty and gentleness more important than power, etc.
Causes	**Sexist power structure** Rowbotham: sexual division of labour. Firestone: male control of female reproduction. Marx (Engels): reserve army of labour.	**Prejudice and ignorance** Tradition, socialisation.	**Biology** Evolution or God has given females genetic tendency to passivity and caring, conscientious disposition.
Solution	**Revolution** Marxist, personal or lesbian? Society must be remade: assumptions re family, carers, careers, politics, etc., reversed.	**Integration** Women to play full part in existing society.	**Apartheid** Women to remain separate but equal.
Action	**Women's liberation** Remove male structures of domination and ideology. Personal – take control of own life. Marxist – as part of proletarian revolution.	**Female participation** Education. Piecemeal legal action Use legal rights to full, e.g. political, nominations or educational opportunities.	**Legal action inappropriate** Safeguard family values.

political rights for women, freedom to pursue any career without discrimination and equal pay for equal work.

Radical feminists would argue that their more moderate sisters mistake the size of the problem in asserting equal status in a male-dominated society. Their analysis of the problem and suggested strategy and tactics vary greatly from one group to another. Thus Marxist feminists tend to follow Engels in seeing the exploitation of women as being part of the capitalist phenomenon of a 'reserve army of labour'. Capitalists exploit an undertrained and underpaid and often part-time female work-force in order to keep the more organised and militant male work-force in order. True emancipation can only come with the triumph of a proletarian revolution – which will wipe away these repressive mechanisms (together with the bourgeois view of the family as male property). Other writers are less convinced that male domination is associated with capitalism, pointing to the recurrence of a sexual division of labour in many non-capitalist societies (Rowbotham,1972) and the power accruing to males until recently from their control of female reproduction (Firestone, 1971).

Most radical feminists have taken a line similar to the anarchists (indeed Emma Goldman (1915) is a pioneer in both movements), that revolution must begin in the private lives of those who are convinced of its desirability. 'The personal is the political' is the slogan of many radical feminists, who argue that the centralised and authoritarian imposition of a way of life is a male style of politics. A tiny minority go one step further and argue that males will never voluntarily give up their power – no ruling class does – so that only in separatist lesbian communities can women achieve equality and freedom.

LIBERALISM

Liberalism may be understood in a broad or a narrower sense. In the broad sense one can argue that liberal ideas of individualism and constitutionalism constitute the basis of a constitutional consensus shared by most of the mainstream parties in the states of the European Union, the United States and many other 'liberal democracies'.

In the narrower sense, liberalism is a doctrine professed by a number of democratic parties distinguished from more conservative/ Christian democrat parties on the right and socialist parties on the left. The Liberal International is a formal expression of this and includes the US Liberal Party and the UK Liberal Democrats. An intermediate use of the term is common in the United States, where people on the left of the two main parties are frequently described as liberals, with the expectation that they favour such causes as internationalism, civil rights and increased government intervention and spending for social welfare. Most liberal parties would be viewed to be on the centre-left of the political spectrum, but some – such as the Liberal Party of Australia and the Liberal Democratic Party in Japan – are considered to be on the centre-right.

A helpful simplification may be to distinguish three phases in the development of liberal ideas. The earliest phase is the establishment of the idea of constitutional government based on individual rights. The United States constitution is a good expression of this, based as it is on the consent of the governed and the entrenchment in the constitution of individual rights. It is a systematic expression of the American colonies' inheritance of the British parliamentary constitutional tradition, and the Founding Fathers explicitly referred to the writings of Locke and to Montesquieu's (1688–1755) interpretation of the British constitution (i.e. the separation of powers).

In the second phase, nineteenth-century liberal writers like Bentham and the Mills (James and his son John Stuart) developed the democratic implications of the experiences of earlier generations. John Stuart Mill's *Essay on Liberty* (1859) makes a case against interference by the state or society in the private lives of individuals and for freedom of expression. This may be thought of the classic liberal value and is encapsulated in the quotation often attributed to Voltaire, 'I disapprove of what you say, but I will defend to the death your right to say it.' The link with capitalism was also made explicit in a defence of doctrines of free trade and the desirability of a minimal state, building upon the writings of economists such as Adam Smith (1723–1790) and Ricardo (1772–1823). Liberals were increasingly seen as the party of the new modernising manufacturing elite opposed to the more conservative landed gentry. In both Europe and North America liberals were increasingly the party of political reform and universal suffrage.

A third phase in the development of liberalism was marked in philosophical terms by the writings of the English 'idealists' (Milne, 1962) – who included F. H. Bradley (1846–1924), Bernard Bosanquet (1848–1923), Josiah Royce (1855–1916) (an American writer with some similar ideas), and most notably T. H. Green (1836–1882) and Leonard Hobhouse (1864–1929). Much of this idealistic writing was a development of the theme evident in the writings of John Stuart Mill: the state exists so as to guarantee a system of rights that will enable individuals to pursue their moral development. These rights must be exercised in such a way as not to prevent others exercising them too. The state may thus intervene, for example to regulate property, in the interests of the development of a common sense of citizenship by all. Green explicitly endorses state intervention to enable the mass of the population to enjoy reasonable standards of health, housing and access to property rights (Green, 1941: 209).

Hobhouse (1964 – originally published in 1911) is a more explicit statement of political liberalism. He identifies liberalism with civil, fiscal, personal, social, economic, domestic, local, racial, national and international and political liberty. He then asserts that 'full liberty implies full equality' and the correctness of distinguishing in terms of taxation between earned and unearned income and between acquired and inherited wealth (Ch. 8).

The third phase of 'social' liberalism is associated in Britain with the political careers, speeches and writings of Lloyd George, John Maynard Keynes and Lord Beveridge. Lloyd George, as chancellor of the exchequer in the pre-First World War liberal government, can be seen as the practical inaugurator of social liberalism with his introduction of both old age pensions and death duties – that is, both state welfare schemes and progressive taxation. Beveridge, in his Second World War coalition government white paper, put forward a blueprint for the modern welfare state in which state-organised 'insurance' schemes and taxation would protect all citizens from the Five Giants of Want, Disease, Ignorance, Squalor and Idleness. Keynes as an economist and administrator successfully argued for the need for government intervention to ensure the efficient working of a capitalist economy. In the United States the inter-war Roosevelt New Deal administration adopted rather pragmatically a similar interventionist approach to the economy and welfare, which has influenced the liberal left ever since.

More recently the immensely influential American liberal philosopher John Rawls in *A Theory of Justice* (1971) provided modern theoretical justification for redistributive activities by the state.

CONSERVATISM

It can be argued that conservatism is more an attitude than a doctrine. However, some components of a basic conservative attitude might be suggested. Pessimism about human nature is often to be discerned, with an associated stress on the need for domestic 'law and order' measures and strong armed forces to repel international threats. The need to support existing spiritual as well as secular authority will also be evident. Nationalism and support for 'family values' will usually also be found.

Rather than a contract between individuals – like a trading agreement – the state is instituted as a partnership between the generations, 'between those who are living and those who are dead', to be approached with reverence.

British Conservatives were much influenced by Disraeli's (1804–1881) doctrine of 'One Nation', popularised in his novel *Sybil* and his political practice as prime minister (1868 and 1874–1880). His idea was that national unity should be preserved through a direct appeal to the interests of the working classes on the part of benevolent Tory governments. In the nineteenth century the Conservatives were still led by a mainly aristocratic leadership which combined ideas of 'noblesse oblige' with an inclination to adopt social measures.

Traditional Conservative suspicion of grand theory may be epitomised by reference to the work of Michael Oakeshott (1901–1990), who suggested that the role of government is:

> To inject into activities of already too passionate men an ingredient of moderation; to restrain, to deflate, to pacify and to reconcile; not to stoke the fires of desire but to damp them down.
>
> (Oakeshott, 1962: 191–192)

In a well-known and rather striking image, Oakeshott further describes the activity of politics as to:

> sail a bottomless and boundless sea; there is neither harbour for shelter nor floor for anchorage, neither starting-place nor appointed destination. The enterprise is to keep afloat on an even keel; the sea is both friend and enemy; and the seamanship consists in using the resources

of a traditional manner of behaviour in order to make a friend of every hostile occasion.

(Oakeshott, 1962: 127)

LIBERTARIANISM

More recently we can identify a neo-liberalism which owes allegiance more to the conservative right than the radical liberal tradition because of the stress on personal freedoms. The theoretical basis is associated with Milton Friedman (1962) and Hayek (1979), who promulgated the importance of the market and a limited role for the state, akin to that of a referee. Politically neo-liberalism was most closely associated with Ronald Reagan's US administration (1980-88) and Margaret Thatcher's Conservative government of 1979–1990.

Robert Nozick (1974) wrote a persuasive riposte to Rawls's work arguing that the results of market forces were a just distribution of resources. The best-selling novelist Ayn Rand exerted enormous influence on the American right with her philosophy of 'objectivism' which advocated 'rational egoism' and the superiority of capitalism as a defence for human rights.

More recently, in the United States, a prominent 'neo-conservative' group supporting the George W. Bush administration and associated with the American Enterprise Institute and the Project for the New American Century have adopted similar economic and nationalist policies. In the US context, conservatism takes a paradoxical form in a belief in the compulsory export of liberal institutions to the South – including Iraq and Afghanistan. The United Nations is the focus for a suspicion of international institutions.

This libertarian sentiment has found voice with the creation in the US of the Tea Party, a fairly loose group of grassroot networks primarily located within the Republican Party. The creation of the movement is primarily a response to President Obama's policies. In 2009 Rick Santelli, a CNBC reporter, delivered a live on-air rant against Obama's mortgage plan, leading to protests which eventually became the Tea Party. Although a fairly informal collection it is possible to identify some core themes of a Tea Party libertarian ideology. As Mead (2011) suggests, this harks back to Andrew Jackson the populist US president (1767–1845), so the Tea Party can be viewed as an outbreak of Jacksonian commonsense against the elite. In terms of precise policies the Tea Party stands for small government, state rights, lower taxes and fiscal responsibility (Barreto *et al.*, 2012). Looking in depth at the views of Tea Party supporters, Perrin *et al.* (2011) have identified four common trends in their beliefs: authoritarianism; fear of change; libertarianism; and nativism. The Tea Party, therefore, appears to be the latest manifestation of a long-standing form of conservatism within the US.

CHRISTIAN DEMOCRACY

In recent years in the US, arguably the strongest organised force on the political right has been Christian fundamentalism, with its emphasis on the so-called 'moral majority' issues of abortion, pornography and so on.

In continental Europe the moderate centre-right position held by the Conservatives in Britain is occupied in many countries by the Christian democrat parties, whose enthusiasm for capitalism is balanced by electoral links to the countryside and by church belief in co-operation and compassion in social affairs. In a number of countries, links with the trade union movement reinforce Christian democrat claims to a centrist rather than conservative/right-wing classification (Michael Smart in Smith, 1989).

The strongest Christian democratic parties seem to be in those Catholic countries where the Church has adopted something of a self-denying ordinance, allowing practical politicians room for manoeuvre. This includes countries such as Italy, Malta, Chile and Venezuela. For simplicity, Protestant democratic parties are not considered here in detail – but they are important in the Netherlands, and of influence in Switzerland and the Nordic countries. The CDU in Germany does include Protestants, but attracts more support from Catholics (Dalton, 1988). Christian democracy has been defined as 'a movement of those who aim to solve – with the aid of Christian principles and "democratic" techniques – that range of temporal problems which the Church has repeatedly and solemnly declared to lie within the "supreme" competence of lay society, and outside direct ecclesiastical control' (Fogarty, 1957: 6). More specifically, Irving (1979: xvii) discerns three basic principles in contemporary European Christian democracy:

> 'Christian principles' (in the sense of a broad commitment to basic human rights, particularly those of the individual); 'democracy' (in the sense of a clear-cut commitment to liberal democracy) and 'integration' (in the dual sense of a commitment to class reconciliation through the concept of the broad-based Volkspartei (people's party)) and to trans-national reconciliation through the strong Christian Democratic commitment to European integration.

As Irving argues (xxi), Christian democrats share conservative values of individualism, respect for property values, anti-communism and dislike of excessive state intervention. However, unlike neo-liberals they have favoured 'concertation' — consultation between government, industry, the trade unions and other interest groups. Muller (2013) offers an explanation of this mixture of ideology, noting that Christian democracy is an attempt to reconcile Christianity with modern democracy.

SOCIALISM AND SOCIAL DEMOCRACY

We have already seen that Marxists regard themselves as socialists. Millions of people, however, remain committed to socialism without regarding themselves as disciples of Marx. For many socialists the doctrine is the opposite of totalitarianism — it is a commitment to values of equality and justice for all. In a Fabian pamphlet Tony Blair wrote of two socialist traditions: a Marxist economic determinist and collectivist tradition, and another 'based on the belief that socialism is a set of values or beliefs — sometimes called ethical socialism' (Blair, 1994: 2). These values he defines as: 'social justice, the equal worth of each citizen, equality of opportunity, community' (p. 4). This latter tradition he sees as predominant in 'European Social Democracy'.

Historically it does seem that a strain of indigenous radicalism often associated with the non-conformist churches is more important than Marxism in the British socialist tradition. The non-conformist churches trained many Labour speakers in the skills of oratory and social organisation. Certainly more important than Marxism has been the influence of a strong trade union and co-operative movement, which, in England, pre-date both Marx and the Labour Party. The Labour Party originated early in the twentieth century as the Labour Representation Committee to represent organised labour in parliament. Only in 1918 did the LRC become the Labour Party, allow individual members and adopt a socialist statement of objectives in clause 4 of its constitution – apparently in an attempt to appeal to middle-class intellectual supporters (McKibbin, 1983).

For many years Labourism might have been defined in terms of a Fabian strategy to bring about the collective management of the economy through a reliance on the power of the collective might of the organised working class. As George Bernard Shaw put it in Fabian Tract 13 (1891), socialism was a doctrine of 'gradualist Collectivism brought about by a strategy of resolute constitutionalism'. In Tony Blair's words, 'the old-style collectivism of several decades ago' is no longer radicalism but 'the neo-conservatism of the left' (Blair, 1994: 7). A similar debate has taken place within many continental European socialist (and, even more, former communist) parties.

Most writers on socialism have agreed that it is about a commitment to equality, but there has been little consensus about the nature of that commitment (Vincent, 1992). Generally speaking, however, democratic socialists have agreed on emphasising equality of rights for all; rejecting the legitimacy of extremist coercive and violent tactics; favouring a liberal democratic state with opportunities for peaceful and constitutional change; and rejecting as unfair, unregulated capitalist economics. The range of opinions within these parameters has been, and remains, a very large one.

COMMUNITARIANISM AND THE 'THIRD WAY'

It will be apparent to most readers that the predominant political style in modern European and North American democracies is what we have called pragmatic rather than radical. Democratic politicians in general seem slow to relate their policy stands to explicit general principles, and appear to be content to manage existing societies rather than to try to fundamentally change them. Few contemporary presidents or prime ministers would be happy to be labelled as Marxists, fascists, radical feminists or ecologists, but tend to cling to the electorally safe centre ground of politics.

Such tendencies have been described as 'The End of Ideology' (Bell, 1960), but this may be a somewhat confusing description. One should distinguish between the somewhat cavalier approach to ideas which is typical of most practical politicians, and the absence of any ideas. Similarly, a period of international confrontation between Marxist-Leninist and liberal democratic/capitalist systems may have come to an end, but this does not mean that new 'ideological' confrontations (for instance on religion, gender and ecology) may not occur.

The possibility of a consolidation of centre streams of thought also seems very likely to the authors; the differences between revisionist democratic socialism, social liberalism, Christian democracy and pragmatic conservatism are surely small compared with the gulf which separates them from some of their unconstitutional radical and authoritarian alternatives.

An illustration of the possibility of such a convergence is the tendency of politicians from a wide variety of formal party backgrounds to endorse the language of 'communitarianism'. Etzioni (1995: ix) suggests that several key Labour, Conservative, and Liberal Democratic figures in the UK, Democrats and Republicans in the US, as well as Christian and Social Democrats in Germany, have all endorsed such ideas.

Etzioni's version of communitarianism accepts the liberal legacy of individual rights and a presumption against extensive state intervention. However, he seeks to balance this with a stress on the need for individuals to accept their duties to the state and community and for the community 'to be responsive to their members and to foster participation and deliberation in social and political life' (p. 254). Sandel (1996: 5) speaks of the need to resurrect the 'Republican' tradition 'that liberty depends on sharing in self-government', which in turn requires 'a knowledge of public affairs and also a sense of belonging, a concern for the whole, a moral bond with the community whose fate is at stake'.

Communitarianism seeks to avoid the clumsy state collectivism of not only Soviet communism but also some versions of British socialism and American liberalism via a 'Third Way'. Bill Clinton popularised the Third Way 'as a combination of small but progressive government, tight financial discipline and a programme to secure economic freedom with social cohesion – countering critics of both "tax and spend" and "permissive" liberalism' (Butler, 2000: 154).

The problem with (or possibly advantage of) the Third Way as a guide to policy is that it lacks specifics. It can be seen as a route to collaboration with liberals, and progressive conservatives and European Christian democrats. It may be questioned, however, whether the doctrine as so far developed has been able to fully confront the economic and social problems of the new globalised economy. Indeed, some have seen it as no more than a public relations fig leaf to cover a naked lack of specific remedies for current problems (Jacques, 1998). Popularised by Tony Giddens as a new form of social democracy, the term 'third way' in the late 1990s and early noughties offered politicians such as Blair, Clinton and Schroeder a way of re-packaging left-of-centre politics. While a policy legacy may last, based around the concept of a stakeholder society, as an ideology the term appears to have had a limited shelf life.

CONCLUSION

Ideology is important as a driver for explaining political behaviour and provides a possible purpose for exercising political power. It provides political actors with a type of compass, so that whatever the precise problem they are faced with, overall principles can guide the direction they should take. Ideology also implies some level of consistency in approach, even if the day-to-day problems are different. So if we were able to whisk forward to today a liberal of the mid-nineteenth century in a time-machine, he/she would broadly understand the tenets of twenty-first-century liberalism – though of course they might be more comfortable with a neo-liberal than a traditional liberal perspective. However, at the same time ideologies evolve step by step over periods of time; thus 1920s Marxism is not exactly the same as Marxism today, though they are recognisably from the same tradition. Moreover, rapid economic, social, technological and environmental change since 1945 has created a host of new political problems, which has encouraged the development of new schools of thought.

FURTHER READING

Dean, J. (2010) *Rethinking Contemporary Feminist Politics*, Basingstoke: Palgrave.

De Crespigny, A. and Minogue, K. (eds.) (1976) *Contemporary Political Philosophers*, London: Methuen.

Dobson, A. (2000) *Green Political Thought: An Introduction*, 3rd edn, London: Routledge.

Eccleshall, R. (2003) *Political Ideologies: An Introduction*, London: Routledge.

Eickelman, D. and Piscatori, J. (1996) *Muslim Politics*, Princeton, NJ: Princeton University Press.

Freeden, M., Sargent, L. and Stears, M. (2013) *The Oxford Handbook of Political Ideologies*, Oxford: Oxford University Press.

Heywood, A. (1998) *Political Ideologies: An Introduction*, 2nd edn, Basingstoke: Macmillan.

Morgan, M. (ed.) (1992) *Classics of Moral and Political Theory*, Indianapolis: Hackett.

Sandel, M. (2012) *What Money Can't Buy: the moral limits of markets*, London: Allen Lane.

WEBSITES

www.politicalcompass.org
Allows you to test where your political affiliations are.
http://typology.people-press.org/typology
Typology created by the US-based Pew Research Center for People and Press.
http://cpi.politics.ox.ac.uk
The Centre for Political Ideologies.
www.catholic.net – Catholic.net
Formerly the Catholic Information Center.
www.islamic-world.net
Including texts of Islamic books & news reports.
www.envirolink.org
Envirolink Network (for ecologists).
www.cddc.vt.edu/feminism/
Feminist theory.

5

STATES

THIS CHAPTER ...

considers the major types of state in the modern world, starting with Crick's distinction between republican, autocratic and totalitarian states. It discusses in more detail the different forms of representative democracy and military and authoritarian government. We also consider the relationship between central, regional and local levels of government within states.

We have already noted that historically states have dominated much of political science's research, analysis and comment. This chapter will, therefore, help us understand political reality in most of the modern world. However, the purpose of this chapter is also to set up some of the remaining chapters where we look at where this orthodoxy is being challenged by pressures both within and beyond states. By the end of this chapter readers will be able to:

- assess the relevance of the state;
- identify the different types of state;
- consider the differences and similarities between democratic and autocratic states;
- introduce different levels of the state.

IS THE STATE NECESSARY?

As we saw in Chapter 3, not all societies have a centralised deci-sion-making apparatus claiming authority over a given territorial area. Thus, the state may be desirable, but it is not, strictly speaking, necessary or inevitable. However, it is difficult to envisage a modern industrial large-scale society functioning without some such mechanism. Yet a small minority – anarchists – advocate precisely this.

Anarchy is derived from the Greek term 'anarchos' which means 'without rulers', so anarchism implies that there is no need for a state. Rather, anarchists are likely to posit the need for a co-operative and non-hierarchical society. Most modern anarchists are anticapitalists focusing on the deficiencies, as they see it, of major corporations and the machinery of the state.

BOX 5.1   DEFINITIONS OF ANARCHISM

(1) 'Absence of government; a state of lawlessness due to the absence or inefficiency of supreme power; political disorder.'

(Shorter Oxford English Dictionary)

(2) 'The Philosophy of a new social order based on liberty unrest-ricted by man-made law; the theory that all forms of govern-ment rest on violence and are therefore wrong and harmful, as well as unnecessary.'

(Goldman, 1915)

(3) 'A doctrine which poses a criticism of existing society, a view of a desirable future society; and a means of passing from one to the other.'

(Woodcock, 1975)

Our first definition in Box 5.1 represents the colloquial meaning of anarchism – supported by few, or no, political theorists but dreaded by conservative politicians as the consequence of illegal popular political action. Arguably it might be more correctly given as a definition of 'anarchy' rather than 'anarchism'.

Emma Goldman's (1869–1940) definition highlights the anarchist's opposing view that order need not be imposed by authority but should stem from unrestricted agreements between free individuals. Writers such as Tolstoy and Kropotkin (1842–1921) would argue that existing states incorporate the systematic use of violence against the population through the police, the prison system and the armed forces. The concept of 'justice' is caricatured by the imprisonment of the poor and defenceless. The concept of 'defence' destroys the lives of millions to defend the interests of the propertied minority. Most anarchists argue that our present wasteful urban industrialised lifestyle should be replaced by a more ascetic and healthy one. Autonomous communes and voluntary literary, educational, artistic and sporting associations would freely exchange goods and services on a non-profit basis.

As Woodcock suggests, a crucial problem for anarchists is how to make the transition to the new state of affairs. Most would advocate simply withdrawing consent from current ways of doing things and immediately practising a new libertarian lifestyle. Hence, a number of anarchists have sought to set up 'communes' independent of current states, while Proudhon (1809–1865) advocated the setting up of an independent banking system based on labour-hours. As Howard Zim puts it:

> The anarchist sees revolutionary change as something immediate, something we must do now, where we live, where we work. It means starting this moment to do away with authoritarian relationships – between men and women, between children and parents, between one kind of worker and another kind. Such revolutionary spirit cannot be crushed like an armed uprising.
>
> (Quoted in Pennock and Chapman, 1978)

A minority of anarchists urge that the state machinery needs to be smashed by armed insurrection. This violent tendency is well illustrated by the following quotation:

> In giving dynamite to the down-trodden millions of the globe, science has done its best work ... a pound of this good stuff beats a bushel of ballots all hollow.
>
> (Johann Most, *Science of Revolutionary Warfare: a Manual of Instruction in the Uses and Preparation of Nitroglycerine, Dynamite, Gun-Cotton, Fulminating Mercury, Bombs, Fuses, Poisons, etc., etc.*, 1885, quoted in Horowitz, 1964: 41–42)

Anarchism as a political movement has had only a small direct practical impact. Perhaps the most influential avowedly anarchist groupings were those in 1930s Spain. However, anarchist thinking influenced Gandhi and the Indian Independence movement, the student movements of the 1960s and many other left-wing protest movements, and is still an influence for contemporary feminist and ecological groups.

TYPES OF STATE

The idea of a state assumes that there is a spatial central authority within formal borders. States vary a great deal in their organisation and in their concept of the role of government. Bernard Crick has suggested a good starting point for the classification of states which brings out some of these differences. He distinguishes between republican, autocratic and totalitarian states:

BOX 5.2   REPUBLICAN, AUTOCRATIC AND TOTALITARIAN STATES

REPUBLICAN

Government as a constitutional process in which disparate group views on the public interest are reconciled through a political process of discussion.

Government may intervene in economic and social affairs to maintain public interest and minimum welfare standards for all.

In 'private affairs' citizens pursue their own happiness without interference.

Examples – eighteenth-century Britain, Classical Athens, modern liberal democracies

AUTOCRATIC

Public interest defined by government. Subjects' involvement in politics seen as suspicious/subversive.

Government's role mainly limited to taxation, foreign policy.

In 'private affairs' citizens pursue their own happiness without interference.

Examples – monarchic governments of the eighteenth century, military regimes

TOTALITARIAN

Government defines public interest that is all-inclusive. Political opposition is treason.
No private sphere – good citizens participate enthusiastically in rebuilding society. Official ideology defines happiness.

Examples – nazi Germany, Stalin's Soviet Union.

(Crick, 2000)

These categories are, however, extremely 'broad brush', as can be seen from the variety of examples quoted for each.

Most modern 'republican' regimes could be described as 'representative democracies' in that they are not only constitutional but also have representative institutions based on universal suffrage (one man or woman, one vote). However, historically there were many states such as England in the eighteenth century that had some respect for individual rights and a constitutional form of government, without being fully democratic. Classical Athens was not in our sense fully 'democratic' since women, slaves and resident foreigners did not vote, although all full citizens could participate directly in debate and vote on matters of public policy. The Greeks too were inclined to see the state as having more of a role in the moral sphere than we are accustomed to in modern democracies. Similarly, Renaissance city states like Venice had participative, but not fully democratic, forms of constitutional rule.

As of 2000 around 63 per cent of modern states can be seen as representative democracies or, in this terminology, republican (Diamond in LeDuc et al., 2002: 211). A more detailed analysis of the degree of democracy in contemporary states can be found at the Country Indicators for Foreign Policy project (www.carleton.ca/cifp). This methodology and data has been modified and updated by the Polity IV Project (www.systemicpeace.org/polity/polity4.htm), which has created a spectrum of governing authority from *fully institutionalised autocracies* through *mixed authority regimes* (termed 'anocracies') to *fully institutionalised democracies*. For example, their 2011 report suggests that since the 1980s the number of autocracies has decreased from over 80 to about 20 worldwide. At the same time the number of anocracies initially increased from 20 and has now flat-lined at around 40–50. They suggest that democracies have gone through a sharp increase, from about 40 to just under 100 in the same period.

Crick's emphasis on the role of an independent private sphere in 'republican' regimes has been echoed in an increasingly strong emphasis in recent years on the importance of the concept of an independent 'civil society' as a mark of a developed liberal democracy. East European writers like Vaclav Havel emphasised the moral case for self-governing social institutions, in contrast to their submergence by the communist regimes they were opposing. This concept from traditional political theory has been further re-emphasised by communitarian thinkers and used extensively by policy-makers in international institutions such as the World Bank (see Axtmann, 2003: 82–92).

Autocratic, or 'authoritarian', regimes were probably more common in the past than today, but they are far from extinct, particularly in the 'South'. Derbyshire and Derbyshire (1991) classified 165 states by regime type and concluded that in the mid-1980s there were 16 'Nationalistic Socialist', 12 'Authoritarian Nationalist', 14 'Military Authoritarian' and 11 'Absolutist' regimes – a total of 53 (or 32 per cent). These regimes were mainly in Africa but there were three from Asia and one each from South America and Oceania. Using Diamond's figures, 72 states were not democratic in 2000 (Diamond in LeDuc *et al.*, 2002: 211).

'Totalitarian' is usually used loosely to describe communist, fascist and racist regimes. But clearly the intention of such a category is to include both extreme right (fascist) and extreme left (communist) regimes. The former Soviet Bloc (eight states in the Derbyshires' study) and apartheid South Africa might have been candidates for this description in the 1980s, representing approximately 5 per cent of states but with a much higher proportion of the world's population. Currently only North Korea, Cuba and arguably China could be described as members of such a category.

DEMOCRACY, THE WELFARE STATE AND THE MARKET

The work of the Derbyshires, Diamond and the Polity IV Project suggest a general trend, with authoritarian states on the decrease, and representative states on the increase in terms of numbers (see Table 5.1). However, we should not see this trend as steady or inevitable; Diamond (2008) noted that between 1974 and 2008 90 countries became democracies, but he referred to a 'democratic recession', with the number of new democracies slowing up because of an authoritarian undertow in some countries. He now suggests that if there is any further growth in democracy it will be in Asia (Diamond, 2012).

We could go further and assert that free elections along with a competitive free economy (modified by some commitment to a welfare state) have become in some sense the norm for a modern state. This combination of representative democracy and capitalism is frequently described as 'liberal democracy' and implies a commitment to democracy, the free market (capitalism) and a minimum standard of social policy. Some countries adopt only parts of this model; for example, China can now be classified as having a capitalist economy but not a democratic political system – the hybrid nature of this economic and political system clearly creates tensions.

The relationship between democracy, capitalism and the welfare state is, therefore, central to the study of politics. It is worth emphasising that this combination of characteristics is historically quite rare and has by no means always been thought to be either desirable or necessary.

Table 5.1 The trend towards democracy, 1974–2000

Year	Number of democracies	Number of countries	Democracies as a percentage
1974	39	142	27.5
1988	66	167	39.5
1991	91	183	49.7
1996	118	191	61.8
2000	120	192	62.5

Source: Larry Diamond (in LeDuc *et al.*, 2002: 211)

Democracy is a concept with a long history, but it comes as a surprise to many modern readers to find that, until the twentieth century, it was more often a term of abuse than praise. In Classical Greece, for instance, where the term originated, it was commonly understood as 'mob rule'. Ancient Greek democracy did not involve elections (officials being selected by lot), and manhood suffrage (i.e. the election of parliaments by all men – but not women) only became a common institution in the nineteenth century. Even John Stuart Mill, the famous liberal philosopher, was concerned about the 'tyranny of the majority'. Britain, France and the United States have only achieved universal suffrage since the end of the Second World War and black voters in the Southern US were effectively disenfranchised until the implementation of the 1968 Civil Rights Act.

It may be useful to briefly define what is meant here by capitalism (see Box 5.3 below).

BOX 5.3   CAPITALISM

'A system of exchange based upon market prices ... in which individuals or combinations of individuals compete with each other to accumulate wealth by buying the rights to use land, labour and capital in order to produce goods and services with the intention of selling them in the market at a profit.'

(Saunders, 1995: 9)

A wide variety of definitions of the 'welfare state' have been put forward, but it is convenient to adopt Johnson's (1987) approach (see Box 5.4).

BOX 5.4   THE WELFARE STATE

A modern liberal democratic industrial state in which the state has intervened to:
1   provide a wide range of social services to the bulk of the population;
2   seek to maintain full employment;

> 3   nationalise or regulate a number of key industries but in which the bulk of the economy remains in the hands of private enterprise.
>
> (After Johnson, 1987)

The welfare state can be viewed as the natural consequence of the extension of democratic ideas to the social and welfare sphere. Thus President Franklin D. Roosevelt proclaimed the Allied war aims to include four freedoms which included freedom from fear and want. In wartime Britain a consensus between parties was evolved on the basis of the Beveridge Report on the need to conquer the 'Five Giants' of want, disease, ignorance, squalor and idleness (Beveridge, 1942).

Despite the apparent coincidence of values between welfarism and democracy, British readers in particular may be surprised to discover that the welfare state cannot be said to have originated with the Labour victory in Britain in 1945. Many of the moves towards a welfare state in Britain took place in the early twentieth century, partly as a reaction to the prior development of welfarism in Bismarck's Germany (an autocratic rather than a liberal democratic state).

Capitalism predated democracy in Britain, while in some parts of the world (e.g. Allende's Chile) the development of liberal democracy has been seen as a distinct menace to capitalism and resisted for this reason. Indeed, to use Greek political terminology, it might be argued that the natural form of government for a capitalist economy (allowing, as it does, the accumulation of large quantities of wealth in relatively few hands) is oligarchy (government by the – rich – few) rather than democracy (government by the – poor – many).

FORMS OF REPRESENTATIVE DEMOCRACY

A key issue in considering the workings of modern democracies is the nature of those governments and the mechanisms for enforcing responsibility of governments to the people. The complex relationships between the elected legislature, the government, and the electorate are summarised in Box 5.5.

BOX 5.5   FORMS OF REPRESENTATIVE DEMOCRACY

PRESIDENTIAL

Popularly elected head of state and government, independent legislature and judiciary.

Examples – US, Latin America

PARLIAMENTARY

Head of state appoints head of government responsible to legislature.

Examples – UK, Sweden, Italy

HYBRID

Directly elected head of state appoints head of government responsible to legislature.

Examples – France, Russia

CONSOCIATIONAL

Minorities have constitutional right to representation in government.

Examples – Switzerland, Northern Ireland

ONE-PARTY

One party legally controls government.

Examples – China, North Korea

The two major types of representative democratic constitution to be found in the world today are the parliamentary and presidential systems. The major features of these are outlined in Table 5.2, which is based on the work of Verney (1959). Derbyshire and Derbyshire (1996: 40) classified 55 states as having parliamentary executives, most of which were Commonwealth members. Presidential systems are those like the United States of America,

Table 5.2 Parliamentary versus presidential systems

	Parliamentary system	*Presidential system*
Assembly	'Parliament'	Assembly only
Executive	Separate heads of state and government	Popularly elected president
Head of state	Appointed by head of state	Also head of state
Appointment of government responsibility	Head of government appoints ministry	President appoints departmental heads
	Government is collectively responsible to assembly	President is responsible to the people
Personnel	Ministers (usually) Parliamentarians	Executive legislative separation
Dissolution of assembly	By head of state on advice of head of government	Not possible

Source: Verney, 1959

with an executive president, and are the most common form of constitutional government, 77 states being classified as limited presidential executives by the Derbyshires. They are found chiefly in the Americas and Africa.

The main differences between the systems may be expressed in terms of the separation and balance of powers. Following Montesquieu's interpretation of the eighteenth-century UK constitution, presidential systems not only divide the powers of government into legislative (law making), executive (law enforcing) and judicial (law interpreting) institutions, but seek to separate these in terms of personnel and balance them against each other. Democratic government is seen in terms of a refusal to concentrate potentially tyrannical power, so that it cannot be used to take away individual rights. Federalism is seen as a further expression of the same approach.

In parliamentary systems the main expression of democracy is seen in the enforcement of the responsibility of the executive to the people through parliament – in practice the independence of the judiciary is accepted, but the executive and legislative powers work in concert as a result of the government's legislative majority.

Not all systems, however, fit easily into one or other of the above constitutional moulds. The Derbyshires found 12 states with what they described as dual executives and we describe here as 'hybrid' systems. For instance, both contemporary France and Russia have adopted some features of each model, with a directly elected president with strong powers who appoints a prime minister to head the administration who is also responsible to parliament. In both cases it seems that the drafters of the constitution anticipated a strong leader (de Gaulle, Putin) faced by a scattering of weak parties. Indeed, the situation in Russia is even more complex: having served two terms as president between 2000 and 2008 and unable to stand again, Vladimir Putin simply swopped jobs and became prime minister, without any apparent loss of powers. The problem with the hybrid system is that the electorate may not elect a legislature sympathetic to the political ideas of the president. In France, on several occasions legislative elections have taken place after the presidential elections and a new and different coalition of political forces has clearly been in the ascendant. The president has usually decided to 'cohabit' with the opposition forces – compromising on policy and government personnel. The alternative is to confront the opposition and cause a constitutional crisis.

Possibly a more radical institutional reinterpretation of democracy can be seen in what is called 'consociational' democracy. In all liberal democratic systems a legitimate role is allotted to minority (opposition) political forces outside of the government. In Britain this is institutionalised in the title Leader of Her Majesty's Opposition. In consociational democracy the attempt is made to ensure that all significant minorities, as well as the majority, are actually represented in government. The best-known and most successful example of this is Switzerland, where the government (the Federal Council) is composed of representatives of all the major parties in parliament in proportion to their strength.

Such an arrangement seems particularly suited to societies that are deeply divided on national, linguistic or religious lines and where important groups may be in a permanent minority. Thus in Switzerland, French, German and Italian speakers, Protestants and Catholics are all automatically represented in the government. A recent attempt to use such a device was South Africa's 1994 constitution in which both the majority black (ANC) and the minority white (Nationalist) populations were guaranteed a role in government at least during a transitional period. In the 1998 Northern

Ireland peace settlement the use of this device was attempted for a second time, failing at first, but reactivated in 2007.

Verney discusses a third major type of democratic constitution: what he terms the 'convention'-style constitution modelled on the revolutionary French Assembly of 1789. The French constitutional tradition emphasised the legitimacy of the sovereign national assembly based on the popular vote. The assembly could not be dissolved and exercised detailed control over the personnel of government drawn from its ranks. Some modern French constitutions (especially the Third Republic from 1870 to 1940) could be described in these terms and the Soviet constitution and many former Eastern Bloc constitutions also appeared to be based on this model.

However, it would be more realistic to describe Soviet-style democracy as one-party democracy, since the legal predominance of the assembly was clearly a fiction that scarcely masked the monopoly of the Communist Party. Only one party-sponsored candidate was presented in each constituency, and all resolutions of parliament were passed unanimously on the initiative of the government/party. The party, in turn, was controlled from the top through 'democratic centralism'. A claim to democracy could only be justified by an appeal to the top party members' superior grasp of 'scientific' socialism, which enabled them to represent the interests of the working masses more certainly than the workers themselves.

Another version of one-party democracy has been put forward in a number of post-colonial regimes. Here a virtually all-encompassing political coalition has been created to fight for independence – often centred on a 'charismatic' popular leader. Not unnaturally the national(ist) party obtains an overwhelming victory at the independence general election. Opposition to the national leader seems like treason. The national party now has a monopoly of the considerable patronage dispensed by the new state. In such circumstances it is not surprising for virtually all opposition to the party to disappear. Indeed, a similar state of affairs occurred in the United States after its national revolution (Lipset, 1979). In many newly independent states ethnic and racial antagonisms constitute both a serious threat to the continued integrity of the state and the natural basis for any multi-party democratic system. In such circumstances the single-party regime may be made a legal as well as a political fact.

The reality of such one-party regimes has differed greatly. In many – such as Nkrumah's Ghana – Marxist rhetoric about the importance of the party masked the reality of its virtual absorption by the government machine (Dowse, 1969). In a few states – such as Tanzania under Julius Nyerere – interesting experiments were attempted to combine the legitimacy and strength of a single national party with opportunities for popular participation through contested primary elections.

Zakaria (1997), in noting the rapid growth of democratic states, identifies two different approaches: liberal democracy and illiberal democracy. With both forms there are elections, but what differentiates them is what happens after an election: in the former there exist bundles of freedoms, but with the latter the government erodes or ignores those freedoms.

It is evident that the vast majority of states in the contemporary world make some sort of constitutional claim to be 'democratic'. Hence the widespread use of elections in autocratic regimes – Golder (2005) found that dictatorships were almost as likely to use elections as democracies.

MILITARY AUTOCRACY

The major undemocratic form in the modern world is military government. Such is the power of the democratic myth that most such regimes represent themselves as transitional – temporary remedies for an unfortunate inadequacy in a preceding nominally democratic regime. Indeed, a key part of the armed forces' temporary assertion to power may be that they claim to be 'non-political', in the sense of both non-partisan and committed to the national interest rather than that of any narrow section of the population. A claim is frequently made for the greater efficiency and incorruptibility of officers (as opposed to civilian politicians) as a united, disciplined, educated and trained modern elite.

Indeed, it is quite common for armies that have intervened in politics to return to the barracks after a period in power when these values come under stress. With the pressure of being forced to make decisions, which will be interpreted as favouring one section of the population or another, conflicts are frequently generated within the military which are not necessarily evident while the army is confined to a technical role. For instance, most Latin American officers have been recruited from white, land-owning groups, and governments dominated by them tend to be unsympathetic to both rural Indian and urban slum-dwelling populations. In Africa regional and tribal conflicts can come rapidly to the fore, as was graphically illustrated in the Nigerian Civil War (1966–1971). Here the military intervened to stop 'tribalism, nepotism and corruption' on the part of civilian democratic politicians, only to preside over more bloodshed and disunity than had ever previously been experienced.

The mechanisms of military intervention vary greatly depending on time and place. In countries such as Turkey and Brazil the army is often seen as having an important 'guarantor' role in relation to the constitution. In the Turkish example this is as the inheritor of the prestige of Atatürk (the founder of modern Turkish nationalism). The army sees itself as entitled to intervene to preserve Atatürk's ideas of secular modern nationalism. In such cases the army may exercise a veto on the participation of some groups in the government, rather than play a direct role. The extreme form of military intervention, in which the head of state and all cabinet posts are taken by officers, the legislature is dismissed and the courts summarily over-ruled, is relatively rare. More commonly a supreme military council or similar body may effectively replace the legislature while the day-to-day government may remain in the hands of a cabinet with civilian participants. Top civil servants may often be deputed to take over roles previously carried out by civilian politicians.

CIVIL AUTOCRACY

Like their military equivalents, few contemporary civilian dictators (autocrats) reject the idea of democracy; most claim either to be democratic rulers or to be preparing the way for democracy when the mess created by the previous corrupt and ineffective regime has been cleared up. Finer (1970) uses the suggestive descriptions of 'facade democracies' and 'quasi-democracies' for regimes of this sort. Meaningful free elections are quite difficult to achieve, so deliberate manipulation of an ostensibly democratic system may help to confuse domestic opposition and satisfy Western aid donors, diplomatic and military allies and investors.

A variety of devices may be used to restrict the impact of elections and opposition criticism. The most obvious stratagems are to continually postpone the next elections having once attained a sort of electoral victory; to ban some opposition parties as 'subversive', 'terrorist', or 'Islamic fundamentalist' and imprison their leading supporters; or to ban all other parties as disruptive to national unity. Slightly less obvious tricks include the deployment of patronage in favour of supporters, discrimination against opponents in relation to employment by the state, and the siting of major public works. Opponents may be prosecuted, censored or physically eliminated. Elections can be held, but under a 'rigged' electoral system.

The constitutional basis of such autocratic regimes is quite variable. In Latin America there is often theoretically a written constitution which the president simply overrides or ignores as convenient. In Africa an original independence constitution based on that of France or of Westminster has more frequently been amended in the name of nationalism to allow the explicit adoption of a single-party model. In some cases what was a military regime has ostensibly been civilianised, with the original military dictator creating a civilian government party to support him. Examples include Colonel Nasser in Egypt, Colonel al-Gadhafi in Libya and Saddam Hussein in Iraq. A few regimes – such as that of the former 'Emperor' Bokassa of the Central African Empire/Republic – are more original in their form.

A probably more significant difference between such regimes is the basis of their political support. As we have seen, traditionally Latin American authoritarian regimes have been supported by landowners, the army and the Church. Regimes in Africa and the Middle East may represent the successors of a coalition of nationalist 'intellectuals' (i.e. a Western-educated minority), who replaced the colonial administrative elite. In Haiti the Duvalier regime was supported by a private gangster army – the Tontons Macoute.

Perhaps related to the question of the social support for the regime are questions regarding the degree of collegiality within the regime and its stability. To the extent that an autocratic regime is built upon one more or less charismatic leader who ruthlessly builds up a personal machine based on patronage, terror and/or personal loyalty, it is likely to be unstable in the long run. The question of succession is clearly a difficult one in such cases, although, as with presidents Duvalier and Kim Il-sung (North Korea), the child of the dead leader may be adopted by the elements that supported the father. When the regime is based on a dominant coalition of social forces, it may have a wider division of power and greater stability. The best example of this is probably that of Mexico, whose PRI (Partido Revolucionari Institucional) dominated the country for most of the twentieth century (until 1997). The PRI clung strongly to the principle that no president should serve more than one six-year term so that no faction within it could overwhelm the others. Despite the name the PRI came to represent a coalition of established local political machines, often with strong bureaucratic, military, agricultural and labour links.

TOTALITARIAN GOVERNMENTS

We saw that Crick defined totalitarianism largely in terms of its all-encompassing role, in contrast to modern republican (or liberal democratic) regimes which leave a much greater area to private initiative and control. The category of 'totalitarian' state has been criticised as too tightly drawn to contain, or at least usefully describe, any modern state. 'Totalitarian' state was not a term coined by Crick, nor do all authors using the term emphasise those elements of Crick's treatment which have been highlighted here.

Other writers (e.g. Friedrich, 1964; Arendt, 1967) have stressed not only the scope of the activities of the totalitarian state but also the similarity of the methods employed by them to control the population. The totalitarian state is seen as one which employs modern technology and techniques of organisation to enforce total control over the lives of the population of a large modern indus-trialised state. Thus, both nazi Germany and the Stalinist Soviet Union employed a single mass party to generate and enforce enthusiasm on the part of the population. Modern communication methods such as newspapers, cinema and radio were monopolised by the regime and used to propagate a 'cult of personality' around the leader. The use of terror – the employment of torture and the mass extermination of whole segments of the population – is also seen as characteristic of such regimes. Although historic dictatorships have also used such methods, this has not usually been on such a scale or so systematically.

Critics of such an approach to the analysis of modern states have variously argued that it seeks to tar all progressive socialist regimes with the Hitler/Stalin brush; that the post-Stalin Soviet Union was a conservative bureaucratic society rather than one based on terror; or even that the concept 'totalitarian' control is better applied to the activities of modern capitalism in creating a consumer society. Thus Marcuse (1964: 13) argues that in modern automated consumer societies:

> the productive apparatus tends to become totalitarian to the extent which it determines not only socially needed occupations, skills and attitudes but also individual needs and aspirations. ... Technology serves to institute new, more effective, and more pleasant forms of social control.

Despite the differences, to the authors it does seem that nazi Germany and Stalin's Soviet Union have much in common and that one can construct an extreme 'ideal type' of government – 'totalitarian' government – which encapsulates their similarities in terms of both all-encompassing scope and ruthless methods. It would not be impossible to imagine, say, an ecological or religious totalitarian regime in the future using modern information tech-nology and psychological and pharmaceutical discoveries for sur-veillance and control to a greater extent than even Hitler or Stalin achieved. What should not be done is to assume that every regime described as communist or fascist shares all these characteristics. In practice there is no clear line of division between autocratic or authoritarian regimes and the more extreme totalitarian variant. Late Soviet or present-day Chinese government could be placed in either category – particularly as market-led economic reform reduces the direct power of the Communist Party.

Logically one can have some sympathy for Marcuse's contention that the capitalist system is moulding everyone's perceptions and behaviour – we may be being 'brain-washed' into becoming good consumers. Thus an analogy is drawn with Hitler's attempt to create pure Aryans or the Soviet Union's programme to create 'New Soviet Man'. His use of 'totalitarian' to describe this

Table 5.3 The characteristics of different states

Democracy	Authoritarianism	Totalitarian
Use of elections	No political dissent	Small elite
A positive norm to use	Use of force	Control of the population
Often associated with capitalism	Can be a façade of democracy	Justification of actions through ideology

phenomenon is however somewhat misleading in that there is no deliberate co-ordinated political direction to this process. Nor are we robbed of our freedom of choice on pain of imprisonment. Alternative life styles are not censored – though they may be swamped.

If nazi and Soviet totalitarianism are essentially historical descriptions of states that no longer exist, a new form of totalitarianism has recently evolved. Singh (2003) notes the importance of the destruction of the Twin Towers in New York on 11 September 2001, with George W. Bush's response being the 'war on terror'. This led German foreign minister Joschka Fischer (2005) to refer to a 'third totalitarianism' replacing the nazi and Soviet versions. Fischer presents this third totalitarianism as based on 'jihadist terrorism', and he suggests that the similarities with the previous two regimes are the aim of global domination and the use of terror. Mozaffari (2007) suggests that Islamism combines a religion and an ideology whose aim, he suggests, is 'conquest of the world by all means'. This implies that the application of totalitarianism is evolving, but as yet it is difficult to view any Islamic state as totalitarian. Perhaps the nearest to this model is Iran – but Islamic Iran is considerably more democratic and constitutional than many states in the Middle East. Alternatively, it is possible that totalitarianism will become a stateless concept.

While it is clear from this discussion that there are variations within Crick's framework, we can highlight in Table 5.3 some key characteristics of democratic, authoritarian and totalitarian states.

ISLAMIC GOVERNMENT: BREAKING THE MOULD?

For many in the South Islam is now increasingly seen as the alternative to capitalism and democracy, but the major problem is to create distinctive and effective economic and political institutions for any proposed Islamic state. A variety of differently governed states such as Iran, Turkey, Afghanistan, Egypt and Sudan have been referred to as Islamic governments, but what does this mean?

While the Qur'anic tradition does have some positive statements to make on economic matters – the immorality of interest payments; the duty to make payments to the poor (zakat) – these have proved difficult to institutionalise in a modern (i.e. capitalist) economic context. Similarly, the Qur'an makes it clear that the ummat (community of the faithful) should be ruled by those faithful to its religious prescriptions and be united and that rulers should listen to the voice of the community – but no concrete political and religious institutions are laid down. The two major Islamic traditions – the Sh'ite and the Sunni – differed early on the succession to the Caliphate (political leadership) (Fischer, 1980). Other differences include the Sh'ite's greater emphasis on the importance of religious scholars and the role of martyrs. The relationship between the strongly developed traditions of Qur'anic law and the modern state, and the role of electoral institutions, are matters of considerable debate within Islamic countries.

In practice contemporary states with a commitment to Islam differ considerably in their political and economic arrangements. For instance Saudi Arabia, several other Sunni-dominated states around the Gulf, Brunei and, to some extent, Jordan retain a dynastic rule in which the leading family of a recently tribal society continues to rule without any great formalisation of constitutional matters. Considerable revenues derived from oil are used in a paternalistic way to ensure the loyalty of the indigenous population – many recent immigrants being denied participation in government and citizenship. Various more or less consultative assemblies have been convened, but they have frequently been dissolved if they have proved overly critical. Social practices vary, but in Saudi Arabia in particular, traditional attitudes towards women, alcohol and the like are strictly enforced through religious courts interpreting the Qur'an in accord with the Wahhabist extreme conservative interpretation of the Sunni tradition. In Afghanistan, similar beliefs culminated in the Taliban regime effectively banning female work, education and even hospital treatment and in the destruction of world famous historic monuments.

In contrast, the Shi'ite state of Iran following a revolution against the Shah of Iran adopted a much more original constitution. Power is divided between a government and a leader, or council of leaders. The government (president, prime minister and cabinet) is based upon an elected national consultative assembly. Islamic scholars head the judicial system, fill the post of commander in chief and vet the suitability of candidates for the presidency. A particular Islamic school of thought is proclaimed to be the official religion of Iran, whilst Zoroastrians, Christians and Jews are the only recognised and tolerated (non-Islamic) religious minorities. The government's responsibility to promote Islam is spelt out, and it has the power to confiscate wealth derived from 'usury, usurpation, bribery', etc. (Article 49 of the Constitution). Legislative power is divided between the National Consultative Council and the Council of Guardians – Islamic scholars who must review legislation to ensure its compatibility with Islam. In practice, since the death of the first revolutionary leader, the Ayatollah Khomeini, considerable tensions have been evident between the more pragmatic and modernising tendencies often centred on the president and the more conservative forces centred on the leadership council. This model of Islamic government may well be less acceptable in areas where the Sunni tradition is stronger and there is not such an established hierarchy of Islamic scholars.

In countries such as Egypt where Islamic forces have been in opposition to a more secular government, they frequently benefit from popular support derived not only from the powerful indigenous traders of the bazaar but also from the beneficiaries of the informal welfare system based on the zakat paid to the mosques and distributed by their leaders. Intellectuals can produce more or less convincing schemes for non-capitalist economic arrangements eschewing the payment of interest. In opposition, Islamic forces may achieve a formidable reputation for discipline and puritanism; this assisted the Taliban faction in Afghanistan towards its initial victory and may have helped the Islamic Brotherhood achieve government in Egypt before it was overthrown by the military in 2013.

So far, however, Islam has proved a useful weapon of opposition to Western influences but has been much less effective in constructing an alternative or discreet model of political and economic management, or in uniting the faithful politically.

THE DIFFERENT LEVELS OF THE STATE

Thus far we have viewed states as large national level organisms, but we also need to recognise that the state is rarely to be found at one level alone. One obvious way to minimise the degree to which state decision-making is seen as remote is to keep the state concerned as small as possible. As we have seen, anarchists advocate dividing the whole world into a network of such voluntary self-governing communities.

The disadvantages of a multitude of small-scale states may include an increased likelihood of inter-state violence. Another problem might be a failure to express larger senses of national or regional identity. Possibly, too, there would be a lack of capacity for large-scale investment necessary for complex transport systems, advanced health, education and research facilities. Manned exploration of outer space and nuclear weaponry would be unlikely in the absence of 'super states' like the US and EU.

The actual distribution of governmental powers between layers of government is somewhat haphazard in practice, with historical influences being very important. In the UK the idea of the sovereignty of the national parliament has contributed to a strong concentration of power at national level. In the United States and in Switzerland, many of the component states or cantons preceded the federal governments and retain exceptionally strong powers. However, the trend in most parts of the world has been towards a greater concentration of powers at the higher levels of government.

Many factors have contributed to this trend towards centralisation. One simple factor is that the central government will normally be the biggest government in the state and therefore contains the greatest concentration of expertise. Control of the major organisations capable of physical harm clearly strengthens central governments. A major factor in most systems is that the higher levels of government usually control the more effective taxing mechanisms – particularly income tax. Clearly, in many areas of government 'economies of scale' mean that large operations can be more efficient than smaller ones.

Opposed to these centralising tendencies are not only democratic considerations, but also the need to deliver policy effectively to citizens where they live. As circumstances will vary from local district to local district, a 'top–down' central solution to a centrally conceived problem may well translate into an inappropriate response to local problems. The idea of 'subsidiarity' can be applied to decide which level of government to allocate powers to. The principle was incorporated in the Maastricht treaty on the future of the European Union of 1991 and advocates that political decisions should always be made at the lowest possible level of government.

The advantages of better democratic control and the greater flexibility of response to local circumstances create a presumption in favour of the lower level. In contemporary Britain, however, governments have interpreted this principle somewhat selectively. There has not been the same emphasis on leaving to local government the maximum decision-making power as the central UK government has asserted in its relations with Europe (see Duff, 1993).

The principle of subsidiarity has been strongly endorsed in twentieth-century papal encyclicals, thus Pius XI in *Quadragesimo Anno* (1931) proclaimed:

It is an injustice, a grave evil and a disturbance of right order for a large and higher organization to arrogate to itself functions which can be performed efficiently by smaller and lower bodies.

Subsidiarity is, therefore, a principle that fits easily with the Christian democratic parties of Europe.

Two further related aspects of the division of powers between levels of government are worth exploration. First, who divides the powers between levels of government? Second, what are the relationships between levels when they are both concerned with an issue? These are summarised in Box 5.6:

BOX 5.6 RELATIONS BETWEEN LEVELS OF GOVERNMENT

In principle a FEDERAL system is one in which the allocation of powers is independent of either level of government in question. Each has its defined sphere of influence, this normally being laid down in a written constitution and interpreted independently (probably by the courts) in case of dispute.

(K. C. Wheare, 1963)

In a system of DEVOLUTION a higher level of government creates and gives powers to a lower (elected) level of government to exercise.

In a system of DECENTRALIZATION subordinate local administrative agencies are created by a central government and may be given some discretion to interpret central policy and consult local opinion.

In a CONFEDERAL system the powers of the higher-level government are granted by the lower-level governments which may withdraw them (as with most international organisations).

(Authors' definitions)

Just over a third of modern liberal democracies have a federal or semi-federal form of organisation, and just over a third have some form of devolution (Keman, 2002). As well as the obvious examples of the US and Germany, there is a wide range, including Austria, Brazil and Ethiopia.

One might expect the lower levels of government in a federal system to act independently of the upper layers. The lower levels in a devolved system may be expected to negotiate a local interpretation of national policies within a framework of national statutory guidance. In decentralised systems the local bureaucrats would merely interpret national policies according to local circumstances. In confederal systems the upper tier would be expected to act according to a consensus of the views of the lower tier.

In practice some measure of co-ordination, co-operation and negotiation between levels seems to emerge. Thus American writers on US federalism have tended to use the term 'co-operative federalism' to indicate the extent to which state authorities have tended to co-operate with federal policy initiatives, partly in order to obtain access to large subsidies from the federal budget. At the extreme, a part of a central bureaucracy may be so much under the influence of a local 'mafia' that national policies conflicting with local interests may be ignored, as in Italy (Banfield and Banfield,

1967). Conversely, as in the former Soviet Union, nominally independent state authorities may be under almost total political control of a centralised political party (Schapiro, 1965). The European Union is a classic example of the fuzzy relationships that can emerge between levels of government.

The institutions of local government often reflect those of central government. Thus, in well-established Western liberal democracies such as France there is a long tradition of local representation and autonomy. In the United States a sturdy tradition of local government was established even in the colonial era, and on this was built the later development of state and national autonomy and democracy. The reverse applies in China and the former Soviet Union, where the mechanisms of national one-party pseudo-democracy were reproduced at local level with large-scale participation masking central dictation of virtually all local decisions and the previously imperial bureaucracies held sway.

In some places, however, there may be conflict between national and local styles of political behaviour, which complicates the establishment of a viable local government system. To give an extreme example, the British in colonial Nigeria set up a system of 'native administration' designed to lead the way to a modern local government system. This was based on modernising and gradually democratising the administration of local 'traditional rulers'. In the north of Nigeria this had the unfortunate effect of reinforcing the power of some of the more conservative elements in a rapidly changing society. In parts of the east of the country, so-called 'warrant chiefs' had to be invented to attempt to impose an authoritarian (colonial) system on what was already an egalitarian society vitally receptive to change (Wraith, in Mackintosh, 1966: 212–267).

The degree to which the structure of local government is determined by central government also varies from state to state. In parts of the United States both the boundaries and internal organisation of local government are almost entirely a matter for local decision. In France all communes are required to have a mayor as chief executive who, while locally elected, also functions as an official of the central government; at departmental and regional level the chief executive is an appointed official of the national ministry of the interior. Communal and departmental boundaries, however, have remained relatively stable and local commitment to them is quite high.

There is also striking variation in the internal organisation of local authorities. The traditional UK arrangement centred around a series of only loosely coordinated committees of elected members, each of which supervised the work of one or more departments headed by professional specialists. In contrast, many US councils have much stronger executives consisting either of professional city managers or directly elected mayors. The French pattern in which the chief executive is provided by the central government is also to be found quite widely – especially in ex-colonial areas. In recent years the British trend has been towards smaller and more tightly co-ordinated committees and a style emphasising the development of a strategic management team of professional officers. In most cases local authorities have moved towards small 'cabinets' of local councillors in parallel with the professional management teams.

Central control of local government may vary from the situation in the United States where the concept is hardly recognised, to situations in some countries in the South where the concept of independent action by local government is similarly virtually unthinkable. An important element in the relationship is the cultural one of the expectations of the parties to the relationship. Another dimension is a legal one. In the United Kingdom until recently the concept of *ultra vires* limited local authorities to those actions explicitly authorised by law (that is, laws passed by the central parliament). On the other hand, the assumption in the United States is that governmental powers not explicitly granted to the centre by the constitution belong to the states or 'the people'. In France, and in many continental European countries, communes are seen as having an inherent right to act on behalf of their inhabitants in the absence of legal restraints.

From a financial point of view, central control over budgets obviously restricts localities. The need for French councils to have their budgets approved by the next highest level of authority used to be regarded as evidence of their relative inferiority by British writers on local government. However, the current system of financing UK local government is based effectively on the central government setting spending limits for local authorities and penalising them through the system of financial grants from the centre if they do not abide by a central civil service judgement of their needs. US local governments seldom have such limitations – although they may be required to submit large-scale borrowing to a referendum of local voters.

Related to this is the important question of the tax base allowed to local government. Again the US freedom to set effective levels of sales and property taxes might be compared favourably with the very limited powers now allowed to UK councils – who cannot even set their own rates of tax on local business premises. Similarly, in many parts of the South the major constraint on the growth of effective local government is the lack of any realistic source of independent income.

The case for more power for local governments than they achieve in most states outside of the US is a persuasive one. The implementation of central policies by local authorities allows local people to make some independent assessment of relative local needs and priorities and allows local circumstances to be taken into account more quickly – more rational policies which suit local needs should ensue. The democratic principle of 'subsidiarity' suggests that local decision-making allows more participation by those affected and citizen education, training and loyalty is facilitated. 'Small is beautiful': the greater the autonomy accorded local authorities, the less central co-ordinating machinery is required. Councils allow the expression of community identity and act as advocates for their communities with other bodies. They present an opportunity for policy and management experimentation, innovation and learning. Division of power in a democracy is desirable: 'Power tends to corrupt, absolute power corrupts absolutely' (Acton, 1887).

CONCLUSION

One new and challenging development in states is the idea of the 'mafia state'. Naim (2012) defines mafia states as ones where government officials and criminals work together and suggests that Kosovo, Bulgaria and Venezuela may be considered as such.

The state is not monologous, that is, found at one level or in one institution alone, rather there are a range of different levels required – local, regional, national and even supra-national. In modern societies with complex economic and social issues a state-less society is probably not desirable or feasible. While anarchism might be attractive for some, it is unlikely to be a viable solution for the problems we face.

In the twenty-first century, representative liberal democracy does appear to be the globally dominant form of government. In many parts of the world, however, the institutions of liberal democracy are still either absent or so recently established that their capacity to endure in the face of economic difficulties, internal corruption, ethnic strife or international confrontation must be seriously open to doubt. Even in those parts of the world where liberal democracy seems more securely established, there are many questions still to be settled as to the units and levels upon which it should operate.

The concept of a state is organic and so it is constantly evolving. Certainly, there now appears to be a caché to the term democracy, as noted by its use where elections are not perhaps as fair and free as they might be. We have also noted primarily an association between representative democracy and capitalism, but Russia and China are two major economic powers which do not easily fit within representative democracy. Moreover, as we shall see in the next chapter, globalisation has raised a number of questions; in part this has led to a strengthening of states, but there are areas where the state has less of a role. If for many centuries the key questions for states were 'internal' such as size, boundaries, political system and who ruled, the 'external' questions concerning transnational matters are growing in importance.

FURTHER READING

Bukay, D. (2007) 'Can there be an Islamic democracy?' *The Middle East Quarterly*, Spring: 71–79.

Hague, R. and Harrop, M. (2004) *Comparative Government and Politics*, 6th edn, Basingstoke: Macmillan.

Journal of Democracy, at www.journalofdemocracy.org.

Miller, D. (1984) *Anarchism*, London: J. M. Dent.

Wilson, D. and Game, C. (2002) *Local Government in the United Kingdom*, 3rd edn, Basingstoke: Palgrave Macmillan.

Zimmerman, J. (1992) *Contemporary American Federalism: The Growth of National Power*, Leicester: Leicester University Press.

WEBSITES

www.cia.gov

CIA: Central Intelligence Agency includes up-to-date statistics in the World Factbook (downloadable free).

www.prio.no/Data/Governance/Vanhanens-index-of-democracy/

Measures the extent of democracy, participation and competition in 187 countries.

www.federalism.ch

Institute of Federalism, Fribourg, Switzerland includes working papers and on-line federalism games.

http://europa.eu/index_en.htm

European Union.

6

GLOBAL

THIS CHAPTER ...

will address, in part, relations between states reflecting the growth since the middle of the twentieth century in both bi-lateral and multi-lateral government relations. In addition, we will look at the growing role of non-governmental international relations in the form of international institutions and multinational corporations (MNCs). Over the past forty to fifty years, non-governmental organisations (NGOs) have played an increasing role, and we shall assess their relationship with states, international institutions and MNCs. We shall revisit some of the themes we have previously highlighted, but illuminated in a global context; for example, the normative nature of international politics and how power is exercised in a global world. What we are increasingly seeing evidence of is that international relations (IR) is key both as an area of study in its own right and as a part of political science.

Up to the nineteenth century foreign affairs primarily meant relations between one state and another or a small, often shifting alliance of a few states. Thus, during the Napoleonic Wars (1803–1815), Russia, Prussia and Austria were at various times in uneasy alliance with France and at others at war with her. Spain even fought both with and against France. This norm of fluid relationships between states all changed after the Great War (1914–1918), with the Versailles Peace Treaty creating an inter-governmental body, the League of Nations. Having suffered such great loss in the fields of Flanders and France, politicians of the leading nations sought to prevent war happening again. However, after some early success in the 1930s, the actions of Japan, Germany and Italy in ignoring it made the League of Nations a 'busted flush'. Learning the lessons after the Second World War, it was replaced by the United Nations, and within Europe the European Community was created as a means of cementing ties between former enemies. Moreover, we have had a proliferation since of political and financial international bodies such as the International Monetary Fund (IMF), North Atlantic Treaty Organisation (NATO) and Non-Aligned Movement (NAM). In addition, organisations such as Oxfam and Médecins Sans Frontières have developed an expertise in addressing particular global problems. By the end of this chapter readers will be able to:

- identify the meaning and importance of globalisation;
- understand some key factors which shape the global political world;
- assess the approaches to international relations;
- evaluate the role of the key actors in global politics.

GLOBALISATION

Marshall McLuhan (1964) popularised the concept of the 'Global Village' in which rapid satellite reporting and transmission of electronic images of events, from the invasion of Baghdad to the Olympic Games, familiarise everyone instantly with the same version of events all over the world. A shared consumption of similar goods such as Nintendo games, Reebok trainers and Coca-Cola is thought to have helped create an international popular (youth) culture. McLuhan was referring to the impact of television, but the existence of the Internet has enhanced the concepts he was talking about in the 1960s and 1970s. Thus online developments such as YouTube, Facebook and Twitter have enabled the creation of interactive global youth networks sharing music, chat and video clips.

Unprecedented levels of international travel have been made possible by modern technological developments. In addition, television documentaries, advertisements and films have all familiarised people all over the globe with the way of life of people in far-away places – especially that of affluent America.

The social and political implications of all this is immensely controversial. In countries as varied as France and Iran many of these developments have been denounced as 'creeping Americanisation'. The growing awareness of standards of living and freedom in the rest of the world was immensely influential in bringing about the end of communism in Eastern Europe.

It is increasingly difficult for national governments to cut their people off from knowledge of developments elsewhere in the globe and this knowledge can be political dynamite. In the US in the 1960s a series of urban riots were said to have been incited by the greater knowledge of the urban poor or the extent of their deprivation as a result of television. The sharing of information amongst citizens, often through the Internet, raises significant issues and tensions for countries. Politically insular countries such as North Korea go to extreme lengths to limit and control access to information from non-state-controlled sources. In a different context China is clearly dealing with the fact that having let the capitalism 'genie out of the bottle', that as consumers get more global market information this may have an impact on internal political demands.

Many of the themes introduced so far are encapsulated in the concept of 'Globalisation' (Luard, 1990; McGrew and Lewis, 1992; Baylis and Smith, 2005). Definitions of globalisation, and attitudes towards the idea, differ radically from writer to writer (see Box 6.1 below).

BOX 6.1   DEFINITIONS OF GLOBALISATION

the removal of barriers to free trade and the closer integration of national economies.

(Stiglitz, 2002: ix)

A historical process involving a fundamental shift or transformation in the spatial scale of human social organization that

> links distant communities and expands the reach of power relations across regions and continents.
>
> (McGrew in Baylis and Smith, 2005: 24)
>
> De-territorialization – or ... the growth of super-territorial relations between people.
>
> (Scholte, 2000: 46)

The authors define globalisation as the thesis that the increasing global interdependence of states, individuals and social and economic organisations is reducing the autonomy of individual states. Box 6.2 summarises some of the factors at work.

BOX 6.2   GLOBALISATION: CHALLENGES TO THE NATION STATE

Internal instability	resulting from mini-nationalisms, ethnicity, etc.
External instability	leading to need for regional global security.
Economic dependence	on global economic and financial organisations.
Social integration	due to development of world standards for human rights, professional behaviour.
Technical integration	means dependence on world communication networks and leading-edge technical developments increases vulnerability.
Ecological interdependence	as threats of pollution, global warming, etc., insoluble within state boundaries.

With the disintegration of the Soviet Bloc and the increasing integration of China into a world capitalist trading system, the political power of multinational companies in a globalised world has become increasingly central and controversial. The rules governing economic relationships between states are increasingly decided through international organisations such as the World Trade Organisation (WTO), the World Bank and the International

Monetary Fund. These in turn are often dominated by the United States and to some extent the European Union, both of which are sympathetic to the interests of multinational companies (Baylis and Smith, 2005: Ch. 14 by Woods).

For instance, Sell (2003) argues that the heads of 12 multinationals successfully lobbied the WTO to mould the Agreement on Trade-Related Aspects of Intellectual Property Rights (TRIPS) in the interests of their companies. This technical-sounding victory has been important in making it difficult for countries in the South to make available generic drugs to treat AIDS or resist the import of genetically modified plant species. Multinational companies have also lobbied hard, via the WTO, to ensure that they are entitled to tender for the provision of privatised government services across the globe.

Guttal (2007) argues that globalisation is economic in nature since it is driven by the needs of a capitalist global market, but that it is essentially a political phenomenon. The exact nature of globalisation is shaped by the actions of, and interactions between, states, international bodies and transnational corporations.

Globalisation as a discrete body of work within political science starts in the 1980s. Held *et al.* (1999) have identified three different approaches to understanding globalisation. The first approach, the globalist, is associated with economic changes having political and cultural implications. The second school of thought is characterised by sceptics who argue that global economy is internationalised rather than actually global. The third approach is favoured by transformationists, who share the sceptics' concerns but at the same time recognise the existence of a complex global world. Whichever way globalisation is interpreted, senior politicians recognise that it is one of the most important issues they have to deal with, be it the Maldives protesting about the effect on them of rising sea levels or how to manage economic recession.

'NORTH' VERSUS 'SOUTH'?

Just as the confrontation between communist 'East' and capitalist 'West' dominated international relations in the second half of the twentieth century, it seems likely that the divisions between 'North' and 'South' will dominate the twenty-first (Brandt, 1980).

'South' refers to what used to be called the 'Third World' or 'developing' or 'underdeveloped' countries. 'Third World' was a useful term since it suggested the geo-strategic truth that such countries were a loose block of states who could play off the capitalist 'West' against the communist 'East' at the United Nations and elsewhere. It seems hardly an appropriate term now, with the virtual disappearance of the second, communist, world. China, which professes to be communist, is of course very much a major – though not yet a super – power. However, it is unlikely to play the same sort of dominating role as the Soviet Union and has adopted many features of the capitalist economic system.

'Developing' is of course a polite euphemism for not yet developed, or 'underdeveloped', but it certainly cannot be taken literally that the rate of economic growth in developing countries is greater than elsewhere. The sad truth is that the whole of Africa on average has actually stayed economically static, or even retreated, in terms of gross national product (GDP) per head over the last three decades, as World Bank statistics show.

The term 'underdeveloped' also carries something of the implication of general inferiority to 'developed' countries, together with an aspiration to emulate them in all respects. To assume that a sub-continent like India, with its artistic and spiritual richness, diversity and long history of civilisation, should aspire to emulate the US is surely to adopt a somewhat limited perspective. Consider the reply attributed to Gandhi on being asked, on a trip abroad, what he thought of 'Western Civilisation': 'I think it would be a good thing!' The simple terms 'rich' and 'poor' states might be adopted as descriptors of the division we are making, but politically and socially an oil-rich sheikhdom might have more in common with its poorer neighbours than with Sweden or Switzerland.

'The South' then is a very loose term to describe the less-industrialised countries of Africa, Asia and Latin America. Although such countries encompass an enormous variety of political, economic and social conditions, we can see that they share some important similarities that may potentially place them in conflict with 'the North'. Beside the general problems inherent in a relatively low average standard of living, most of these countries share an experience of colonial subordination to the North (often exacerbated by racialism), and a continuing position of economic subordination to a world market dominated by Northern interests.

There is the potential for this economic disparity to have major political impact as the world struggles with issues which can only be addressed globally. As Yazdani and Dola (2013) note, many of the environmental issues have been created by industrialised nations over the past two hundred years, yet many countries in the South are both particularly vulnerable to climate change and unable to do much to address it on their own. Another issue is population growth: in the lifetime of the authors the world's population has grown from six billion to seven billion; this has primarily been driven by population growth in the South rather than the North. No single country can deal alone with the causes and consequences of such issues.

In most areas of the South the institutions of a modern independent state are relatively new (although most parts of the South contain civilised cultures dating back as far as, or further than, those of Europe). New state institutions and old social values can sometimes conflict. In other cases, rapid industrialisation and new waves of migration have created new ethnically mixed communities which can be difficult to govern – or easy to disrupt with irresponsible political agitation. Transition towards new styles of government and the lack of an established democratic tradition have helped generate greater political instability on the whole than in the North. Both military governments and experiments with single-party government are much more common in the South than the North.

Having made some generalisations about the politics of the South, it is worth cautioning readers against accepting too readily generalisations put forward by Northern commentators. The employment of huge generalisations about the 'rationality' of Western forms of political organisation (Parsons, 1957) and the prevalence of 'kleptocracy' – government by thieves – in the South (Andreski, 1968) may, on occasion, be little more than a mask for sophisticated ethnocentrism. It is worth bearing in mind that, as we have seen, ethnic conflicts can be found in US cities, in Northern Ireland and in the former Yugoslavia as well as in Africa or the Indian subcontinent. Corruption, too, can be observed on a large scale in apparently stable and rapidly growing political and economic systems such as the nineteenth-century US or twentieth-century Japan.

The range of social, political and economic systems to be found in the South means that the prognosis for the future of these countries may well be equally varied. Already states like South Korea, Singapore and Taiwan (the 'Newly Industrialised Countries' – NICs – of South East Asia) seem to have achieved massive, if not uninterrupted, economic growth. Japan has moved rapidly up the 'league tables' of social and political indicators. Conversely, parts of the UK seem to be taking on many of the social and economic characteristics of the South – for instance acting as a reservoir of cheap labour for the assembly plants of multinational enterprises (some of which are Korean and Japanese).

Rather than concentrating on the domestic political systems of the South, it may be more relevant to consider the extent to which the South faces a common economic and political environment which has the potential to drive the states of the South together in alliance against the North (Box 6.3).

BOX 6.3 NORTH VERSUS SOUTH: A MAJOR FAULT LINE IN INTERNATIONAL RELATIONS?

Consider such issues such as:

Southern indebtedness to Northern banks;

adverse movements in the terms of trade for the primary products of the South;

Northern monopolisation of intellectual property rights and information resources;

the activities of (Northern) multinational enterprises;

destruction of the planetary environment in the interest of Northern consumption.

Many of these issues were raised by the report of the Independent Commission on International Development Issues (Brandt, 1980). The likelihood of such a development must depend upon the extent to which the South feels deliberately excluded from the affluent economies of the North. Conversely, the degree to which it is thought possible that individual countries will gradually be able to participate in the benefits of Northern affluence will reduce instability. The dangers of the situation may be emphasised by a quotation from the Brandt report: 'It is a terrible irony that the most dynamic and rapid transfer of highly sophisticated equipment and technology from rich to poor countries has been in the machinery of death' (Brandt, 1980: 14).

BRICS

Alternatives to the North versus South hypothesis have been presented. In the 1980s there were the 'tiger' economies of the Far East, the term being normally applied to Singapore, Taiwan, Hong Kong and South Korea. These countries enjoyed significant economic growth for a number of years, primarily through manufacturing, and although these nations are still relatively wealthy, they have joined rather than replaced the economic dominance of the traditional Western nations. Moreover, their growth has not significantly increased their global political influence.

A more recent, and probably tenable, alternative consists of the so-called BRIC countries – Brazil, Russia, India and China. These present a completely different proposition to the 'Four Little Tigers' noted above, partly because of history but primarily due to their geographic size, population size and access to raw materials. Collectively they account for approximately a quarter of the world's landmass and some 40 per cent of its population. In 2010 this acronym was enlarged to BRICS with the addition of South Africa.

The term BRIC was devised in 2001 by economist Jim O'Neil in a paper, 'The World Needs Better Economic BRICs', where he argued that due to their demographic and economic potential they could dominate the world by 2050. The implication of this politically is that American hegemony may be replaced by one based around these initially four now five disparate countries. Their (potential) political impact derives from their economic size.

Although based in four continents (Europe, Asia, South America and Africa) there is some co-operation between the five countries. The heads of state meet annually for a summit, and they have agreed some joint activity. For example, at the Fifth BRICS

Summit held in South Africa in 2013 they agreed to establish a new development bank and a Think Tanks Council to develop policy and that the next Director-General of the World Trade Organisation (WTO) should come from a developing nation (www.brics5.co.za). That five heads of state will give up the time for such a meeting suggests that they believe the BRICS concept has some domestic and probably international relevance.

Kirton and Bracht (2013) suggest that at present there are two interpretations of the possible political impact of the BRICS. The first is that they will work increasingly closely and replace the current international status quo. The second is that they will merely join the developed powers and lead to a second 'scramble for Africa', which might explain why South Africa was invited.

Whatever the political objectives of the BRICS their supremacy is not guaranteed. Their political impact is largely based on their economies and, as noted by Sharma (2012), it is difficult to maintain economic growth for a decade or more. However, irrespective of what happens economically, it is in the realm of politics that the future impact of the BRICS will be determined. Despite the beginnings of collaboration they are not yet a coherent alliance working together. Perhaps more importantly, they have very different political cultures that make closer cooperation as a political club fraught with issues, and there are question marks over the long-term stability of each of their political systems.

A major limitation to the potential political influence of the BRICS is the inequality in economic resources; many commentators believe that China is the only one of the five that matters. For example, Rothkopf (2009) wrote: 'Without China, the BRICS are just the BRI, a bland, soft cheese that is primarily known for the whine [sic] that goes with it. China is the muscle of the group and the Chinese know it.' According to this analysis BRICS is essentially a vehicle for increasing the economic and political power of one nation state, supporting Kirton and Bracht's second hypothesis.

While clearly the BRICS may or may not have a significant impact in the future, Armijo (2007) has provided a possible framework for explaining how new and old political dominances may react to each other. Armijo identifies hard power based on the size of a country, its economy and military abilities, and soft power based on people liking your language and your views and identify-ing with your culture. This implies that were the BRICS to replace America as economic, military and economic *inter pares* at some point in the future, this could still leave room for an Anglo-Saxon cultural impact.

POLITICS BEYOND THE STATE: INTERNATIONAL INSTITUTIONS

We saw in the previous chapter that the state is considered to be the unit orthodoxy for most of the world, and consequently it is no surprise that it extends to international relations. The origin of this is believed to be the Treaty of Westphalia which ended the Thirty Years War in 1648 and in which the signatories (all European) recognised the sovereignty of other states. What has become known as the Westphalian model, therefore, implied that the state and not individual rulers took precedence. Though Tilly (1994) has suggested that in Europe the dominance of the Westphalian state is now over.

Formal and informal relationships, alliances and treaties between rulers and countries, have existed for centuries. But these have normally been bilateral discussions that are based on negotiations between two or more participants and essentially temporary. As noted earlier, it was not really until the twentieth century that an impetus for a different approach arose. The introduction of some form of international arbitration body is, therefore, a recent and challenging innovation which has a limited historical basis.

The United Nations (www.un.org/en/) is an international orga-nisation founded in 1945 by 51 countries committed to maintaining international peace and security, developing friendly relations among nations and promoting social progress, better living standards and human rights. It now has 193 member states and the UN can take action on a wide range of issues and provide a forum for members to voice their views through its various bodies and committees.

The four main purposes of the UN are:

- to keep peace throughout the world;
- to develop friendly relations among nations;

- to help nations work together to improve the lives of poor people, conquer hunger, disease and illiteracy, and encourage respect for each other's rights and freedoms;
- to be a centre for harmonising the actions of nations to achieve these goals.

The Secretary-General is the 'chief administrative officer' of the UN. The current secretary-general, and the eighth occupant of the post, is Ban Ki-moon of the Republic of Korea, who took office on 1 January 2007. He plays a number of roles and is essentially the chief executive and the symbolic figurehead of the organisation. Table 6.1 outlines the five main organs of the UN that shape its decisions and actions (we have not included the Trustees Council which is suspended because it has no trust territories to administer).

The United Nations building is in New York and there have been some accusations that having the UN based in New York has given the US undue opportunity to influence its agenda. But conversely the US has had to accept on their shores people they would not normally allow in. For example, some 200 senior members of the ruling ZANU PF party in Zimbabwe are banned from having any dealings with several countries, including the US, but this sanction does not apply when they officially visit for UN business.

The United Nations General Assembly is in many ways an unconvincing 'world parliament' since it is based on the equal representation of giant countries (in population terms) such as Brazil and Russia and mini-states like the Gambia and Luxembourg. Nor can a body which allowed dictators like 'Papa Doc' Duvalier of Haiti or General Amin of Uganda to misrepresent the populations they terrorised be viewed as possessing great legitimacy. The Security Council can be seen as a potential world 'government'. Its inclusion of 'permanent members' (US, China, Russia, Britain, and France – each with a veto over any decision by the Council) may have the merit of political realism, in that the UN cannot be expected to act effectively without 'Great Power' agreement. Alas, until the 1990s the Cold War meant that virtually all effective action by the UN was stillborn. Even now, with apparently greater international consensus, although humanitarian action in the former Yugoslavia, Liberia and the Congo has been possible, the UN is handicapped by the lack of effective executive apparatus and in

Table 6.1 The main organs of the UN

Body	Membership	Role	Power
General Assembly	All 193 members. Each member has one vote.	The main deliberative, policymaking and representative organ of the United Nations.	Decisions on important questions, such as those on peace and security, admission of new members and budgetary matters, require a two-thirds majority. Decisions on other questions are by simple majority.
Security Council	The Council is composed of 15 members – five permanent members: China, France, Russia, US, UK; ten non-permanent members elected for two-year terms by the General Assembly.	Primary responsibility for maintaining international peace and security to the Security Council, which may meet whenever peace is threatened.	• economic sanctions, arms embargoes, financial penalties and restrictions, and travel bans; • severance of diplomatic relations; • blockade; • collective military action.
Economic and Social Council	The Council's 54 member governments are elected by the General Assembly for overlapping three-year terms. Seats on the Council are allotted based on geographical representation, with 14 allocated to African states, 11 to Asian states, six to Eastern European states, ten to Latin American and Caribbean states, and 13 to Western European and other states.	Discusses, debates and makes recommendations for the world's social, economic and environmental problems.	Holds annual ministerial reviews and a biennial Development Cooperation Forum.
International Court of Justice	15 judges, elected for terms of nine years, sitting in The Hague in Holland.	The principal judicial arm of the UN.	To settle, in accordance with international law, legal disputes submitted to it by states and to give advisory opinions on legal questions referred to it by authorised United Nations organs and specialised agencies.
Secretariat	Headed by the Secretary-General with some 43,000 staff around the world.	Carries out the day-to-day work of the UN.	It gives advice to the other main organs.

2003 splits in the Security Council once more prevented effective action against Iraq. Long delays in taking humanitarian action in the Darfur region of the Sudan were accounted for partly by UN weakness against any recalcitrant sovereign state and partly by Chinese oil interests.

The response from the international community to the fact that chemical weapons were used during the Syrian civil war is an example of the role *realpolitik* plays in UN policy-making. Russia and the US appeared to be heading for an impasse which would have prevented any coherent UN response. A possible solution came seemingly by accident out of a press conference Secretary of State John Kerry gave in London, when an apparently throw-away comment that Syria could avoid a US military strike if it handed over its chemical weapons stockpile was seized upon by international statesmen and became the basis of a new policy.

However, focusing on major political decisions at the summit level of international organisations may well be a misleading guide to their importance and potential. The examples of NATO, the European Union (EU) and OPEC (the Organisation of Petroleum Exporting Countries) suggest that, when international organisations serve what is seen as a clear and necessary purpose, genuine and effective multinational cooperation is possible. These are of considerable interest in that they have exercised powers that are commonly seen as fundamental to 'sovereign states' on a collective basis.

Another example of the way international bodies are working effectively in the modern world is to consider such obscure agencies as the International Standards Organisation (ISO) or the International Telecommunications Union (ITU). Bodies like these hammer out essential technical agreements which enable telephones across the world to operate as one vast international network. This enables computer manufacturers on opposite sides of the globe to manufacture equipment which will work together, and agree on common scientific units in which new discoveries can be expressed.

There has been since 1945 a proliferation of the number and types of international institutions. Table 6.2 highlights a fairly random selection with a range of membership and purposes.

In trying to understand how international institutions work two main approaches dominate: the realist and the institutionalist. The former is probably the dominant paradigm and suggests that

Table 6.2 International institutions

Organisation	Membership	Purpose	Impact
Intergovernmental Panel on Climate Change	Composed of representatives selected by governments and organisations.	Publishes special reports.	Agenda setting. Awarded the Nobel Peace Prize in 2008.
International Atomic Energy Agency	159 states are members.	To promote the peaceful use of nuclear energy and inhibit its use for any military purpose.	Helps countries develop and manage their nuclear industries safely.
International Monetary Fund	188 countries.	Working to foster global monetary co-operation, secure financial stability, facilitate international trade, promote high employment and sustainable economic growth, and reduce poverty around the world.	As a major lender it can have a major impact on the world's economy.Its advice can also affect individual state economic policies.
OPEC (Organisation of Petroleum Exporting Countries)	Twelve members (six from the Middle East, four from Africa and two from South America).	Its mission is to co-ordinate and unify the petroleum policies of its member countries and ensure the stabilisation of oil markets in order to secure an efficient, economic and regular supply of petroleum to consumers, a steady income to producers and a fair return on capital for those investing in the petroleum industry.	As it represents some of the biggest oil producers in the world, its decisions can affect the supply and price of oil worldwide.
International Criminal Court	122 states are party to it.	The court of last resort for prosecution of genocide, war crimes and crimes against humanity.	High-profile and often notorious cases are dealt with here.

(Continued on p.148)

Table 6.2 (continued)

Organisation	Membership	Purpose	Impact
International Whaling Commission	88 states.	Charged with the conservation of whales and the management of whaling.	Addresses key issues to help in recovery of whale populations. In 1986 introduced zero catch limits for commercial whaling.
International Hydrographic Organisation	80 maritime states.	Intergovernmental consultative and technical organisation to support safety of navigation and the protection of the marine environment.	Ensures conformity in nautical charts.
African Union	54 African states.	The main objectives of the OAU are to rid the continent of the remaining vestiges of colonisation and apartheid; to promote unity and solidarity among African states; to co-ordinate and intensify co-operation for development; to safeguard the sovereignty and territorial integrity of member states; and to promote international co-operation within the framework of the United Nations.	Involved in a number of high-profile political crises such as the Libyan civil war.
Alliance of Small Island States	44 states and observers, drawn from all oceans and regions of the world.	A coalition of small island and low-lying coastal countries that share similar development challenges and concerns about the environment. It functions primarily as an *ad hoc* lobby and negotiating voice within the United Nations system.	Seeks to set the environmental agenda.

governments engage in those international activities that meet their rational self-interest. This implies that international relations is a zero-sum game: there are winners and losers. Though as Lieb (2004) notes when looking at Iceland's decision to join NATO (North Atlantic Treaty Organisation), this can be a complex matter – Iceland had a potential fishing 'issue' with the UK, one of the other signatories. The institutionalist approach often associated with Keohane and Nye (1989) suggests that international institutions act as independent variables which can influence state policy and behaviour. This might, therefore, explain why nations might take a cooperative, non-zero-sum approach to their participation in international institutions. The proponents of this approach point to the joint work on environmental issues which need not always be explained by self-interest.

A third approach is provided by Risse-Kappen (1995), who argues that internal domestic factors can shape foreign policy and participation in international organisations. He suggests that the domestic structure is affected by the nature of a country's political institutions, societal structure and the policy networks that exist between the state and society. Therefore, some countries are more likely to have internal actors which shape their involvement with international institutions.

EUROPEAN POLITICAL INSTITUTIONS

The growing importance of European institutions for so many countries and their unusual nature compared with the parliamentary and presidential models discussed earlier justifies some further discussion here. By 'European institutions' we mean those associated with the European Union. However, it should be noted that there are also many separate international bodies which may cover more of Europe. These include the European Court of Human Rights, the European Parliamentary Union and technical bodies such as the European Organisation for Nuclear Research (CERN).

The European Union is an interesting example of the processes of political change. It has developed from an organisation to co-ordinate iron and steel production in six countries to a potential continental superpower in less than fifty years. For the most part this has been a story of building alliances around common interests, trading advantages against disadvantages and seeking accommodations where national interests have conflicted. The original group of six members has expanded to 28, with more waiting to join, and it has become a potential superpower in its own right.

The initial creation of the European Economic Community (EEC) can be seen as a pragmatic bargain struck with an eye to a perhaps nobler vision. The creation of the EEC was part of a process in which the French government accepted the rehabilitation of (Western) Germany within the democratic community of nations in return for a measure of economic integration regarding basic industries and co-operation over defence issues through NATO. Thus, no German attempt to independently dominate Europe militarily and economically would be feasible. Although the details of the Treaty of Rome were fairly prosaic, behind it lay the vision of Jean Monet's Action Committee for a United States of Europe.

It is significant that most of the states which 'joined Europe' between 1957 and the early 1990s shared a vision of a united and democratic Europe – the idea of Europe as a political symbol. For instance, Spain, Portugal and Greece all joined what was by then known as the European Community after periods of authoritarian dictatorship, seeing it as a significant move towards joining the political mainstream of European development. Similarly, former Eastern Bloc countries such as Poland, Slovakia and Hungary, which became members in 2004, clearly wished to assert their commitment to a long-term future as part of a united and democratic Europe. There are at least 11 countries which, to varying degrees, are currently interested in joining, and negotiations are on-going with, for instance, Turkey, Montenegro and Iceland.

In contrast, the British application to join was defended domestically even by its proponents as a sensible economic move much more than a political one. Even proponents of joining the EEC asserted that the UK could still maintain its special political relationships with the US and the Commonwealth and that parliamentary sovereignty was undiminished by the move. Long after Brussels dropped the middle 'E' in EEC, the British government retained it. In the circumstances it is understandable that France's president, de Gaulle, vetoed Britain's first application to join on the grounds that Britain would be an American Trojan horse undermining European unity.

Since joining, Britain has played a somewhat ambivalent role. Under Mrs Thatcher's leadership, despite expressions of reservation on the political front, Britain did show some enthusiasm for the creation of a 'single European market'. The removal of obstacles to trade in order to create a 'level playing field' throughout Europe fitted the free-market economic policies of the Thatcher government and therefore permitted a temporarily strengthened legislative procedure to be introduced for the purpose.

The Maastricht agreement of 1991 reinforced the ambivalence of British government policies. There was a renewed nominal commitment to greater European unity and the creation of a single European currency, the strengthening of the powers of the European Parliament and of European institutions vis-à-vis domestic ones. But this was combined with a UK opt-out from the Social Charter and single currency provisions and the securing of general assent to the principle of subsidiarity. This inherent tension is to be currently found within the Conservative–Liberal Democrat coalition, with growing pressure within the Conservative Party for a referendum on whether or not to stay in the European Union.

The most distinctive features of the European Community include the existence of a dual executive with a complicated system of legislation by delegation and the co-existence of elements characteristic of both federal states and intergovernmental organisations.

The 'dual executive' comprises the Council of Ministers and the European Commission. The Council of Ministers consists of ministers from the member states' national governments, their votes normally weighted roughly according to the population of each state (but with smaller independent states over-represented). Ministers vote as representatives of their governments. The final policy decisions are made this way. The European commissioners are appointed for a fixed period of five years from each member state but are supposed to act as a single body from a European perspective. Each commissioner heads one part of the European civil service, such as energy, trade or climate action. There are currently 28 commissioners, which include the president (Manuel Barroso 2010–2014) and eight vice presidents. Jointly they propose legislation to the European Parliament and to the Council of Ministers and are responsible for the execution of policies decided by them.

The legislative process is uniquely complicated. It starts with extensive consultation by the commissioners, who may call upon formal advisory councils including those of employers, trade unionists and others from all over Europe. After approval by the European Parliament through an elaborate committee system and in full session, proposals go to the Council of Ministers. At present most proposals require a 'qualified majority' of votes to be approved (requiring the support of most of the larger states). Most important European legislation takes the form of 'directives' which require national parliaments to pass legislation for their implementation by a certain date, thus effectively adding a further stage to the process. Should national legislation not be sufficient to implement a directive, then the Commission would have to take the national government concerned before the European Court. In the event of disagreement between Commission, Parliament and Council, measures may shuttle between them and special majorities may be required to override recalcitrant parties.

In many – but not all – matters the Council of Ministers has the final say. In this respect the EU is like a conventional international organisation. But in having a directly elected parliament with substantial budgetary powers and a court of justice with authority to decide appeals from national courts on the interpretation of 'community' law, it is a similar position to a federal state.

Since the Maastricht agreement of 1991, these 'community' arrangements for co-operation on a wide range of economic matters have been supplemented by the so-called second and third 'pillars' of co-operation: direct intergovernmental agreements on a common foreign and security policy and on justice and home affairs (e.g. co-operation to catch international drug rings and illegal immigration). The three pillars together constitute the European Union.

In the long run, crucial technological developments are likely to require substantial investment, probably by multinational companies and states with massive economic resources. In effect, only the United States and, possibly, Japan and China have political and economic systems with large-enough tax bases and consumer markets to independently develop massive technological innovations such as space research, genetic engineering or super computer networks with built-in artificial intelligence. Individual European countries left to compete on their own (with the possible exception of Germany, now it is united) will become (as to some extent they already are) merely important subsidiary areas for competition between US and Japanese 'multinationals'. Only if Europe is a real single market and its research and development effort is genuinely pooled can it hope to remain an area where first-rate scientific, technological and hence industrial development on a substantial scale takes place.

The European Parliament based in Strasbourg has 766 members (MEPs); each is elected for a five-year term by universal suffrage. There is not one electoral system used by all; rather, each country selects its own means of voting in line with certain wider principles such as equality of the sexes and proportional representation. Seats are allocated on the basis of the population of each member state, with MEPs grouped together around political affinity, not nationality, as one of seven political groups. MEPs divide their time between their constituencies, Strasbourg – where 12 plenary sittings a year are held – and Brussels, where they attend additional plenary sittings as well as committee and political group meetings. The European Parliament is led by a president who oversees its work.

Originally more of a consultative body, the powers of the European Parliament have grown, especially since the 2009 Lisbon Treaty. Like many legislatures, the prime role of the European Parliament is now not to initiate legislation, but it does have the power – jointly with the Council of Ministers – to decide on the allocation of the EU budget and the right to approve or reject international agreements. Twenty standing committees help to develop legislation. A significant physical organisation has been created in a relatively short space of time.

Politically, the existence of a directly elected European Parliament can hardly be reversed. Given the dominant traditions of representative democracy the European executive must, in the long term, become responsible to it. A democratically constituted European executive will find itself the focus for enormous expectations for a peaceful, prosperous and united Europe. Already the EU has been expected to play a peace-making role in the former Yugoslavia – even though Yugoslavia has never been a part of the EU.

Thus far no independent state has joined and then left the European Union or any of its predecessor forms, though some states that gained independence from a larger state have done so. Thus, Greenland joined in 1973 as part of Denmark, but when it gained independence from Denmark in 1985 it decided to leave. Whether it should withdraw has occasionally been a political issue for the United Kingdom, and indeed the right to secede is written into the European Union articles. However, this move is unlikely since the majority of the UK's trade is with the EU and virtually all the inward investment it attracts is because Britain is inside the EU trading area. As the euro becomes better established, London may find it difficult to remain the primary European financial centre if sterling is retained.

An analogy can be drawn between current European developments and American history in the period 1776–1789. Following the Declaration of Independence in 1776 the 13 former American colonies agreed to a 'confederation'. Because of an insistence on the sovereignty of the individual states, Congress was without adequate executive, judicial or financial machinery with which to attempt to manage the security and economy of North America. Congress's failure to meet the expectations its very existence generated led to the adoption of the present constitution in 1789.

Similarly, the prospect of the accession of ten additional countries to the Union and a 'democratic deficit' in existing institutions led to the formation of a European Constitutional Convention which reported in 2003 and led to the proposal of a new constitution for Europe in 2004. This included a declaration of rights, a strengthened presidency of the Council of Ministers, changes in the numbers of commissioners for each state and more decision-making by a qualified majority (on a modified basis) in the Council of Ministers.

The defeat of referenda on the proposed constitution in France and the Netherlands slowed the reform process, but it seems likely that some of the measures proposed in the constitution – including the strengthening of the presidency and moves to include more policy areas in weighted majority decision-making – will be adopted piecemeal.

NON-GOVERNMENTAL ORGANISATIONS (NGOs)

NGOs have played an increasing role in international affairs. They are independent actors which provide advice, support and solutions to problems in areas such as disasters, health, education, human rights and environmental issues. Probably because of the insight, skills and credibility their experience gives them, many NGOs have also been asked by states to become involved in international institutions. For example, NGOs are able to attend the ministerial conferences organised by the World Trade Organisation (WTO) – several hundred had accreditation for the 2013 Bali meeting. The growth of NGOs reflects both the top-down encouragement of states and a bottom-up response to socio-economic factors.

While the assumption is that NGOs play a role by influencing primarily state-based institutions, NGOs have increasingly targeted the behaviour of commercial operations. Spar and La Mure (2003) highlight the example of the impact of the Free Burma Coalition, which successfully encouraged a number of companies to change their policies in dealing with Burma. The lesson they drew was that the success of such lobbying depended upon the impact on the bottom line of profitability.

The role that NGOs are playing in international affairs raises a key question concerning their impact on states. They can be viewed as a means of creating an increasingly borderless world: Teegan *et al.* (2004) suggest that the existence of NGOs is a challenge to states as they can support weaker states by lobbying against more powerful ones. Whereas Raustiala (1997) believes that by adding new skills and resources NGOs actually enhance states by enabling them to achieve their goals.

THE IMPACT OF MULTINATIONAL ENTERPRISES

The importance of multinational enterprises in the modern world is difficult to over-estimate. Some of these firms have a greater financial turnover than the gross domestic product of a medium-size state (see Table 6.3).

Thus, the 'economy' of South Africa, a BRICS member, is roughly the same size as that of the major UK oil company, while a small Caribbean country, St Kitts and Nevis, has less than 1 per cent of the revenue of Apple.

In addition, many of these corporations control vital economic resources such as oil (the 'Seven Sisters': Exxon, Texaco and BP), banking (Bank of America, HSBC and JPMorgan Chase) and

Table 6.3 Multinationals and countries compared

State or Company	Sales revenue or GDP ($ billion)	Company national HQ
USA	15,648	
China	83,583	
Japan	59,597	
Germany	33,995	
UK	24,351	
Brazil	22,526	
India	18,417	
Wal-Mart Stores	4,690	US
Royal Dutch Shell	4,670	Netherlands
BP	3,701	UK
South Africa	3,383	
PetroChina	3,081	China
Latvia	2,832	
Apple	1,641	US
Allianz	1,401	Germany
Morocco	959	
Haiti	783	
Samoa	71	
St Kitts & Nevis	7	

Source: Compiled by the authors from World Development Indicators Database, World Bank, November 2013 and the Forbes Global 2000, November 2013.
Note: GDP = Gross Domestic Product

computing (Microsoft, Intel and IBM). In some cases the world price of an entire commodity may be under the control of a multinational enterprise (e.g. De Beers and diamonds).

Virtually all multinational enterprises are clearly based in one host country, with the majority of shareholders and senior personnel from that country. (The few exceptions include Anglo-Dutch operations such as Unilever and Royal Dutch Shell.) Operations in specific countries may, however, be minority-owned and largely staffed by local personnel. Since our last edition there has been a growth in the size of companies from China such as ICBC, China Construction Bank and Agricultural Bank of China, which are now challenging the dominance of US-based companies. Ten out of the 20 biggest multinationals in 2012 on the Forbes list were of US origin, five were from China, and Russia and the UK provided two each.

In bargaining with governments in the South, a multinational enterprise is a sophisticated, rich organisation bargaining with a poorer and less skilled, less well-informed one. This can be illustrated by the problems even large Southern countries such as South Africa and India have had in their relations with multinational pharmaceutical companies in relation to drugs to treat HIV/AIDS (Seckinelgin, 2007).

Even in bargaining with a middle-rank power like France, a large Japanese or American corporation has very considerable negotiating power since it has the alternative of setting up elsewhere within the European Union and exporting to France from there. Even a US corporation dealing with its own government can channel its funds and development projects 'off-shore' to lower labour-cost countries or tax havens.

In the past, multinational enterprises often ran virtually independent operations in separate countries (e.g. Ford in US, Germany, Australia). But they are now increasingly pursuing integrated global strategies in which financial resources can be swapped around the world and production is planned centrally, with resources coming from the cheapest country relevant to the market in mind while profits are channelled to the most tax-efficient point. This is only possible due to a sophisticated global use of information technology, including the Internet (see Tansey, 2002).

NON-WESTERN INTERNATIONAL RELATIONS

One of the key arguments between commentators over a 50-year period has concerned transnational international relations theory. Lucian Pye writing in 1958 assumed that there were separate Western and non-Western political processes which reflected differences in culture, history and civilisation. Diamant (1959) accepted this broad hypothesis but critiqued it by suggesting that some of Pye's non-Western political processes are found in Western societies. Similarly, Puchala (1997) assumes that it is possible to distinguish between Western and non-Western ways of looking at the world, but added the idea that this was not just a matter between states – there could be immigrant enclaves within Western states with different values and ways of seeing the world.

History, especially that of the last four centuries, has clearly shaped the non-Western viewpoint due to the impact of imperialism.

Puchala suggests that the Western approach is dominated by the Westphalian state-based approach, whereas this is of less relevance to non-Western countries because many of their current state boundaries were drawn up in colonial times. Thus, the focus in non-Western countries is on ideas and ideologies rather than power and wealth.

However, Puchala did not pull together exactly where such a non-Western body of thought was to be found. Such an attempt has been made by Acharya and Buzan (2007), who argue for its location in Asia because of this area's long-standing history with distinct international relations and it is the location of the only concentration of power and wealth comparable to that of the West. They identify four sources of a discrete Asian international relations theory:

1 classical Asian traditions deriving from philosophers such as Sun Tze and Confucius;
2 the foreign policy attitudes of Asian leaders such as Gandhi, Mao and Sukarno. They cite the non-alignment movement set up by Nehru in the 1950s and adopted by Asian and African nations;
3 the application of Western international theory to an Asian context;
4 Asian international theoretical work in an Asian setting.

Chen (2011) rejects Acharya and Buzan's hypothesis on the basis that there cannot be a separate Asian international relations theory until the hegemony of the Western epistemology is replaced by a non-Western one. That any attempt at creating an Asian, or any other non-Western, approach will fail because it will be framed by imperialism. Chen, therefore, focuses on the overriding importance of removing the Western hegemony of international relations thought, rather than attempting to create at this stage a discrete non-Western approach.

Although Puchala, Acharya and Buzan and Chen adopt different viewpoints, they share one common characteristic. They all assume that international relations theory is normative, centrally shaped by the colonial behaviour since the sixteenth century of primarily European nations.

CONCLUSION

International relations have changed significantly since 1945. We have witnessed more determined attempts to create international bodies, such as the UN, and a number of new regional or global institutions. These have provided many states with a voice, but at the same time we have witnessed the growth in the representation of non-state players, primarily MNCs and NGOs, which have changed the nature of some global debates. We have also observed changes in the major state powers – where the US has remained constant as a superpower, the Soviet Bloc is now no more. Many individual European states have been gradually declining, though the EU as a collective has the potential to be a superpower. Countries in Asia have grown in economic importance, especially Japan and China.

Given the importance of assessing who is up and who is down in global power terms, it is no surprise that much of the analysis of global politics has a normative element. For many commentators this reflects the impact of colonial expansion by European countries in centuries past. At points it has reflected ideological issues such as whether communism was the way forward or not. While much of international relations study reflects individual state power, we have also witnessed the salience of essentially global issues such as environmentalism.

FURTHER READING

Keohane, R. (1988) 'International institutions: two approaches', *International Studies Quarterly*, 32 (4): 379–396.
Martell, L. (2007) 'The third wave in globalisation theory', *International Studies Review*, 9 (2): 173–196.
Peterson, J. and Shackleton, M. (2006) *The Institutions of the European Union*, Oxford: Oxford University Press.

WEBSITES

http://ec.europa.eu/commission_2010-2014/members/index_en.htm
Lists the members of the EU Commission.
www.europarl.europa.eu/portal/en

Details of the working of the European Parliament.
www.forbes.com/lists
Database of multinational enterprises, the rich, etc.
www.polity.co.uk/global
Globalisation debate, with good links.
www.worldbank.org
Useful source of global statistics on economy and governance.
www.cfr.org
Influential US Council on Foreign Relations.
www.isn.ch
Security and global politics from a Swiss/European perspective; note excellent links pages.
www.globalpolicy.org
Monitors United Nations policy-making, with good resources and links on globalisation, etc.
www.globalisation.eu
From a European free market think tank.
www.brics.utoronto.ca/
University of Toronto BRICS research centre.

MECHANISMS

THIS CHAPTER ...

will assess how government and governing are operated within liberal democracies, by looking at how decisions are made and how the voice of individuals and groups of citizens can be heard. One historical approach to understanding this process has been the idea of four estates of power. The origins of this can be traced back to medieval Europe, when the first estate was the Church in the form of the clergy. The second estate was the monarchy in the form of kings and queens, and included aristocrats such as dukes and lords. The third estate was made up of what can be referred to as commoners and included working men, peasants, serfs and whoever was at the bottom of society, though this estate eventually built up political influence in connection with the growing electoral franchise. These three estates existed in some relationship of co-operation and conflict for several centuries. Then in the eighteenth and nineteenth centuries they were joined by a fourth estate – the media in the form of newspapers, the role of which was to act as a neutral check against unacceptable behaviour by the first and second estates. The media could highlight and question abuses of power by the elites, though it would be wrong to overstate this role. To varying degrees commentators still apply these four estates to analysis of the body politic.

This chapter will focus less on wider ideals and more on the practicalities. We will look at the institutions and political machinery that exist – how is the political process enacted, how do people have their views heard, and how formally are we governed in liberal democracies? By the end of this chapter readers will be able to:

- understand how individuals' rights are maintained;
- assess the application of a separation of powers;
- identify the key institutions of governing in liberal democracies;
- evaluate the role of key 'actors' in the political process.

CONSTITUTIONS AND CONSTITUTIONALISM

Wheare (1951) makes it clear that there are two main under-standings of 'constitution': first, as the fundamental political institutions of a country; second, as a written document which usually defines both the institutions and the rights of the citizens of the state. The United Kingdom does not have the latter – although there are various legal documents such as the Magna Carta (1215) and the Bill of Rights (1689) which are seen as helping to define its constitutional arrangements. The so-called 'unwritten' constitution is one of the distinctive features of only a few democracies, which include the UK, Israel and New Zealand.

Liberal democratic constitutions usually have a variety of political functions to perform. First, a symbolic and legitimising role in asserting and demonstrating the democratic credentials of the political system concerned. Second, they are usually intended to protect and conserve the fundamental political institutions they define and establish how they may be legitimately changed. Third, they are intended to protect the fundamental rights of individual citizens. Constitutions are not 'dry' pieces of paper: they shape the political process as well as defining individual liberties.

More generally, from broadly conservative and liberal perspectives, it may be said that constitutional government means the 'government of laws and not of men' (from the 1780 Massachusetts Constitution) and that constitutions exist to limit the power of the government in the interests of individual rights. Conversely, some socialist and radical interpretations lay greater stress on the idea that constitutions empower democratic governments to change society to achieve a more just social order.

Where written constitutions exist, they often mark a revolutionary change in the political system – that is, they may be originally written in circumstances which favour a radical interpretation of constitutions. As the document ages, the interpretation may become more conservative and legalistic. Britain's unwritten constitution is usually defended as fulfilling the purpose of a constitution more effectively than (more recent) written constitutions. However, this has become a matter of considerable debate in Britain in recent years.

The symbolic role of the constitutional document is often of considerable importance. The United States' constitution, for instance, is treated with some reverence. The first act of each president is to take the oath or affirmation: 'I will faithfully execute the Office of President of the United States, and will to the best of my ability, preserve, protect and defend the Constitution of the United States.' Similarly, the French Declaration of the Rights of Man has a key role in French political culture.

However, the existence of a constitution does not automatically guarantee freedoms. Many post-colonial nations initially adopted the Westminster model, but gradually over a number of years they developed their own constitutions. For example, as noted by Mellor (1990), Kiribati in the Pacific took the basic Westminster model but added its own unique cultural aspects to it. This might, in part, explain why this fairly small and remote island state has had relative stability since it gained independence from the UK in 1979 (though it is worth noting that Kiribati is highly vulnerable to rises in sea level and may disappear).

It is often argued that Britain is unusual in embodying much of its constitution in 'conventions' – generally accepted rules that are not part of the law. These are seen as a more flexible way of expressing the constitution than a written legal document. However, conventions are, in fact, found in any mature constitutional system. For instance, in the US, conventions surrounding the operation of the Electoral College have effectively transformed what the founders intended as an indirect election of the president into a national popular vote.

RIGHTS AND CONSTITUTIONS

Most written constitutions incorporate some sort of declaration of the rights of citizens of the country concerned. However, there is an important distinction to be drawn between a mere declaration intended as a guide to politicians – and perhaps for judges to consider in their interpretation of laws – and a justiciable 'bill of rights' which is seen as a binding part of the constitution, superior in status to ordinary law and superseding it in case of conflict. A declaration may be of some symbolic political usefulness, but a bill of rights is clearly more likely to be directly useful to ordinary citizens who consider their rights have been taken away or abused by the executive or legislature.

In the US there is a long history of judicial use of the federal constitution to declare invalid both acts of the president and federal legislation ('judicial review'). The main parts of the constitution which have been used in this way are the first ten amendments to the constitution (which include the rights to free speech and assembly as well as, more controversially, rights against self-incrimination and the right to bear arms). Also important are the Civil War amendments (13–15) against slavery and racial discrimination. These clauses are still frequently invoked against state and local authorities. There are many examples of brave decisions by the Supreme Court defending individual rights in this way, but also of decisions by the Court to prevent progressive social measures being implemented in the name of property rights. The political and social climate of the times has clearly influenced court decisions on many occasions: for instance, in 1896 (Plessey v. Ferguson), when it declared that 'separate but equal' facilities for Negroes on a railway train were constitutional. And again in 1954 in Brown v. Board of Education of Topeka, when it declared that separate educational facilities for blacks could not, in fact, be equal. A bill of rights takes power away from elected politicians (and bureaucrats) and can transfer it to lawyers.

Dicey (1959) and other traditionalist British constitutionalists have preferred to rest their hopes for the protection of individual rights on a widespread attachment by all Britons to their ancient 'common law' rights. These are reaffirmed in historical documents such as Magna Carta and the Bill of Rights, but not legally entrenched by them against later legislation. Asserting the responsibility of the executive to the popularly elected 'Commons' for all its actions is seen as a major guarantee of rights for the individual. MPs have traditionally been prepared to defend the rights of their constituents – of any party affiliation – by interrogating ministers on their behalf in the Commons. Certain features of common law have been seen as offering better protection to individuals than either American constitutional guarantees or continental systems of special administrative courts. These features include the right to trial by jury, the right to silence in court and under police interrogation, and the writ (now judicial order) of habeas corpus ('produce the body').

Britain does not have its own detailed declaration of rights (the Bill of Rights is a more limited document than the name might suggest), but it is a signatory to both the UN and European declarations of human rights. The European document has a commission and court to interpret it. It may be significant that the British government has been the subject of more actions than any other signatory (perhaps because of the relative lack of legal remedies within the UK until the 1998 Human Rights Act gave power to British courts to draw attention to such breaches). As a conventional international organisation, however, the European Court of Human Rights (which is not a part of the European Union machinery) cannot enforce its judgements in Britain but must rely on shaming the British Government and legislature into action if it finds against UK authorities.

One Scandinavian institution which has been adopted in Britain to help defend individual rights against administrative error or invasion is a parliamentary commissioner for administration (the 'Ombudsman'), who can independently investigate actions by government departments in cases of apparent 'maladministration'. (Similar ombudsmen have since been introduced in Britain for the health service, local government, banking, insurance and building societies.) This innovation was originally opposed as a breach of British parliamentary traditions, but this was overcome by having the ombudsmen report to a parliamentary select committee.

The major limitations to the power of the British parliamentary Ombudsman are that their jurisdiction is restricted to errors of administration by a department for which a minister is responsible and the Ombudsman can only recommend remedial action to the minister. An 'unfair' piece of delegated legislation would be outside the Ombudsman's jurisdiction. In Sweden, where the office of ombudsman originated, they have much stronger powers to insist on remedies and all government documents being open to inspection.

In much of continental Europe the tradition stretching back to administrative reforms introduced in 1804 by Napoleon is for there to be a separate set of administrative courts. While these were intended originally to be more sympathetic to the executive than ordinary local courts, they have now developed a sturdy judicial independence combined with considerable administrative expertise. In France, for instance, top graduates of the École National d'Administration (ENA) aspire to become members of the Council of State, which is the superior administrative court. The ENA is perhaps the most prestigious postgraduate-level educational institution in the country.

THE SEPARATION OF POWERS

The separation of powers identifies the three main branches of government and is designed so that no single branch can dominate. It was designed to create various balances and checks to avoid the abuse of power. The equilateral triangle in Figure 7.1 implies equality between the three branches, whereas the other image suggests that what is more likely is that the executive will dominate and the other two branches, if not subservient, will probably have less power.

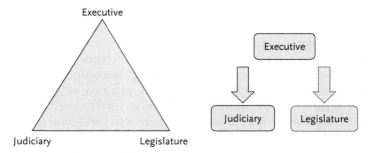

Figure 7.1 The separation of powers

THE EXECUTIVE

The executive, in the broad sense, includes the head of state, the political members of the government and the civil servants who staff the offices of state. It not only enforces the laws but also proposes changes in them to the legislature, and it conducts foreign relations. Less formally, the executive must often act to symbolise the unity of the country and provide leadership within the political system.

Different systems differ greatly in how roles are distributed within the executive, and indeed how large the executive is and, therefore, how many people control the levers of power. As we have seen, formal head of state duties such as convening and dissolving the legislature, receiving distinguished visitors, presenting honours and decorations, signing legislation into law, opening new buildings and the like, may be reserved to a hereditary sovereign or a distinguished retired 'statesman'. Such kings, queens, presidents or governors customarily lead uneventful (but comfortable) lives. In times of crisis, however, they may have to arbitrate on which leading politician is most likely to command a parliamentary majority if the current prime minister loses the confidence of the legislature.

Alternately, such largely symbolic roles may be combined with the job of leading the day-to-day government of the country. Where the symbolic and real leadership are combined (as in the US presidency) this may give the head of government a boost in his or her relationships with other national politicians. However, placing a practising politician in such a powerful position may increase the possibility of misbehaviour by the head of state and the consequent disillusionment of the citizenry, as the problems of presidents Nixon and Clinton indicate.

Another important difference between executives is in the mechanisms whereby their responsibility to the nation is expressed and how they are selected. The presidential model with direct selection by popular vote of the head of government increases the democratic legitimacy of the executive and helps to ensure that each head of government constructs a majority national coalition of supporters. The 'downside' of such an arrangement is that such figures cannot be easily removed should they lose touch with their constituencies. In the US, Congress can impeach the president only in the event of gross misconduct and with great legal difficulty. In parliamentary systems the prime ministers may be less well known and supported, but can only retain office for as long as they command a legislative majority. If no obvious national majority exists then a process of bargaining between parties in the legislature can produce one.

The number of political posts (that is, jobs to which politicians are appointed by the head of government) in the national executive may vary from something like 5,000 posts in the US to approximately a hundred ministers and 98 ministerial special advisers in Britain in 2013. Clearly, the fewer the number of 'political' posts, the more top civil service jobs are likely to have a policy content. Virtually all systems have a large civil service of permanent state employees recruited on 'merit' (normally via special competitive examinations or on the basis of professional or academic qualifications). Their role will vary from country to country. The British Civil Service is relatively unusual in its degree of unity, with a stress on 'generalist' administrators who may move from department to department. In France and the United States, for instance, there is a greater tendency to recruit say agronomists for the Agriculture Department, accountants for the Audit Department and so on.

It is also usual for modern executives to have some rule-making powers – 'delegated legislation' in the UK, 'decrees' in some continental European systems. These would normally cover detailed technical matters like the construction and use regulations for motor vehicles, or the approving of by-laws by local authorities. As well as sponsoring a legislative programme, the executive often has a veto through a requirement that the head of state must sign each law for it to be valid.

THE LEGISLATURE

Legislatures in virtually all systems have a formal role in making laws and have powers to investigate and, to some degree, control or influence the executive. A major element in this is usually the need for annual financial revenues and expenditures to be approved.

All legislatures work through a committee system – the more effective the legislature, the stronger and more complex this tends to be. They usually also work through some variant of the UK system of three 'readings' of proposed legislation ('bills') in full session, and a committee stage. In many legislatures, but not usually in Westminster-style parliaments, the committee stage of the process is the most significant and takes place before the main debates in permanent specialised committees. In the Westminster model the committee stage usually takes place in specially set up ('ad hoc') 'standing committees', while separate 'select committees' review areas of administration and finance.

The effectiveness of such committees and of legislators generally is also related to the number of support staff and ancillary facilities available. Congress employs thousands of administrators, researchers, and clerks as well as having a library which contains virtually all copyrighted material published in the US and much material from overseas. The European Parliament is also well staffed – although part of the staffing is explained by the requirements of translation and its operating in both Brussels and Strasbourg. In contrast, MPs at Westminster until recently found it difficult to even secure a desk for themselves, but do now have better office facilities in an expensive new building and an annual allowance sufficient to employ a handful of staff. Elected representatives have increasingly become professional politicians.

Historically the Anglo-American principle of 'No taxation without representation' has been of great importance in establishing legislative power over the executive. The need for the executive to apply for annual approval for most of its expenditure still dominates the legislative calendar in the UK, with many key debates being on 'supply days'. However, detailed financial reviews now mainly take place in select committees, and the existence of a more or less automatic government legislative majority has weakened the effective financial power of parliament over the executive. In the US there is much more struggle for control over budgetary matters, with Congress extracting political concessions on a regular basis in exchange for appropriations. It is worth remarking that the European Parliament has now asserted more control over the European Union budget than in the past – thus marking a movement towards full legislative status.

Legislative oversight and investigation of the activities of the executive vary both in extent, depth and form. Parliamentary systems have the advantage that ministers as members of the legislature are in daily contact with 'backbench' MPs. In the UK particularly there is a well-developed tradition of MPs addressing oral questions to ministers (including the prime minister) in full sessions ('on the floor') of the House of Commons. In contrast, in the US the president normally only appears once a year to give the State of the Union address. However, US congressional committee investigations are probably more probing than those of Westminster (where the government has a built-in majority on each committee) and the president faces frequent media interrogation at press conferences.

In the UK there was a concern that parliament was becoming a mere rubber stamp, but as Rush (2001) and Norton (2005) have noted, since the 1960s there has been the rise of a scrutiny role. A number of reforms to the committee structure and the resources available to MPs have enabled parliament to challenge government policy and actions.

Most legislatures are 'bicameral' – they have two 'houses'. In almost all the 'lower' house (popularly elected by universal suffrage in geographical constituencies) is the one which has ultimate power and is the house to which (in parliamentary systems) the government is responsible. In federal systems the upper house represents the constituent states; in many other systems it is indirectly elected via panels of local government councillors. Other strange variants are to be found such as two university representatives in the Seanad Eireann, the Irish Senate.

The United States is unusual in that, if anything, the Senate (consisting of two senators from each of the 50 states) is the most important chamber. In practice the crucial decisions on legislation arise from bargaining between a joint committee of both houses and the president.

One of the key questions asked about elected representatives is 'Who do they represent?' One school of thought suggests that elected representatives are 'mandated' to vote in line with their party's electoral pledges to the majority of their constituency. However, the Burkean tradition, based on the thoughts of Edmund Burke, MP for Bristol in the eighteenth century, rejects this and suggests that elected representatives are independent and should weigh up the arguments for and against on policy issues. The reality is that elected representatives are influenced by a number of factors, including their own party, pressure groups, constituents and the media.

THE JUDICIARY

All liberal democracies endorse the principle of an independent judiciary, but they vary as to the degree of power judges may exercise in constitutional matters.

UK judges are formally amongst the least powerful in being limited by the prerogative powers of the Crown, the doctrine of the sovereignty of parliament, the lack of an enforceable declaration of rights (until 1998), and a tradition of deference to the executive in such matters as official secrecy and executive discretion. A further cause for concern is the secret process by which judges are appointed by the government of the day. 'Democratic' elements of the British system include the jury system, the presumption of the innocence of the accused and that only activity formally proscribed by law can be illegal. In this 'common law' system, highly professional lawyers interpret legislation according to the precedents set in previous cases.

US (and many Commonwealth) judges, while still operating a common law system, are in a much stronger position in that they have established powers of 'judicial review' of legislative and executive action in the light of a constitution which includes a bill of rights for individuals. In the US the political importance of federal judges is recognised by constitutional guarantees of independence once appointed, and an open and rigorous appointment process including endorsement by the Senate and hearings before its Judiciary Committee. At state and local level a separate judicial system operates in a similar way, except that in some areas judges are elected (generally in non-partisan elections) for fixed periods.

In the continental (Napoleonic) tradition, administrative courts often independently exercise a degree of control over executive action without parallel in Britain. The legal system in continental European countries usually goes back to Roman law as modified by Napoleonic reforms. It places more stress on general principles (such as respect for constitutionally recognised rights) and less on precedent. Trials are more of an inquisitorial process controlled by the judge, and less of a confrontation between defence and prosecution lawyers. Separate constitutional courts to review the constitutionality of laws or government decrees are also to be found in a number of states.

The traditional model of a separation of powers assumes that the three branches of government have freedom of action within a state. However, as we have seen in Chapter 6, a range of international institutions exist which can have some effect on their independence. Within Europe the impact of these bodies is fairly obvious since we have a transnational legislature, judiciary and executive, but the existence of international courts and the UN can also have an impact. The separation of powers, a largely eighteenth-century concept, is evolving due to globalisation.

THE PROCESS OF POLITICS

ELECTIONS

In modern liberal democracies the concept of democracy is often thought to centre primarily on the opportunity it gives for citizens to freely choose their rulers at periodic intervals, rather than make governmental decisions for themselves. In other words, we have a representative rather than participatory democracy, so elections take on great symbolic importance.

Free elections do seem to be something which cannot be dispensed with in a democracy – and an institution which is more difficult to implement than those who take it for granted might suspect (McKenzie, 1958). A secret ballot, freedom from blatant election bribery, parties free to campaign anywhere in the country, and a reasonably unbiased electoral system seem simple and obvious devices in those countries which have achieved them. However, experience in Eastern Europe and Africa, Asia and Latin America in recent years has shown how difficult such conditions are to achieve.

Many discussions of liberal democracy place great emphasis on the range of electoral systems used – for example, the merits of 'proportional representation' versus 'majoritarian' systems. Fascinating though the topic may be for some, it seems much less fundamentally important than many of the less discussed issues involved in achieving free elections which we have just considered.

In fact, few electoral systems are either based simply on a single-member constituency, 'first-past-the post' system traditionally used in British general elections, or on a national constituency divided proportionally between the parties, as in Israel. Many single-member constituency systems incorporate ways of ensuring (or increasing the likelihood of) a majority at constituency level. Thus France has a second ballot in any constituency in which no candidate gains an overall majority. The US has a preliminary ('Primary') election within each of the two major parties, so only two serious candidates are likely to emerge for the election proper. In Australia voters record preferences for candidates in order that the votes of the weaker candidates can be transferred until one candidate obtains a majority. Most 'proportional' systems have area or regional (rather than national) constituencies; several combine single-member constituencies with a national 'pooling system' (e.g. Germany and in elections for the Scottish Parliament and Welsh Assembly). Almost all have a minimum quota of votes to obtain seats in the legislature.

It is worth echoing the conclusion of Rae's (1967) study: that all existing electoral systems are less than perfectly proportional (even Israel has a minimum vote quota for a party to be represented in parliament) and that the major factor affecting proportionality is the size of the constituency employed. To achieve perfect proportionality between seats allocated in parliament and votes for each national party a single national constituency would have to be employed. However, the cost of this might well be thought too high in terms of breaking the links between individual voters and specific representatives – and the power it would give to national party organisations in determining candidates' places on the national list.

Relatively less proportional systems, like Britain's, may be defended as yielding strong or stable government. In recent years the authors have felt that 'strong' government has come to mean a government which is rather too unrepresentative and unresponsive, a criticism levelled at both the Thatcher and Blair administrations. Yet the result of the 2010 general election was to create a coalition, as the majoritarian electoral system had not delivered a majority to one party. Certainly, however, the viability of the executive produced by the system must be weighed in assessing such systems, alongside the links to constituencies and the proportionality of the legislature. To some degree the assessment of electoral systems must depend upon current political circumstances and the political preferences of the assessor.

The electoral system is at the heart of the credibility (legitimacy) of modern democracies, so it is important to try to establish as broad a consensus as possible about the system employed. A situation such as that in post-war France, in which major changes of government bring about a consequent change in the electoral system, are liable to breed cynicism and apathy on the part of the electorate (Campbell, 1965).

POLITICAL PARTIES

BOX 7.1   POLITICAL PARTIES

Political parties may be thought of as organised social groups that seek to wholly or partially take over the government of a country, usually by contesting elections.

While there were clearly factions centred upon individual politicians in ancient times, the idea of a modern political party is believed to have started in England with the Glorious Revolution of 1688 and the actions towards Catholics of the king, Charles II (Abbott, 1918). Those who agreed with the king became known as the Tories, and those who opposed him the Whigs. Indeed, these two parties dominated until the middle of the nineteenth century, when they metamorphosed into the Conservative and Liberal parties respectively. In America we do not see parties until the 1780s/1790s and the emergence of the Federalists and Anti-Federalists. In both England and the US the creation of political parties is linked to differing views within the political elite as to how government should be run.

Political parties seek to take power for their leading members, either for its own sake (the psychological, social and economic rewards of office), on behalf of some social group (e.g. workers, farmers, protestants), or with some ideological objective in mind (e.g. national independence, socialism). The names of parties are often a poor guide to their objectives, and it is also worth stressing that most – probably all – parties are coalitions of people with different goals in mind.

In most liberal democratic countries, the main obvious function of political parties is to contest elections – selecting candidates in constituencies, canvassing and organising voters, composing and delivering election addresses in local constituencies and running local and national media campaigns. By offering voters candidates with commitments to certain policies (especially as identified by the national leadership) they make elections a choice by electors of public policies as well as the selection of representatives. Parties are a means by which the political elite can be chosen.

To understand such parties it is necessary to distinguish between the roles of voluntary members in the constituencies, activists and professionals who are employed by the local or national parties, and the full-time paid and elected representatives.

The ordinary members play only a small role in the electoral process. Occasionally they may act as 'tellers' at polling stations or deliver leaflets in their street. The activists who run constituency parties, act as local councillors and attend conferences or conventions, can communicate what they see as local 'grassroots' feeling to their local legislators or at national party meetings (conventions, conferences, assemblies, etc.). As noted by Jackson (2009), party conferences are now primarily festivals of politics rather than policy-making bodies. In the US the only real – though very important – function of the national party conventions is the selection of presidential candidates.

Lilleker and Jackson (2014) seek to explain the interaction between party members and political parties by applying Christopher et al.'s (2002) loyalty ladder. They suggest that individuals are targeted by parties as prospects and gradually 'move up the rungs of the ladder' by developing their relationship with the party, so that they may eventually become evangelists and activists for the party.

In Britain, party professionals play only a small political role. At a local level they are almost exclusively concerned with keeping the party machine going (and paying their own salaries). At a national level, headquarter professionals vary in that they are officially responsible to the (parliamentary) party leader in the Conservative Party but to the mass party executive in Labour and the Liberal Democrats. In the US there are few significant party employees because the political system is a candidate not a party one. Consequently, each politician employs their own *ad hoc* group of image consultants, pollsters, public relations specialists and the like.

In practice, in virtually all liberal democracies, nationally elected politicians firmly control the national party machinery. In Britain, the parliamentary party (i.e. its members in the House of Commons) constitutes the core of the party and, for the government party in particular, is an important centre for duplex flows of information. Information is exchanged between MPs (members of parliament) and government members, interest group representatives, party activists and ordinary 'constituents'. Government backbench MPs seek to increase their chances of re-election by popularising the government's message to the electorate and by alerting government 'Whips' to potential and actual problems. In the US, incumbent Congressmen (and women) are at an enormous advantage in having sizeable professional staffs, free postage and travel facilities and the opportunity to do individual constituents favours and build up goodwill.

In US parties, and in more conservative parties in Europe, there are often few party activists to contest for control of the party machinery with elected officials and those who have, or hope to, benefit from their patronage. European socialist, Christian democratic and, to some extent, liberal parties may have larger numbers of activists, some of whom may be ideologically committed 'militants' with strong policy views. While useful as enthusiastic canvassers or lickers of envelopes, such militants may be, from the professional's point of view, a source of internal conflict and resistance to the perhaps inevitable compromises of democratic politics. From time to time, however, they may serve to inject an element of idealism and dynamic change into political systems.

PRESSURE GROUPS

We have considered democratic government in terms of the extent of popular participation in government, the degree to which the people can influence the choice of governors and the form which democratic institutions might take. Arguably more important than any of these, however, is the responsiveness of government to people's views and interests and even its ability to leave well alone (to respect their rights). While in part the means by which an individual's voice is heard is through contact with elected representatives, pressure groups now increasingly help give a voice to those who may previously have felt that they were not being heard.

It is impossible to pinpoint the earliest pressure groups, though looking just at the UK we can see phenomena such as Magna Carta and the 1689 Bill of Rights which imply shifts in society even if they do not exactly signify a formal pressure group. However, we can see evidence of organisations displaying some of the traits of pressure groups as we now understand them in Victorian Britain. For example, in 1839 the Anti-Corn Law League was formed to oppose the existing protectionist system concerning the import of cheap wheat. The repeal of the laws in 1846 represented a success for the new power base of manufacturers over the old power base of the landowners. However, it was not until the 1950s and 1960s in America, the UK and Europe that we see the growth of organised pressure groups, often initially campaigning against bad practice by governments or businesses.

BOX 7.2   PRESSURE OR INTEREST GROUPS

A pressure or interest group is a formal social group that pursues a particular cause or interest which differs from a political party in seeking only to influence government – not become a formal part of it.

A pressure group can be said to be in the business of political communication. 'Interest group' may be the better term since it may well seek to influence the government more by persuasion and information than by threats of political reward or penalty. However, it would be surprising if interest groups were not listened to more closely if they represent large numbers of voters (trade unions), influential 'opinion formers' (doctors) or wealthy actual or potential contributors to candidate or party funds than if they have little significance.

Pressure groups can be divided into at least two different types. Sectional groups exist to further the interests of particular sections of society, such as trade unions, employers and particular professions. Cause groups seek to promote particular beliefs, attitudes or principles, such as Greenpeace, Amnesty International and the Red Cross. A common typology for understanding pressure groups is Wyn Grant's (2000) insider–outsider status. Insider groups are normally incorporated into the relevant policy-making community and so have formal and informal contact with decision-makers in government. The decision-makers believe that these groups have a role to play in policy-making. By comparison, outsider groups are not consulted on policy as a matter of course. They may have contact with decision-makers, but they are not incorporated into the policy-making process. Most outsiders want insider status, but occasionally they want to remain an outsider so they have more freedom to criticise the government; Greenpeace would be in this category.

Where the interest is a professional or business one, the group concerned may well have both specialised expertise which government policy-makers might wish to draw upon and the capacity to aid the acceptance and implementation of the policy. Thus, doctors' representatives (notably the American and British Medical associations) will usually be drawn into making health policy and will often then help win acceptance within the health professions for an agreed policy to be implemented by their members. Most democratic governments tend to consult such groups and try to win them over to their policies.

In Britain, the links between Whitehall and such producer interest groups are institutionalised in the practice of each sector of industry having an official 'sponsoring' department. It is standard for such groups to be represented on official advisory committees and for their leaders and administrators to be on first-name terms with the corresponding higher civil servants. This can often be facilitated through unofficial communication patterns such as lunches and regular telephone calls.

In the UK, trade unions have generally speaking (i.e. post-1945) been seen within this framework as groups which are automatically consulted, whose prominent leaders finish up in the House of Lords and are appointed to QUANGOs, etc. This was so under Conservative administrations such as those of Edward Heath and Harold Macmillan. In Labour administrations they have benefited from the historic link between the various wings of the Labour 'movement'. In the past it was not unknown for trade union leaders to be appointed to Labour cabinets. For example, Richard Marsh was a trade union official in the 1950s, got elected as an MP and was secretary of state for transport in the 1960s. Conversely, some on both left and right have argued that trades union leaders have often been too pliant towards 'their' Labour governments – sacrificing their members' economic interests to the political success of the party.

In all democratic systems, non-producer interest groups – residents affected by planning proposals, consumers of both private and public goods and services, housewives, carers and so-called 'cause' groups which operate more altruistically on behalf of others – seem less effective than producer groups. Such groups may only hear of legislative or administrative decisions after they have been made, rather than while they are being considered. This then makes it much more difficult – if not impossible – to influence the relevant decisions. Even trying to amend a bill in parliament when it is still under consideration is a relatively late stage to try to affect events. By that time the prestige of the government may have been attached to the bill and amendments may affect compromises reached between civil servants or ministers and other more established groups.

The rise in prominence of professional lobbyists has highlighted the importance of informal links between politicians, government officials, parties, the media and interest groups. The more policy is made in private at the pre-legislative stage by informal coteries of political advisors, professional lobbyists retained by wealthier and established groups, and small factions of politicians who are in favour with the head of government, the less responsive and democratic it will seem. If some lobby groups attain preferential access to government through financial support to parties or by retaining well-connected professionals, then this clearly constitutes a move away from pluralism towards elitism in the political system.

THE MASS MEDIA

BOX 7.3   THE MEDIA

The mass media is a collective term for the technology and form for communicating information which includes broadcast (television and radio), press (newspapers and magazines) and the Internet.

If the media do not know what the government is doing then clearly it cannot be reported to the electorate. Democratic countries vary greatly in the access and information reporters and citizens can obtain regarding government decision-making. At one extreme the Swedish tradition of 'open government' requires virtually all decision-making to be publicly documented. At the other, in the past the British tradition of official secrecy has made the assumption that executive deliberations will be kept private unless a positive decision has been made to release information. The US has adopted the opposite assumption with its Freedom of Information Act which requires Federal government agencies to reveal any document at the request of any enquirer unless reasons such as national security or personal confidentiality can be plausibly advanced against this. In Britain a non-statutory Code of Practice on Access to Government Information (April 1994) rather half-heartedly moved in the open government direction. It allowed for numerous exceptions – including advice to ministers and anything that could be the subject of a public enquiry. The Blair government was pledged to introduce a stronger statutory measure, but the legislation that resulted (the Freedom of Information Act 2000) has been criticised as weaker than the Code of Practice. The act has been implemented slowly and without enthusiasm.

The extent to which journalists have a tradition of, and are rewarded for, hard-hitting investigative journalism is also of importance. In the US there is a long tradition of such 'muckraking' journalism, culminating in the 'Watergate' investigations of Bernstein and Woodward (1974) that contributed to the ignominious resignation of President Nixon. Recent revelations by the *New York Times* and the *Guardian* of the role of the intelligence services in intercepting Internet communications may be seen in the same light.

The idea of the fourth estate suggests that the role of the media is neutral, but in reality various parts of the media have their own agenda. This bias is important because the media is believed to have an impact by setting the agenda; indeed, this is believed to be its key influence. As initially noted by Cohen (1963) the media cannot tell the public what to think, but it can tell them what to think about. This agenda-setting role creates awareness of an issue, which may shape public opinion and ultimately impact on public policy.

Press freedom has been viewed as central to the functionality of democracy, a counterweight allowing citizens to know what governments may not want them to know. This can be perhaps best summed up by Lord Northcliffe, one of the original press barons, who stated: 'News is what somebody somewhere wants to suppress; all the rest is advertising.' In the political sphere this implies that politicians sometimes have to be 'encouraged' to reveal the full facts. Politicians themselves have normally been supporters of press freedom, but in recent years this has come to be challenged, particularly in the years since 9/11 – the assumption being that in a 'war' situation the role of the media is to support the government. It is fair to say that not all journalists accept that this is their role during war, and probably even fewer would consider themselves to be currently working in a time of war. The UK has largely relied on self-policing, with a code of practice and the Press Complaints Commission. However, in October 2013 the government introduced significant change, with a new cross-party Royal Charter on press regulation. This charter will lead to the creation of a new press regulator. While clearly this relates to UK-specific issues such as phone-hacking, as we shall see in Chapter 9 it should also be viewed within the context of changing international affairs following 9/11.

The Frankfurt School associated with Theodor Adorno, Max Horkheimer and Herbert Marcuse was a left-wing body of intellectuals who could not understand why fascism had become so popular in Italy, Germany and Spain. Their explanation was that the mass media acted as a 'subtle narcotic' which pacified the masses and that fascists used the media to manipulate the working class by providing them with entertainment, popular culture and propaganda. Such an analysis is sometimes referred to as the hypodermic needle model because it suggested ideas were injected straight into individuals.

The first empirical research to assess the impact of the media on politics was when Lazarsfeld *et al.* (1944) studied the 1940 US presidential election. They found that the hypodermic needle did not work – that the process of media impact on politics was more complex. Interpersonal communications was important, with news about the election sought out by a minority of opinion leaders, who in turn influenced their family and friends who were less interested in the election. This so-called two-step flow model of the media's impact was refined by Robinson (1976) to the multi-step flow model. This suggested that information flows through a group using a series of opinion formers.

POLITICAL COMMUNICATION

In the US the differences between parties have long been less marked than in Europe, and the system of primary elections for major party nominations encourages candidates to sell themselves as individuals rather than party ideological standard-bearers. It is not surprising that the use of techniques from commercial marketing and public relations should have been pioneered in politics. These techniques have now crossed the Atlantic, with Britain's Labour Party 'rebranding' itself as 'New Labour' and even the redoubtable former Conservative prime minister Mrs Thatcher consulting image consultants on how to dress and speak. More recently, the Conservative Party leader, David Cameron, has also been trying to actively 'woo' key supporters using marketing techniques. And we find that campaigning 'gurus' are hired to work in elections in a number of different countries.

Observation of this trend has led to a disagreement over its explanation. One view is that the increased application of commercial communication practice within the political arena reflects an Americanisation – that because America is the dominant political power, the use of new techniques are pioneered there and then exported to other countries. This is therefore a very top-down analysis. Plasser (2002) on the other hand has suggested that there is evidence of a more bottom-up process, culturally linked to different countries' experiences and systems. Thus, countries in Europe such as Germany adapt wider lessons to their own context. However, what does appear to be agreed is that changes in political campaigning practice are having an impact on political structures.

Is this merely a (perhaps unfortunate) change of style or something much more significant? Jennifer Lees-Marshment (2001) argues that Labour did much more than adopt new techniques. The party, in common with many other Western political parties, changed its approach first from that of an old-style 'product-orientated' party to that of a sales-orientated party and finally to that of a market-orientated party (see Table 7.1).

Table 7.1 Political marketing and New Labour

Type of party	What they do	New Labour examples
Product-orientated	Party does what it thinks is best (improving policy product).	Unilateralism and socialism.
Sales-orientated	Focusing on hard sell for the product.	New logo, slicker party political broadcasts, rapid rebuttal.
Market-orientated	Giving the consumer what they want.	Focus groups, policy adjustment; no tax rises or sleaze.

Source: Based on Lees-Marchment, 2001

The growth of political marketing implies that politics is less about campaigning for what ideology a politician believes is right for society and more about finding out what the electorate wants. This implies that selling politics is akin to selling baked beans (Kotler, 1975). This is a controversial view and not all commentators – especially not those within the political science field – would agree with it.

The growth of spin and an increased emphasis on presentation did not just happen – it has been driven by the development of the permanent campaign. The phrase 'permanent campaign' was coined in 1980 by Sidney Blumenthal. Up to this point the orthodox view was that there was a distinction between campaigning and the business of governing. However, Ornstein and Mann (2000) have suggested that such separation in politicians' behaviour before and after an election has been blurred, so that now, 'Every day is Election Day' (Heclo, 2000: 17). Coleman (2005) has suggested that the existence of the permanent campaign has resulted in 'permanent communication', whereby political actors seek to dominate the political agenda every day through every available communication channel.

In order to win the media battle every day, governments, political parties and other political actors have increasingly relied on media management to dominate the news agenda. This is a competitive process in which the protagonists are always looking for new techniques and technologies to gain an advantage. While the permanent campaign was initially assumed to be limited to the industrialised and democratic North, Conaghan and de la Torre (2008) found evidence that it was also applied by Rafael Correa, president of Ecuador.

The ever-increasing reliance on media management has fundamentally changed the relationship between politicians and the media. One school of thought suggests that the control of mass communication by the elite has led to a 'public relations state' (Deacon and Golding, 1994). Another view is that whereas journalists were deferential to politicians in the 1950s, they are now contemptuous of them (Barnett, 2002; McNair, 2003). A worsening relationship between journalists and politicians cannot help the transmission to citizens of political communications.

THE INTERNET

What we now know as the Internet owes its origins to political events. Two in particular had a major impact: first, in 1957 the Soviet Union launched the first satellite (Sputnik 1) into space, second, the Bay of Pigs crisis in 1962 almost led to World War Three. This concentrated military and political minds in the US, wondering how they would communicate and govern in a post-apocalyptic world following a nuclear war. The answer, in part, was to communicate by computers, and this led to the creation in the 1960s of the military-led APANET. This was the forerunner of the Internet.

The Internet uses electronic digital technology and enables ordinary users to transmit as well as receive information. Potentially every home becomes a broadcasting studio able to transmit its own political messages, as well as to respond interactively to broadcasts by others. Thus we have multiplex flows with complex networks being developed.

The Internet, especially websites, has been used extensively by political parties and candidates in their campaigns. It is widely believed to have helped the former professional wrestler Jesse Ventura win the governorship of Minnesota in 1998 and Roh Moo-Hyun the South Korean presidential election in 2002. Early in the 2004 US presidential campaign Democrat Howard Dean's supporters mainly organised themselves through a 'meetup' Internet site (www.meetup.com) rather than waiting for professional centralised organisation. John McCain in the 2000 campaign raised 2.6 million dollars over the Internet (Parkinson, 2003). Virtually all parties and interest groups have web pages. The game changer was believed, by many, to be Barack Obama's use of the Internet in the 2008 presidential election. However, it would be wrong to over-emphasise the impact of the Internet as a vote-winner. As Lilleker and Jackson (2011) suggest, the Internet is better as an organisational tool building resources via the mobilising of activists and fundraising than persuading voters.

Potentially the Internet may have a still more radical impact in enabling the rapid construction of new networks of people and groups (Castells, 2002). In the period before the invasion of Iraq in 2003, demonstrations and petitions in the UK of a size unprecedented in modern times seem to have been largely organised through *ad hoc* 'Stop the War' websites. More sensitively, terrorist organisations such as Al-Qaeda have turned to the Internet as a powerful internal and external communication tool.

In many ways the Internet seems to be an inherently democratic and participative medium. This does not prevent the technology from being employed to great effect by governments and corporations to sell their products, services and ideas. However, the networked structure of the technology makes it more difficult for governments to control than conventional broadcast media (Tansey, 2002).

There are a plethora of online tools that can be utilised by political actors. Since the 2004 US presidential election political weblogs have attracted a lot of attention. As personal individual diaries they have tended to be influential in political structures where the candidate and not the party controls election campaigns. For organisations such as political parties, a weblog creates a potential problem because an amorphous structure cannot provide a personal diary (Jackson, 2006). The strength of a political weblog is that it enables like-minded people to share ideas (Sunstein, 2004), and some act as 'focal points' (Drezner and Farrell, 2004) around which influential people congregate. Weblogs have both provided an alternative to the traditional media, and some have suggested bloggers are a fifth estate, but it is also increasingly a means by which that media communicates.

In recent years the focus has been increasingly on the impact of social media. Political actors have adopted social networking sites such as Facebook, file-sharing sites such as YouTube and micro-blogging sites such as Twitter. Such tools inherently encourage dialogue and there was some hope that they might enhance democracy, but the evidence is that this has not been their prime effect (Jackson and Lilleker, 2009a, 2012). Rather, these tools have been used to mobilise supporters for election campaigns (Lilleker and Jackson, 2011). Moreover, this campaigning use has not been restricted to traditional political elites in the North, previously excluded groups have used Twitter and Facebook for example in the Ukraine, Egypt and Iran.

CONCLUSION

When we look at the mechanisms in operation in liberal democ-racies we can identify four separate, but interrelated, factors that shape them. First, the structures in place which create the required framework; thus, constitutions play an important role because they articulate important principles and are often backed up by legislative authority. The separation of powers, although not always equal, can also establish important checks and balances. Second, the instru-ments in use, of which elections are probably the most important. We then need to understand the key actors, such as individual politicians, political parties and pressure groups. The last factor is the role that communication plays within the system. This can be direct, between political actors and citizens and between political actors, or indirect through the media. What we understand by liberal democracy and, especially, good governance, is shaped by the interaction between the rulers and the ruled, with the media possibly playing a neutral or biased role.

FURTHER READING

Bogdanor, V. (1988) *Constitutions in Democratic Politics*, Aldershot: Gower.

Carter, A. and Stokes, G. (2002) *Democratic Theory Today*, Cambridge: Polity Press.

Castells, M. (2002) *The Rise of the Network Society*, Oxford: Blackwell.

Farrell, D. (2001) *Electoral Systems: A Comparative Introduction*, Basingstoke: Palgrave.

Jones, N. (1996) *Soundbites and Spin Doctors*, London: Indigo.

King, A. (2001) *Does the United Kingdom Still Have a Constitution?* London: Sweet & Maxwell.

Lees-Marshment, J. (ed.) (2012) *The Routledge Handbook of Political Marketing*, London: Routledge.

Louw, E. (2010) *The Media and the Political Process*, London: Sage.

McQuail, D. (2010), *McQuail's Mass Communication Theory*, London: Sage.

Oates, S. (2008) *Introduction to Media and Politics*, London: Sage.

WEBSITES

www.opendemocracy.net
An online think tank committed to promoting human rights and democracy worldwide.

www.constitution.org/liberlib.htm
Liberty Library of Government Classics includes full texts of constitutions from that of Hammurabi (1780 BC) to the present day.

www.museum.tv/archives/etv/P/htmlP/politicalpro/politicalpro.htm
The Museum of Broadcast Communications looks at the impact of political processes on the development of television in the US.

www.hansardsociety.org.uk
The Hansard Society is a charity which seeks to promote effective parliamentary democracy.

http://darrenlilleker.blogspot.com
Musings on political communication.

www.ucl.ac.uk/constitution-unit
The Constitution Unit (mainly UK).

www.parliament.uk
Houses of Parliament home page.

www.whitehouse.gov
US presidency.

www.aei.org
American Enterprise Institute (neo-conservative think tank).

www.PoliticsOnline.com
Information on the Internet and politics.

www.mori.com
Leading public opinion-polling organisation.

8

POLICIES

THIS CHAPTER ...

considers how, in liberal democracies, public policies should be made and implemented, how they are actually made, and the problems of evaluating the public policy process. One of the key themes of this book is the purpose of politics, which is very much a macro-level concern. This chapter will take a very different tack and focus on the nitty gritty level, effectively the minutiae of politics: making policy. In the previous chapter we looked at how individual decision-makers are chosen and the means by which a range of interests get their voice heard. This chapter will take this process to the next stage and look at how these various groups are able to convert their ideals, or serve their interests, through change in the form of policies. There is – or there should be – a clear link with Chapter 4 on ideology, as we are now looking at how political actors seek to use their overall principles or philosophies to drive action. Having general beliefs about how society should develop is merely an intellectual pursuit unless it is backed up by policies designed to bring about the required change.

One of the growing concerns of political science involves the idea of governance, and this concept applies to much of what we have already discussed in terms of how governments are chosen, operate and replaced. However, many commentators particularly focus on the policy field: for example, how does a government make good decisions and ones that reflect the views of society? Indeed, the World Bank (http://info.worldbank.org/governance/wgi/index.aspx#home) produces the Worldwide Governance Indicators (WGI), a research dataset summarising the quality of governance provided. To make this assessment the World Bank uses six indicators, all of which relate to policies in some way, with two relating overtly to the policy-making capabilities of each country. 'Government effectiveness' looks at the quality of policy formulation and implementation, and 'regulatory quality' looks at the perception of the ability of government to introduce sound policies. Policy-making in terms of both process and outcome should be at the heart of the body politic.

Before any such discussion about the precise nature of policy-making, however, it is important to consider the extent to which the state – especially national government – should make decisions on behalf of the whole community. Finally, we return to the extent to which it is possible and desirable for the individual to influence political policies and events. By the end of this chapter readers will be able to:

- identify some of the problems associated with policy-making;
- evaluate how policy is made;
- assess why different policy-making processes are used;
- consider the factors which shape a government's ability to implement its policies.

PUBLIC POLICY PROBLEMS AND SOLUTIONS

Writing in a US context, Bachrach and Baratz (1970) stress the domination of WASPs (white Anglo-Saxon Protestants) in setting the political agenda. In Britain we could perhaps go further and suggest that the 'chattering classes' – the media, academic and professional sectors and the civil service – which dominate politics are still predominantly London-resident public school/Oxford or Cambridge arts graduates and the like. What such people define as urgent problems are not necessarily the same as what people who left school at the minimum leaving age, are employed in manual jobs (or are unemployed) and live in Lancashire or Scotland would put in that category.

Similarly, the 'same' problem may be understood in radically different terms from different perspectives. Thus, the existence of increasing numbers of young unmarried mothers can be seen primarily as a symptom of Britain's moral decline; a serious threat to the social security budget; a consequence of the failure of sex education; or a symptom of the emergence of a deprived underclass on Britain's former council estates. Alternately, it may not be regarded as a problem at all but merely an outcome of changing individual moral choices. Indeed, some would see the phenomenon as a welcome sign of inevitable progress towards the extinction of the bourgeois/patriarchal family.

Naturally, 'solutions' are an equally contentious matter. Using our example – does this mean no more premarital sex; fathers supporting financially all their biological children; no more 'unprotected' premarital sex; full employment and community renewal in deprived areas; or abandoning the expectation that all children are brought up in two-parent families? The terminology of 'problem' and 'solution', as de Jouvenal (1963) points out, may also introduce a misleading mathematical analogy, indicating that reasoning will lead us to a unique resolution of a defined problem. One might more sensibly speak of managing a situation.

Further consideration of this 'problem' will make clear another vital point about the nature of policy-making. In the example we can see that the same problem has been viewed through different ideological spectacles (libertarian, socialist, liberal and feminist). It is also clear that different perspectives are to some extent a question of whose eyes we are looking through: the moralising detached observer, the tax-payer, the sympathetic outsider, the mothers, fathers or children concerned, fellow residents of 'sink' estates, etc.? In short, political conflicts are as much about the interests of groups of people as they are about power struggles, ideas or social management.

THE CHOICE OF SOCIAL DECISION-MAKING MECHANISMS

Not every social problem is perceived as a public policy problem. Choices may be left to be resolved through the market mechanism, or informally through families and social networks. In political argument this choice of social decision-making mechanisms is often debated in terms of simple dichotomies (Box 8.1); in other cases it may be taken for granted that only one mechanism is appropriate.

BOX 8.1: CHOICE OF SOCIAL DECISION-MAKING MECHANISM

From the right:
Individual freedom = Consumer sovereignty = Good
versus State decision-making = Bureaucracy = Bad

From the left:
Social decision-making by welfare state = Democracy = Good
versus Market decision-making = Capitalism = Exploitation = Bad

---

The approach we have adopted here suggests a more pragmatic approach, in which it is appropriate to consider the issue, the time and the place before deciding which way social decisions should be resolved. In addition to pure market or pure state systems, it is clear that a mixed system – where the market is regulated and adjusted by the state (the so-called 'social market') – is often a viable alternative to consider. Mixed systems combine a free market in consumer goods with a commitment to social objectives such as equality of opportunity, as well as political measures to prevent the undue dominance of elites. Nor should the role of voluntary co-operation through family and neighbourhood networks or more formal organisations be neglected.

In deciding the appropriate role of the state, important considerations are: how far is it likely to reach a more rational decision than the market; how far can it effectively involve ordinary citizens in the decision-making process; and whether the increased costs of such decision-making are justified by any improvement in its quality? We might also ask, bearing in mind the concept of subsidiarity, at what level should a decision be made?

THE CASE FOR THE MARKET

If the state is seeking to promote (following Jeremy Bentham) 'the greatest happiness of the greatest number', it should not lose sight of the fact that only individuals can judge their own happiness.

The argument of the early economists (since endorsed by fashionable neo-liberal conservative commentators such as Milton Friedman (Friedman and Friedman, 1980) and Hayek (1979)) is that with only a finite amount of real resources, a centralised deployment of resources by the state will almost certainly result in waste. If we each have an equal amount of real resources with which to achieve satisfaction, some will achieve most satisfaction from buying fishing rods or fashionable clothes, others from the purchase of fast cars or the consumption of malt whisky. For the state to allocate everyone equal amounts of fishing equipment, cars, clothes and whisky and proceed on the assumption that all citizens want the same things will lead to dissatisfaction and waste. Thus fishing enthusiasts may find the concrete they wanted to be used to dam a river has been used to construct a bridge over it to somewhere they did not wish to go. Fashion enthusiasts may find themselves allocated rayon trousers when they aspired to a woollen kilt (or whatever is fashionable at the time). Sporting motorists may be issued with Trabant motor cars incapable of reaching the speeds they wish to attain, while teetotallers throw away in disgust an allocation of malt whisky which their neighbours would savour with relish. The state cannot achieve the level of information and efficiency required to satisfy individual consumer needs.

If this account of a fully centralised planned economy be dismissed as an exaggerated fantasy, an examination of the experience of the Soviet economy suggests it is not so far from the truth (Nove, 1980). While in the Soviet model in the Stalinist era consumers were paid in money and could dispose of their incomes largely as they pleased, the goods available in the shops were determined by the operation of a somewhat arbitrary national plan, and prices bore little relationship to the cost of production. Since managers were rewarded for over-fulfilling their plan quotas rather than making a profit but might well not have official access to the necessary raw materials, they resorted to such expedients as making all their shoes in small sizes so as to minimise the use of raw materials. That large-footed customers could not obtain shoes and shops were congested with unsold small sizes would be of no significance. Conversely, housing was rented and cheap – but there was no incentive to build more housing and gross overcrowding resulted.

The argument is, therefore, that a free market economy enables individuals to allocate resources in such a way as to maximise everyone's satisfaction. The introduction of a market economy in which all are free to spend their money income as they please enables a painless 'swap' of the whisky ration for fishing tackle. Factories manufacturing rayon trousers when such items are out of fashion will go out of business, to be replaced by weavers of kilts (or whatever is currently in demand). Further, the sports car enthusiast may give up his/her leisure to earn extra resources in (say) overtime payments in order to secure a faster car, while the keen angler may decide to live simply in a remote area on the proceeds of only part-time employment. As Adam Smith described, the 'invisible hand' of the market balances supply and demand to the satisfaction of all in the market place.

As global economic systems, capitalism and state planning have influenced international relations. This can be between systems, such as during the Cold War when the West and the Soviet Bloc argued which economic system was the more efficient and effective. There are also subtle differences of emphasis and tone within the proponents of particular systems. For example, since the 1980s the US and UK have taken a more 'market economy' approach to capitalism and Germany and France have taken a more 'statist' approach. Both approaches agree on the need for a capitalist economy, but in the 'market economy' approach the state seeks to take less of a role, whereas in the 'statist' approach governments try to adopt a more direct management role in the operation of capitalism. One of the interesting outcomes of the 2012 French presidential election is that the winner, socialist François Hollande, has to struggle to combine policies that encourage economic prosperity with those that maintain social justice.

PROBLEMS OF MARKET DECISION-MAKING

With its superior productivity and response to consumer demand, the market mechanism might appear to have justified itself. Yet the inadequacies of raw capitalism seem hardly less than those of raw centralised planning.

The problem is that the accumulation of profit over time in the hands of successful 'entrepreneurs' leads to a grossly unfair distribution of resources. This is particularly the case when wealth is inherited – the result being an arbitrary distribution of purchasing power and consumer satisfaction. In many cases the distribution of wealth is the consequence of obscure historical events in periods when the market system hardly functioned. Consider the English aristocrats who continue to own a totally disproportionate share of the land, or, for that matter, the superior share of the earth's resources owned by the current generation of North Americans.

Further distortions in the market mechanism, familiar to all economists, include the absence in many industries and places of the 'perfect competition' assumed in the model of the market mechanism explained by Adam Smith and generally expected by its political proponents. That is, for consumers to obtain the goods that will maximise their satisfaction in return for their expenditure, it is necessary for them to have full knowledge of the goods and prices available. It is also required that new entrepreneurs be able to enter the market freely whenever exceptional profits are being made in an industry. The number of producers is also assumed to be so large they cannot affect the market price. In reality, markets are almost always 'imperfect' in that consumers are misled by advertising; new competition faces considerable barriers to entry into the market; and governments may subsidise domestic producers and tax or obstruct foreign competition. Thus the state is often forced to intervene to re-establish a competitive environment.

In a purely capitalist system, the producer is responsible only for staying within the law and maximising profits for shareholders. Thus for neo-liberals such as Friedman the 'business of business is business', therefore the role of the state is to act as a referee when/if firms break the law. As Peach (1987) notes this approach assumes that companies' social responsibility extends to little more than employing people and encouraging economic growth. Competitive forces are thought to ensure that individual consumer needs are met. However, it may be that the costs to the community of some productive activities will not be reflected in the costs producers (and ultimately consumers) pay. For instance, a factory may pollute its environment or workers in distant markets may be exploited. This may lead to a severe misallocation of resources. This often leads to demands for government intervention and/or for businesses to adopt a socially responsible attitude towards all the 'stakeholders' affected by them.

VOLUNTARY ORGANISATIONS

So far, we have examined this question largely as if there were only two alternative modes of social action – decisions are taken either by individuals through the market mechanism or by 'the state'. This is clearly an oversimplification.

In the first place it has to be emphasised that much 'individual' decision-making is not market-orientated but reflects patterns of social co-operation which are more altruistic than the sort of bargaining for individual advantage which is normally associated with the market. People seek not only their own satisfaction but that of their family, their neighbours and various community groupings with which they identify, and they may sacrifice immediate self-interest to causes as varied as vegetarianism, conservation or world government.

The idea that market decision-making is a form of individual choice is also an oversimplification. Individuals are generally confronted with alternatives that are the result of social processes over which they have little control. Many consumers, unlike affluent minorities in highly industrialised countries, have little 'discretionary income' with which to exercise choice. 'Consumer sovereignty' may seem a poor joke to many in Africa, India and China and of limited relevance to those living on social security benefits in more affluent countries. Discretion on the supply side of the economy seems still less real for the many individuals with limited marketable skills, little or no capital and few employment opportunities.

Social co-operation on a voluntary basis, especially between relatives and neighbours, is clearly an older and more basic form of human behaviour than market behaviour. There have been perhaps Utopian attempts to set up local communities according to such principles right up to the present day. For example, the early *kibbutzim* in Israel developed a system of co-operative labour and communal living arrangements. In social policy, the importance of family ties and behaviour should not be underestimated – even in modern communities in which work, leisure and spiritual activities which were previously family-based may now be carried on outside the family home.

In the present context, however, it is vital to consider the role of voluntary sector organisations in carrying out activities that might otherwise be the subject of market or government determination. Churches are an interesting example of voluntary organisations, since, as we have seen, in earlier times they have frequently had a legal monopoly of matters that are now seen as predominantly for the state or the individual. For members of these bodies their decisions may retain a greater legitimacy than those of the state. Churches retain a commitment to charitable works and to influencing government policy on 'moral' issues from contraception to debt relief for countries of the South.

More generally, a whole range of voluntary organisations carry out co-operative activities which enable their members to achieve satisfaction with little reference to either the market or the state sector. Examples include: leisure groups such as football clubs or rambler groups, educational groups such as play schools and Franco-British University of the Third Age movements. Economic activities such as providing food or clothing may take place via allotment and knitting societies. Some of the oldest voluntary groups provide welfare services to their members (friendly societies, the Masons, alumni associations). The Royal National Lifeboat Institution is an interesting example of the provision of what might be expected to be a state-financed 'Public Good' (a free public emergency sea rescue service).

Most voluntary organisations, however, do relate to the state, in one or both of two ways. First, they may provide services to the community in collaboration with the government – and increasingly often as contractors to it. Thus, in Britain, the Women's Royal Voluntary Service often delivers 'meals on wheels' to social service department clients. National Health Service hospitals are supported by the League of Friends, who may raise additional funds for specialist equipment, visit lonely patients or drive outpatients to the hospital. The National Society for the Prevention of Cruelty to Children has special legal powers in its work of protecting children. Citizens' Advice bureaux, staffed by volunteers, are usually financed by local councils.

Second, many voluntary organisations lobby the state to pass legislation or spend money on causes helpful to their client group. Thus the Royal Society for the Prevention of Cruelty to Animals is a major source of legislation in the United Kingdom pertaining to animal safety. Veterans' groups and the National Rifle Association are very influential in US legislation.

The voluntary sector is viewed by some politicians as a means of combining the best features of the welfare state and the market. For example, recent governments in the United Kingdom have increasingly encouraged both commercial and voluntary sectors to get involved in the provision of what were previously monopoly state social services. For instance, getting the volunteer, commercial and state sectors involved in policy implementation was a key part of both Labour's 'Third Way' and the Conservative Party's 'Big Society'. Therefore, using the voluntary sector can be applied to ideologies of both left and right. While the state continues to fund services, the actual provision of services such as health and community care is increasingly delivered by the voluntary and private sectors. The advantage for a government, especially a neo-liberal one, is that the state does not need to provide the service.

THE POLICY PROCESS

Hogwood and Gunn (1984) offer a useful model of the policy process, which takes into account some of the points we discussed above. They offer it not as a description or prescription of what happens in every case, but as a framework for understanding what does or does not happen in each particular case. Each of these stages is potentially of key importance in deciding the outcome of a policy process:

> ### BOX 8.2   HOGWOOD AND GUNN'S MODEL OF THE POLICY PROCESS
>
> 1   Deciding to decide (issue search or agenda-setting)
> 2   Deciding how to decide
> 3   Issue definition
> 4   Forecasting

In comparison with the rational-comprehensive model, this formulation has some important and desirable features: it sees policy-making as a more or less continuous process; it stresses political issues of agenda-setting, decision process and definition; and it does not take the implementation of the decision for granted.

In particular, items 1 and 9 in the model rightly suggest that policy-making is an extended process in which certain issues are picked out for attention, may be approached in different ways during the process of decision and implementation, and then may be subsumed into debates on other issues as time goes by.

Rather than a one-off decision on values, we have already stressed the extent to which policy-making often reflects compromises on the values of different groups. These groups, in turn, may define 'the problem' in different ways. As we saw earlier, the question of whether a problem should be dealt with by the state, the market, voluntary action or whatever is a crucial part of many contemporary policy discussions.

Diez (2013) provides an interesting framework for understanding successful policy campaigns. Looking at the adoption of same-sex union legislation in Buenos Aires and Mexico City, Diez found the presence in both cases of three factors. The first of these was the existence of effective pressure groups that acted as advocates; then the appropriate framing of their messages to appeal to decision-makers; and finally the existence of a political opportunity (which for one of the cases was immediate and for the other took six years). This framework can help explain the role of non-state actors in policy-making.

One popular approach for explaining policy-making processes is the idea of policy communities. The original idea as presented by Richardson and Jordan (1979) suggested that the explanation of policy-making was to be found within key organisations rather than party manifestos. For example, Wray (2009) looked at how tourism policy-making was a complex process – multi-layered and involving cross-sectional issues. The concept of policy communities has been expanded to include territory, not just sector, thus Keating *et al.* (2009) look at how this has been framed around devolution. Policy communities are now also believed to extend internationally: Stone (2008) identified transnational policy communities.

In policy communities the government plays the dominant role, but an alternative approach has identified the existence of policy networks. This is where policy-making is influenced by public and private organisations that are outside government control. For example, Braun (2009) found that the European Union emissions trading scheme was a result of the sharing of trading emissions knowledge by a policy network.

One of the questions often asked about the policy-making process is: what drives the government to work with groups? One view is that ideology is the prime factor, that governments want to work with those they feel an affinity with. An alternative view focuses on the power they have – that is, that a government deals with those with greatest influence in a field. Looking at regional planning in California, Henry (2011) found that policy groups were formed around ideology.

BOX 8.3   POLICY COMMUNITIES

A network of organisations which due to their expertise or political 'muscle' are formally consulted in the policy-making process by government bodies. There is a level of interdependence and negotiation.

Policy communities and networks are probably more applicable to liberal democracies. Looking at a more authoritarian political system, Zhu (2012) suggests that in China a policy entrepreneur can play a central role in policy-making. Zhu assessed housing reform in one province and concluded that the policy entrepreneur, a local government official, was able to identify the problems, build coalitions and set an example. For China a top-down approach based on a powerful champion may be more applicable than the more pluralist policy-community style.

Policy-making should be about making good policy; this in part implies a wide ownership, but it also requires the provision and understanding of appropriate information. Bryson *et al.* (2010) looked at the immunisation policies of 140 countries and found the importance of information provided by the World Health Organisation.

IMPLEMENTING PUBLIC POLICY

Partly as a consequence of the extended time policy-making takes and the partial nature of the consensus built up behind many policies, it cannot be assumed that decisions once made will automatically be implemented. Many agencies, firms and levels of government may be involved in realising a decision initially taken at one level of the state machinery. The outcome may not be recognisable to the initial policy-makers. The consequences of the policies adopted may not, in fact, be as predicted by the original analysis upon which the policy was based. For these reasons it is sensible that policy-makers set up mechanisms to monitor the success or failure of their policies so that they may be adapted, refined, or indeed abandoned as appropriate.

Public policy is often discussed almost entirely from a central government perspective. A problem is identified, a 'solution' propounded, after which the solution to the problem is assumed to be the effective and efficient implementation of the policy at local level. Indeed, many commentators on public policy – especially in the national press – scarcely consider the possibility of a gap between policy prescription and its implementation. Yet, most public policies are implemented by local agencies at various distances from the central government.

Hood (1976) introduced the concept of 'perfect implementation' for a state of affairs in which central policy-makers' prescriptions were perfectly realised. The likelihood of such an eventuality in the real world is remote. For instance, studies by the UK National Audit Office show that social security payments, being paid through local branches of a central ministry on the basis of relatively clear and unambiguous rules enforced through a single bureaucracy, suffer from a 35 per cent error rate. In the case of the Child Support Agency, its first annual report referred to a study by its chief child support officer who found, of 1,380 assessments checked, only 25 per cent were judged correct, 39 per cent were found to be incorrect, while in 35 per cent of cases insufficient information was recorded to tell if the assessment was right or wrong. When policies are implemented through a series of agencies, each of which expects to have some influence on the nature and interpretation of the policy, then clearly 'perfect implementation' becomes still less likely. Inter-organisational bargaining will doubtless affect the outcomes of policies, and with different agencies in different parts of the country considerably different outcomes may result (see Figure 8.1).

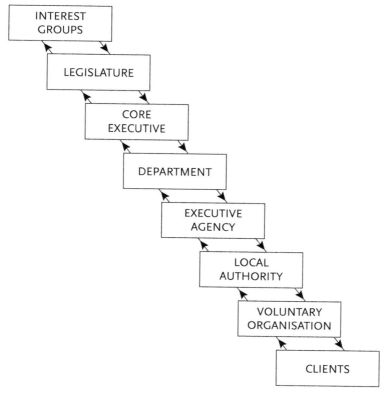

Figure 8.1 Levels of inter-organisational bargaining

Pressman and Wildavsky (1973), looking at the implementation of federal policies in Oakland, California, found that if a series of administrative agreements or clearance stages are necessary for implementation, even with 99 per cent of agreement at each 'clearance', overall probability of perfect implementation falls below 50 per cent after 68 clearances.

Is 'perfect implementation' always desirable? Local conditions may differ radically from those that central policy-makers had in mind in formulating their response to 'the' problem. Barrett and Fudge (1981) attack the traditional British 'top-down' approach to public problem-solving, arguing that local communities can deploy scarce resources much more effectively to meet their real need rather than the centrally perceived 'problem'. Lindblom (1959) defended incrementalism as a policy-making procedure in cases where it is difficult to define a clear consensus on policy goals and circumstances are rapidly changing – as is the case with much public policy. If the central policy is a radical one then the analysis of Bachrach and Baratz (1970) referred to earlier may well help to explain its non-implementation. Equally, any central government may find local areas (particularly those controlled by a different political party or candidate) will stonewall on the implementation of economic and fiscal policies, with severe impact on the local economy.

In some cases it may even be that policies are not intended to be implemented. Edelman's (1977) study of political language has emphasised the symbolic function of many policy declarations. A fine-sounding policy may have its origins in a political compromise at central level which was acceptable *because* it was too vague to be implemented unambiguously. In a nice twist, in the UK the almost anti-politics Monster Raving Loony Party was the first to call for passports for pets, and now a form of legislation has been enacted.

'Perfect implementation' then is not necessarily desirable – and certainly not inevitable. To overcome the barriers to implementation may well be costly in both communication effort and need to offer sanctions/inducements to the implementer. Following R. E. Neustadt (1960), implementation seems to require that:

1 An unambiguous signal of required behaviour must reach local implementer and be understood.

2 Either (a) they must want to conform to the new policy and have the power to implement it, or (b) costs of non-implementations must be made to clearly exceed benefits of inertia.

One theory which has gained interest as a means of implementing policy change is Thaler and Sunstein's (2008) 'nudge'. They consider how psychology and behavioural patterns can have an impact. They suggest that this can lead to policy changes which support libertarian paternalism, and so quickly gained the interest of the neo-liberal right. In 2010 the Cameron government in the UK set up within the Cabinet Office the behavioural insights team (www.gov.uk/government/organisations/behavioural-insights-team), commonly referred to as the 'nudge unit'. It is designed to find ways of improving individual behaviour in fields such as health, taxation and house insulation.

MANAGING LOCAL PUBLIC POLICY

It may be helpful to expand upon the previous section by looking briefly at the implementation of public policy from the point of the local managers of such a service. This may help to add a realistic perspective to the problems of implementing policy prescriptions. Although such managers are in very varied circumstances we can point to some likely common characteristics: they are in a multiple series of bargaining relationships as suggested by Figure 8.2;

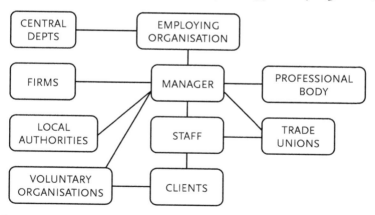

Figure 8.2 Managing local public service provision

they have limited time and information sources, many tasks and limited resources.

A minor example of this would be one of the authors' research on the Youth Training Scheme (Tansey, 1989) in which training officers within organisations were seen as having to negotiate with:

- personnel and finance directors for permission to run/finance the scheme;
- departmental heads to offer worthwhile placements for trainees;
- Manpower Service Commission (a quango) representatives to approve the scheme;
- Careers Service (local government) officials to publicise and recruit for the scheme;
- technical college course tutors on the content of off-the-job training;
- industrial training boards (more quangos) on the acceptability of the training for apprenticeship purposes;
- the trainees themselves in respect of their behaviour.

Some major variables which may affect managers' capacity to take an independent view of how policy should be implemented will include their relationship to – and distance from – clients, their relationship to local authorities/central departments and the degree of their dependence on firms/voluntary organisations for resources.

MULTI-LEVEL GOVERNANCE

Two major factors have helped to extend and complicate the chain of relationships involved in policy implementation in recent years. One is the trend towards multi-level government, the second is the trend away from monolithic government departments that both decide policy and manage the nation-wide delivery of public services towards a reliance on a network of agencies, public, voluntary and private, for local delivery. Indeed, with regard to the latter, Cairney (2011) suggests that though the UK has had a highly centralised approach to policy-making, the Conservative Party's 'Big Society' concept is moving the UK towards a more decentralised approach. This implies a link between ideology and policy-making.

Neo-conservative thinkers have influenced many democratic governments towards attempting to restrict the institutions of government into a role of regulating and co-ordinating the delivery of public services, rather than undertaking their supply directly. Coupling these trends together, the term 'multi-level governance' may help to encapsulate recent trends (see Pierre and Stoker, 2002).

'Governance' is a fashionable but tricky word that can be used in a variety of different ways. Rhodes (1996) suggests at least six major uses of the term. Strictly one might argue it refers broadly to 'the process of making collective decisions in a more or less binding way' (Keman, 2002: 260). Hence, it could encompass decision-making through the market, by networks of voluntary co-operation or by bargaining by government. In practice it is often used to emphasise that public policies are increasingly implemented in a pragmatic way through a network of organisations which must then be managed professionally: 'Governance is about managing networks' (Rhodes, 1996: 658).

A moderate and extremely influential version of this approach is to be found in the work of the US writers Osborne and Gaebler (1992), who argued that approaches to the delivery of public services should be rethought along the lines of ten principles (Box 8.4).

BOX 8.4 TEN PRINCIPLES FOR RE-INVENTING GOVERNMENT

Entrepreneurial public organisations should:

1 steer more than they row;
2 empower communities rather than simply deliver services;
3 encourage competition rather than monopoly;
4 be driven by their missions not rules;
5 fund outcomes not inputs;
6 meet customer, not bureaucratic, needs;
7 earn as well as spend;
8 prevent rather than cure;
9 decentralise authority;
10 lever the market place rather than spend on public programmes.

(Osborne and Gaebler, 1992)

Despite the prevalence in the everyday lives of many of the Internet, this technology has not yet had a noticeable effect on governance. Themistocleous *et al.* (2012) have posited a model of e-participation, but note that citizens have not yet shown an interest in a bottom-up form of governance.

In the UK Margaret Thatcher was successful in cutting the size of the civil service, privatised many nationalised industries, introduced requirements for contracting out as many central and local government functions as possible, and began the process of subdividing existing departments of state into business units ('executive agencies'). The overwhelming majority of public servants in the United Kingdom are now in executive agencies, national or local quangos such as National Health Service Trusts, or working for local government. Additionally, many posts which were formerly in the civil service or part of a nationalised industry are now in the private sector.

Although Labour in opposition opposed many of these developments, New Labour governments endorsed 'public–private partnerships' as being a pragmatic way of ensuring the efficient delivery of public services. In the white paper 'Modernising Government' (1999) and in the reforms of the NHS, they placed more emphasis on achieving user-centred targets and less on cut-throat competition and financial economy. The mechanism of contractual delivery of public services by private companies in collaboration with public sector commissioning agencies has remained prominent. Gordon Brown continued the project of reducing the size of the civil service, announcing a reduction of 104,000 posts in July 2004. In 2010 the agreement setting up the Conservative–Liberal coalition outlined the requirement of some 100,000 civil service job losses. According to civil service unions, the response to this has been an exodus of senior civil servants due to low morale (Hope, 2012). Table 8.1 shows that government intent in reducing numbers is a slow process, though across time UK governments want a smaller, more streamlined and commercially aware civil service.

Recent agreements by the World Trade Organisation require all signatory states to open up the market for government services to international tender. This, and the accession of the former Eastern Bloc countries to the European Union, has meant

Table 8.1 Civil Service employment

Year	Headcount
2009	524,400
2010	527,500
2011	498,400
2012	463,800
2013	448,800

Source: Annual Civil Service Employment Survey (http://www.nomisweb.co.uk/articles/780.aspx)

that privatisation and public–private partnerships have become a worldwide trend.

NON-WESTERN POLICY-MAKING

What we have covered so far considers either generic rules for policy-making and implementation or specifically relates to industrialised Western nations. However, as noted in Chapter 6, what applies to the North might not always operate in the same way elsewhere. In large parts of Asia, Africa and Latin America we can possibly identify a non-Western approach to policy-making, or at least a recognition that what works in the North need not automatically work in the South. As noted by Horowitz (1989), the key difference in policy-making between North and South relates to different systemic frameworks, such as the institutions involved, the range of participants and access to resources.

Another key difference which explains policy outcomes is culture. Thus, Lin and Rantalaiho (2003) examined the role of a collective versus an individualist approach in family policy. They found that in Scandinavia there was a consensus for sharing the costs of childcare which was reflected in a strong policy function. Whereas in Confucian Asia childcare is considered a private affair, so the social policy function was weaker.

There is some evidence that industrialised nations and some international institutions assume that the processes that work for them will automatically work to solve the different problems the South faces. For example, Ochieng (2007) suggests that there has long been a tradition of agricultural innovation in Africa, but that policy alternatives from external policy stakeholders such as the World Bank can relegate good ideas from internal stakeholders. Therefore, external factors and the requirements of aid programmes can shape policy-making.

Also looking at policy-making in Kenya, Norton-Griffiths (2010) suggests that not only international institutions but also NGOs impact on internal policy-making. With both wildlife conservation and national land policy Norton-Griffiths found that foreign NGOs were involved in the formulation of domestic policy-making which led to legislative changes.

Ochieng and Norton-Griffiths's research argues that many international organisations seek to impose their own approach – typically one linked to the market. However, Gore (2000) argues that a non-Western alternative approach, a 'Southern consensus', is being formed which focuses on the impact of development on people's lives. However, we are yet to see concrete evidence of any resultant change in policy-making.

Although we have seen the impact of international players on domestic policy, we suggest that public policy-making is still largely heterogeneous; there is not a single homogenous approach. For example, looking at taxation policy in South America, Hart (2010) found that while international economic forces did have an impact, party ideology of the government was a good predictor of tax policy, implying the supremacy of domestic considerations.

EVALUATING PUBLIC POLICY

Evaluation of decision-making processes on public policy can concentrate on either procedural or substantive issues. From a procedural point of view, we can ask whether the process of making the decision accords with the evaluative criteria to be applied. For example, was the decision taken in a democratic manner, or did the decision-maker consider all rational alternatives and cost them? From a substantive point of view we can ask was the result 'correct', set against appropriate criteria in terms of its outcome? The criteria employed may be many and various – ethical, economic, ecological, egalitarian, etc. – but ultimately the question is, were the decision-makers' objectives achieved?

Assuming we have defined our values and specifying objectives, using Lindblom's terminology, it may be possible to assess decision-making in a less controversial way. Here we offer some more 'managerial' concepts for evaluating policy-making (Box 8.5)

BOX 8.5   THE THREE 'E'S: EFFICIENCY, ECONOMY, EFFECTIVENESS

Efficiency can be seen as something like the physicists' definition of 'the ratio of useful work to energy expended' (*Shorter Oxford English Dictionary*: Addenda). Thus, given fixed resources and a fixed objective, efficiency can be seen as achieving the maximum effect in the desired direction. The emphasis is often on implementing planned actions to specification.

Economy is clearly closely related to efficiency, but is more likely to be expressed in financial terms. It can be seen as employing minimum resources to achieve a fixed objective. It is more likely to encompass costing of alternative ways to achieve an objective.

Effectiveness can then be seen as including the choice of objectives in order to realise the values desired. The emphasis here is not on the volume of work done but the overall impact of the work done. In economists' terms, has utility been maximised?

The three concepts can thus be seen as occupying a hierarchical relationship, with efficiency the most limited concept, economy a somewhat broader one, and effectiveness the most comprehensive. Economy in public administration may be interpreted irrationally as merely minimising financial expenditure on a particular budget. If, however, a reduction in expenditure means that the department or organisation fails to achieve its objective, or if, for instance, refusal to buy capital equipment means that expensive staff time is not made good use of, then such behaviour is far from economical in the true sense.

MONITORING PERFORMANCE IN PUBLIC POLICY

Any rational monitoring and evaluation of public policy needs to measure as precisely as possible how far objectives are being achieved. In the absence of a general-purpose measure of efficiency, such as profitability in the private sector, then the output of public sector organisations can only be measured in more specific terms related to their objectives. In principle the establishment of 'performance indicators' seems unexceptionable. The attempt to define performance indicators has, however, become more controversial and central to the political process in Britain in the light of a number of political developments. These developments include the role of such indicators as part of the privatisation process; their use in the context of 'citizen's charters'; and their role in public sector pay bargaining.

In the privatisation process, performance indicators are important in defining the standard of service to be expected from the privatised service provider. Merely specifying a maximum level of profits or prices could encourage the provider to produce a substandard service (perhaps with minimal investment) allowing exploitation of a monopoly position. Thus an electricity company is required to restore any interruptions to supply to at least 85 per cent of domestic customers within three hours (Southern Electric, 1994: 7). Such indicators can then be policed by an independent regulator (in this case the Director General of Electricity Supply), with 'league tables' of the efficiency of each supplier being compilable and the possibility of the removal of franchises from non-performing companies.

One of the major problems may be that those aspects of performance which are most easily quantified are not necessarily the most significant parts of the public sector organisation or individual's work. Yet, particularly where managers' pay or career success are felt to be crucially affected by them, such performance indicators may come to be 'the tail that wags the corporate dog'. Thus, if police officers and forces are judged by the crime clear-up rate, crime prevention and developing good community relations may be neglected. Such statistics may also be subject to manipulation – in our example, criminals may be induced to confess to a string of unsolved crimes they did not commit, or 'unsolvable' crimes may not be recorded.

Another example of the problems inherent in the use of such performance indicators can be seen in the publication of school league tables of examination and test performances. The problem here is that the environmental differences between schools are neglected – together with the pupils' starting points. Some attempts have been made to assess the 'value' added by schools, but these have received much less attention than the crude and misleading headline figures.

EVALUATING POLICY OUTCOMES: THE DISTRIBUTION OF WEALTH AND INCOME

We shall discuss briefly here the outcomes of public policies in modern welfare states in terms of equality and justice.

Consider, by way of example, the distribution of wealth and income. In contemporary Britain, the official statistics on the distribution of marketable wealth are as follows:

Table 8.2 Marketable wealth in Britain

	1976	1986	1996	2003	2010
	%	%	%	%	%
Most wealthy 10%	50	50	52	53	44
Least wealthy 50%	8	10	7	7	10

Source: Office for National Statistics, 2012

In other developed countries published statistics suggest a similar distribution of both income and wealth. The most striking inequalities, however, can be seen if figures from less-developed economies are taken into account, as Table 8.3 suggests. Moreover, these bald figures hide longer-term trends, so that the percentage in South Asia is essentially the same as in 2001, marginally higher in Sub-Saharan Africa, and significantly lower in East Asia.

From a socialist point of view, such statistics suggest that policies attempting equity between individuals in the UK (and similar economies such as those of the EU and the US) will have to abandon the market mechanism altogether and distribute benefits

Table 8.3 World population below the international poverty line (2010)

	Percentage of population	Number of people
All developing countries	21	1.2 billion
South Asia	31	507 million
Sub-Saharan Africa	48	414 million
East Asia	12	251 million

Source: World Bank Estimate based on population living on below $1.25 per day in Poverty and Social Impact Analysis (http://www.worldbank.org/en/topic/poverty/overview).

direct without regard to ability to pay. It is in this context, also, that some radical socialist critiques of piecemeal welfare reforms become intelligible. Such massive inequalities are felt to be incompatible with equal rights for all in a democratic society.

A liberal approach might be to adopt some form of means testing or redistribute income on a large scale, perhaps through a 'negative income tax' scheme instead of social security and means-tested benefits. In such a scheme a minimum standard of living is guaranteed to all, with a minimum of stigmatising special treatment for the poor, by paying out income through the same machinery which collects taxes on the basis of one declaration of income and circumstances for everyone. Solutions are sought which preserve the individual freedom associated with market mechanisms, while treating all citizens by consistent rules.

From a conservative point of view, an uneven distribution of capital may merely be seen as enabling worthwhile investments to be made and the result of rewards of previous risk-taking and effort. Providing the income of the bottom 20 per cent of the population is judged to be above an adequate 'safety net' level, the existence of unequal incomes is not seen as a problem for social and economic policy.

It is often thought that the 'welfare state', through both progressive taxation and the redistributive effect of its 'universal' social services, has radically affected the distribution of income and wealth (especially the former after tax and benefits). A considerable academic literature exists on this (concentrating, though, on the tax element of the equation). Summarising this, brutally the overall conclusion seems to be that taxation has had surprisingly little effect – other than to redistribute within social classes. Perhaps surprisingly, it seems that the social services have also had virtually no redistributive effect between classes, as LeGrand (1982) shows. In Britain, working-class gains from unemployment benefits have been counterbalanced by middle-class gains from post-school-leaving-age educational benefits – with the middle classes showing a greater capacity to benefit from the National Health Service.

The global inequalities referred to seem difficult to address in a world divided into sovereign states and employing a capitalist economic trading system. The rules governing finance, trade and aid are clearly less than ideal in terms of promoting equality. More important still, it might be argued, is the lack of any real commitment by either ordinary people or politicians in richer states to make extensive sacrifices to achieve greater justice and equality across the globe. The reluctance of US voters to give up gas-guzzling automobiles which help to create global warming – thus ruining the environment of Bangladeshi coastal farmers and flooding low-lying Pacific islands – seems to support this. On the other hand, the partially successful movement for a moratorium on the public debts of the poorest countries gives cause to hope that a sense of a global community is emerging. Colas (2002) highlighted the need for a sense of 'international civil society' to be developed in a globalised world. Social movements of ordinary citizens must develop to balance the power of multinational enterprises and governmental organisations.

Thus, in the end, any discussion of public policy is likely to return to the ideological differences explored in more depth in Chapter 4. Individual choices on political values cannot be avoided in evaluating public policy. However, the potential for consensus can be underestimated since many enlightened social policies (e.g. effective health and educational services) are both good for the individuals they benefit and contribute to the efficiency of the overall economy.

THE POLITICAL POLICY-MAKING PROCESS

This chapter has largely focused on what might be termed 'macro'-level policy-making in terms of how governments make and implement policy. But this can be shaped by 'micro'-level policy decisions made by individual politicians (in weak-party systems) or political parties (in strong-party systems). These political actors develop and present the suite of policies they believe will be electorally successful.

The micro-policy process is not just about the end result of producing the policies but also about the process itself and what that says about that political organisation. After four successive election defeats (1979, 1983, 1987 and 1992), the Labour Party in the mid-1990s felt it had to change how it decided party policy as well as the actual policies themselves. Under Tony Blair's guidance the Labour Party streamlined the policy process by significantly reducing the number of people who were consulted. At the same time Labour made use of political marketing techniques such as focus groups to obtain feedback from voters (Wring, 2007). The effect of these changes was to strengthen the position of the Labour Party leadership on policy-making. The Blair and Brown administrations continued this centralised approach.

After the election losses of 1997 and 2005, the Conservative Party did not particularly change their policy-making process, but as Norton (2008) noted, David Cameron stressed broad values and, where he has looked at policy, has introduced new areas of concern such as the environment. Thus, the focus has been more on the purpose and presentation of policy than the process of constructing it.

CONCLUSION

When we are looking at policy we need to focus on three related areas: the policy-making process, the policy itself, and how it is implemented. We are, therefore, interested in both the process and the outcome. Candidates and parties have used changes to the first two as a means of presenting an image to voters which they hope makes them more electable.

There are at least three themes which we can identify in policy-making. First, there are players ranging from government, pressure groups, the commercial world and voluntary organisations which are involved. In each country the exact nature of and relationship between these players will vary. Second, there is a clear link to ideology: not only is policy shaped by broader principles but policy-makers group together in comfortable policy zones based on a shared philosophy. Third, the growth of globalisation has been accompanied by an international aspect to policy-making. This is in part due to the nature of the problems, but also the introduction of international players which have a voice. Policy is at the heart of day-to-day politics.

FURTHER READING

Dorey, M. (2005) *Policy Making in Britain: An Introduction*, London: Sage.

Hill, M. (1997) *The Policy Process in the Modern State*, London: Prentice Hall.

Roe, M. (2013) *Maritime Governance and Policy Making*, London: Springer.

Smith, C. (2010) *Writing Public Policy: A Practical Guide to Communicating in the Policy Making Process*, Oxford: Oxford University Press.

Stevens, J. (1993) *The Economics of Collective Choice*, Oxford: Westview.

Wallace, H., Wallace, W. and Pollack, M. (2005) *Policy Making in the European Union*, Oxford: Oxford University Press.

Young, M. (1961) *The Rise of the Meritocracy 1870–2033*, Harmondsworth, Middlesex: Penguin.

WEBSITES

http://thomas.loc.gov/

THOMAS – US legislative information, with link to Library of Congress, etc.

http://lib.umich.edu/govdocs

University of Michigan Documents Center – government resources online.

www.gpoaccess.gov/index.html

GPO access – US Government Printing Office, with the full text of many US government documents.

www.crossover-project.eu/ProjectHome.aspx

Policy-making project looking at policy Web 2.0.

9

CHALLENGES

THIS CHAPTER ...

will focus on a range of challenges that democratic government faces. We are to some degree crystal ball-gazing as to how democratic politics may evolve. As we saw in Chapter 5, the basis of what we understand by democracy starts with Athens over two millennia ago. Then in the sixteenth and seventeenth centuries philosophers such as Locke, Paine and Hobbes began to address ideas of governance and helped shape the debate. Their focus was on the role of the monarchy, the rights of individuals and the beginning of discussions about representative government. In the eighteenth and nineteenth centuries more overt thought was given to what we now consider democracy, though it was not always viewed that way by the authors. Writers such as Thomas Jefferson, de Tocqueville and J. S. Mill looked at governance and justified practical ideas we recognise today such as 'inalienable rights' and the 'separation of powers'. The initial construct of the mechanisms of what we now understand to be democratic institutions have existed for some time. Thus Iceland's *althing* dates from the tenth century, parliaments are identifiable in France, England and Spain by the thirteenth century and the House of Burgesses of Virginia created in 1619 is probably the first representative body in the New

World. However, it is valid to ask if a political world created by (it has been argued) the American Revolution, the French Revolution and the industrial revolution is still relevant today. Maybe the economic, social, environmental and technological construct of the twenty-first century requires a shake-up of democratic government.

This chapter will consider the key problems which provide the context shaping any discussion about the future of democracy. These issues shape not just what governments decide to do, but also who makes those decisions and how they make them. They include the impact of population growth and migration patterns, the 'War on Terror' and rapid technological and scientific change. By the end of this chapter students will be able to:

- identify the key current issues shaping the future of democratic government;
- consider how the concept of democracy might be evolving;
- assess the applicability of e-democracy and e-representation.

A CRISIS IN DEMOCRATIC POLITICS?

In 1992 Fukuyama predicted that the end of the Cold War which resulted from the break-up of the Soviet Bloc meant that Western-style liberal democracy had triumphed. However, some twenty years later democracy faces some important challenges from both within and without. The concept both as an ideal and a form of government is clearly evolving, with the voice of new players being heard. For example, if BRICS are the next power bloc (and the authors have some doubts about this), we note that one of them would not claim to be a democracy, two provide a democratic cloak of elections but not everything else we might expect, and the remaining two have social and economic issues the handling of which present a challenge to democratic politicians. In addition to such pressures for change from the rising nations, older established democracies will also shape the future. Ostrom (2000) drew a very interesting parallel with family businesses and suggested that it is during the third and subsequent generations that problems arise. This implies that many democracies are now at a highly vulnerable stage. Ostrom argues that within mature democracies there needs to be continuous civic engagement, intellectual struggle and vigilance.

We introduced in Chapter 1 the concept of depoliticisation when discussing the value of politics. We now return to this debate because, as Kettell (2008) suggests, depoliticisation is a means for explaining a system of governance which seeks to reduce democratic content. As a result it is potentially a serious threat to democracy.

As a deliberate state strategy for political management, depoliticisation is a component of neo-liberalism. Political managers, be they politicians or senior officials, ostensibly remove themselves from controlling key economic issues, leaving it up to professionals and the market. But at the same time they may retain some control of the issue behind the scenes. Thus they try to avoid any potential negative backlash for having to take controversial political decisions. This is a difficult manoeuvre to pull off.

In the UK there is evidence that governments of all flavours may be pursuing a depoliticisation strategy. The Conservative government of the 1990s separated out the technical aspects of the exchange rate mechanism from the thorny political decision of whether to join the euro or not (Kettell, 2008). The Labour government also adopted this ploy for economic policy-making (Burnham, 2001; James, 2010). The potential impact of relying on the market is that it downplays the role of political participation by citizens and replaces it, in principle, with that of the consumer.

Dahl (2000) identifies a paradox in democracy – namely, that even though citizens in Western democracies may have declining confidence in some democratic institutions, they still have a strong attachment to the desirability of democracy as a form of government. His explanation for this paradox is that there are two dimensions to democracy – one an ideal and the other a set of institutions – and it is possible to be loyal to both at the same time.

One important debate for democracy involves the question of what influences individual behaviour, and one possible answer is political culture. This idea was first associated with Gabriel Almond (1956), and it suggests that individuals' actions are shaped by shared values, beliefs and preferences to be found within society. Elazer (1972) identified three different political cultures in America:

1   Moral political culture – society is more important than the individual
2   Individual political culture – private concerns are more important than public concerns
3   Traditional political culture – family and friends play a key role in shaping political views.

Elazer identified different parts of the US demonstrating these three separate cultures. Fisher (2010) applied Elazer's typology to the 2008 Democratic presidential primaries, and found that Obama won 76 per cent of the states classified as 'moralistic', whereas the 'individualistic' and 'traditionalist' were evenly split between Obama and Clinton.

An alternative to political culture is rational choice theory, which argues that individual political attitudes and behaviour are influenced by the political context. Thus, Pateman (1971) suggests that it is political elites, class and institutions which play a key role, rather than a shared culture. This debate suggests that democratic governments are faced with two alternatives: either respond to bottom-up pressures or offer clear top-down guidance.

Civic engagement is where citizens participate in civil society, for instance by being a trade union member, organising a youth group or belonging to a charity. Together such disparate activities comprise social capital in terms of the overall well-being of society, and so act as a social bond (Norris and Curtice, 2004). Putnam (2000) suggests that civic engagement is the invisible cement which brings together different communities within one overall social infrastructure. Although civic activity may be non-political, it does imply an interest in public affairs, the very basis upon which politics is founded.

The orthodox view is that over the past thirty years there has been a general deterioration in civic engagement in liberal democracies. It is suggested that this has been especially acute among younger people and the better educated (Putnam, 2000). One clear manifestation of this, it is maintained, has been a general decline in voting turnout in many Western countries. This it can be argued represents either political apathy regarding liberal-democracy or a sense of alienation, especially among the young.

A number of different explanations for a growing sense of civic disillusionment have been put forward. One view is that a crisis in liberalism has created the growth of individualism, which undermines the connective nature of civic engagement (Mazzoleni, 2000). An alternative view suggests that it is the communication process, in the form of political marketing, which has led to a focus on the individual at the expense of society (Putnam, 2000). However, not all commentators believe that these developments suggest civic engagement is in decline. Rather, Scammell (2001) argues that one type of civic engagement is being replaced by another, which is increasingly based around consumption. Consumer behaviour is increasingly adding to civic participation through its focus on environmental and ethical concerns and the consequent growth of 'accelerated pluralism' (Moloney, 2006). Communication by politicians therefore needs to reflect the fact that the recipient is the citizen-consumer, not the citizen-voter.

An alternative view is suggested by Bennett *et al.* (2011), who argue that many young people engage in civic engagement in social networking sites, but in a different way to traditional engagement. Therefore, to reach young audiences organisations need to adjust how they communicate online to encourage more engagement.

ENVIRONMENTAL ISSUES

Scientific evidence strongly suggests that one of the more pressing issues facing humankind is the impact of our activities on the planet. Concerns about global warming, greenhouse gases, the melting of the polar icecaps and our food chain are now recognised as important to political decision-making (for more information see the Intergovernmental Panel on Climate Change report via www.ipcc.ch). While clearly such global environmental problems are relevant to all countries irrespective of political system, we can see that they present specific problems for liberal democracies.

The very nature of pluralism that gives voice to a range of interests may be preventing the creation of a determined consensus-driving state and international decisions. White and Hooke (2004) note that scientists and environmentalists have successfully gained public interest, which has in turn meant that decision-makers have considered a raft of environmental issues. Indeed, some governments have sought to pressure other more powerful states into action. For example, in October 2009 the Maldives government held their Cabinet meeting underwater in the sea, with all ministers wearing scuba diving equipment to highlight the effect of global warming on their low-lying nation. However, White and Hooke note that the result of activity by campaigners has been a 'frothing' of political debate and a paralysis of political action. Vested and competing interests may be preventing decision-making at national and global levels – one illustration of this being the decades of hesitation on the construction of additional runways for London airports.

One of the key political issues within the whole environmental debate is whose fault it is and whose responsibility it is to fix the mess. Given that the data suggest the environmental problems coincided with the industrial revolution, it may not appear unreasonable that those who became industrialised more recently indicate that the older industrialised nations (broadly what we have referred to as the North) have a duty to change their behaviour first and to a greater extent. In reply the North may argue that the seriousness of the situation is such that all countries need to change their behaviour.

This debate, which has been going back and forth, highlights the related issue of inequality. We have noted that globalisation is based upon a capitalist market system, but an important question is whether liberal democracy is facilitating increased economic inequality between and within countries. If so, it is logical to assume that at some point in the future this will lead to political conflict, and the possible overthrow of democratic governments.

There is no consensus as to whether economic inequality is growing. Qureshi and Wen (2008) looked at cross-country data and suggested that location and access to capital are the main determinants of inequality, so globalisation was not a significant factor in cross-country inequality. However, Spence (2011) noted that greater global competition has led in the last decade to increased inequality in the US, with the highly educated enjoying more opportunities and the less educated facing declining employment prospects and income. A more complex situation has been identified in Brazil, where Castilho *et al.* (2011) found that trade liberalisation contributes to greater inequality and poverty in urban areas but decreasing inequality and poverty in rural areas. Therefore, possible solutions to one problem – environmental crisis – could exacerbate another problem – inequality.

POPULATION CHANGE

As long ago as the eighteenth century the Reverend Thomas Malthus warned of the dangers of population growth, arguing that eventually the food supply will not be enough for everyone to be fed. At the time he wrote 'An Essay on the Principle of Population' there were approximately one billion people alive; now there are seven billion. Population growth is clearly an exacerbating factor in such environmental issues as how we feed ourselves, produce energy and dispose of waste. It also raises unique problems such as access to other resources and the interaction between different communities.

Population growth in itself need not be inherently bad, but if it is excessive, in the wrong geographical areas and leads to unsustainable urbanisation density, it can be. A government may decide that population control is a good thing for the country, but individual citizens may continue to choose to have more children than the government wants. Solutions are not easy to achieve, and for liberal democracies raise ideological issues concerning individual freedom. Governments have attempted a variety of means to stem too much growth; an example from the second most populated country in the world serves as a warning for democracy. In 1976 Sanjay the son of the Indian prime minister Indira Gandhi introduced a forced sterilisation programme which targeted men with three children (Mehta, 2012). This policy occurred during the two years of declared national emergency, at a point when normal democratic politics was not fully functioning, but it does raise the question of how a political system based on individual freedom can/should apply illiberal policies. An alternative scenario is population growth in the future becoming such a critical issue that governments have to consider draconian curbs on reproduction, which would have a significant effect on what democracy stands for and perhaps dilute the liberal aspect.

The issue facing politicians and political systems is not only the exact number of people in any country but also migration trends. Migration has always occurred, but Castles and Miller (2003) note that there has been an increase in the number of countries of origin and destination and that migration has become more politicised, affecting relationships between and within states. There are clearly great benefits for the host country of immigration, but if numbers are deemed too high, this could lead to resource-based issues such as the cost of policing, health and education gaining traction in the public consciousness. It also raises a politically more controversial and emotive issue – namely, whether multiculturalism should be a government goal.

RELIGIOUS AND ETHNIC CONFLICT

Important factors shape whether ethnicity becomes a political issue; these include relative size and economic and political influence. Thus, a small group occupying an unimportant but useful economic role (e.g. Chinese or Indians running take-aways and restaurants) in an otherwise undivided community may be almost invisible. A similar-sized group owning a large part of the land on which the majority community lives and farms (e.g. 'European' farmers formerly in Zimbabwe) may be extremely visible and vulnerable to political pressure. Another factor may be the degree of linguistic, cultural and religious differences between groups – the greater the differences, the less easy it may be for the groups to communicate, integrate and negotiate.

Religious and linguistic differences serve to heighten awareness of local loyalties and, indeed, lead to different perceptions of national identity. Thus in Northern Ireland, Quebec and Kosovo, some inhabitants (Protestants, English-speakers and Serbian-speaking Orthodox) may see themselves as inhabitants of a locality within a currently constituted state (the United Kingdom, Canada or Serbia). Others (Catholics, French-speakers, Albanian-speaking Muslims) may feel loyalty to a different national identity – either to another state (Ireland, Albania) or to the region as an independent entity (Quebec, Kosovo).

It can be argued that many conflicts which appear to be religious in nature have little to do with theological considerations. Thus divisions between Catholics and Protestants in Northern Ireland appear to relate to economic and political opportunities. The origins of struggle can be seen historically in the British crown allocating land to Protestant settlers from the mainland. Current differences are much more about nationality than theological concepts such as transubstantiation or papal authority.

Similarly, divisions between Palestinians and Israelis may be seen as an Islamic/Jewish conflict but more realistically as a conflict between rival national groups for land and resources. In fact, many of the founders of Zionism were secular rather than orthodox Jews, and the many ultra-orthodox Jews refuse to serve in the Israeli army. Correspondingly, Palestinian Christians (a small minority) have generally aligned themselves with their Muslim Arab compatriots.

Another striking example of the extent to which religion may be a dependent variable in social and political conflict is the trend in modern India for political leaders of lower-caste groups to urge their followers to convert to Buddhism. This is urged not for theological reasons but in order to escape their low prestige and influence in traditional Hindu society. However, it is clear that religious, linguistic, tribal and other ethnic factors loom large in the construction of many people's political identity – but to different degrees at different times and places, depending on the political environment.

An important psychological and political factor seems to be the 'racial' identity of the ethnic groups concerned. By 'racial' is meant the existence of real or assumed visible physical differences – particularly in skin colour – between the groups. Such differences are socially rather than biologically defined. For instance, most US 'blacks' would be regarded as 'whites' in tropical Africa; most South African 'whites' probably have some 'black' ancestry. In essence the major socially defined 'racial' division is that between 'whites' and 'non-whites'.

The importance of the distinction between black and white 'races' seems to link quite clearly with our inheritance from the period of European imperialism in which a racial justification was advanced for both slavery and colonialism. The subjection of black slaves and the conquest of the Caribbean and North America had to be justified in terms of the superiority of white Christian civilisation over the alleged barbarity of the 'natives'.

The importance of racism is dramatically illustrated if we consider the history of ethnic relations in US cities. Waves of ethnic groups – Irish, Russian, Italian, Jewish, Puerto Rican – have arrived successively in many American cities to go through similar processes of accommodation, integration and assimilation. At first such groups have been accommodated in the worst city-centre slums, in multiple-occupation 'tenements'. They have taken the worst-paid, lowest-status jobs and usually formed isolated groups seeking help from already established members of their own community.

However, such groups have gradually assimilated to the American 'way of life'. First, they have become politically organised – their votes and bargaining power were sought by others, than by members of their own community. Next, second- and third-generation immigrants have sought acceptance in the wider American society by anglicising names, obtaining college education and moving out into the affluent suburbs. Integration has gradually occurred partly through the new immigrant group accepting American values and citizenship, but also on the basis of America accepting a rich kaleidoscope of cultural traditions and religious beliefs within society. The power of many 'immigrant' groups has been comfortably accepted in many respects – consider the giant St Patrick's Day parade every year in New York and the political power of the Kennedy family. While Catholicism was, at first, regarded as a badge of inferior immigrant status and, as late as the 1920s, Al Smith's candidacy for the presidency may have been defeated by a Protestant backlash, it is now just one more fully acceptable denomination of Christianity (Jones, 1960).

In contrast to this, the Afro-American group was one of the first to arrive in what is now the United States. Yet it has been the last to achieve anything near equal status with the WASP (white Anglo-Saxon Protestant) majority. Even after emancipation in 1865 they remained the victims of massive social and political discrimination. Although they long ago lost their specific African languages and cultures, they have contributed greatly to the development of a distinctive American culture and interbred extensively with the white population. However, it was only with the Civil Rights Act of 1965 that they can be said to have achieved anything near full and effective citizenship.

WAR ON TERROR

As we have noted in Chapter 5, the concept of terrorism is highly subjective: one person's terrorist is another person's freedom fighter. One of the classic examples is Nelson Mandela, who was convicted in 1962 of committing sabotage, yet when the apartheid system which jailed him was dismantled he became president of South Africa (1994–1999). When he died in 2013, 91 world leaders attended his memorial service.

The use of violence by political actors to further their interests is not new. For example, during the 1970s and 1980s there was a series of bombings, plane hijackings and murder committed on behalf of a range of groupings. Those such as ETA in the Basque region of France and Spain, the IRA in Northern Ireland and the PLO in Palestine were essentially nationalists seeking independence from another country. Others such as the Shining Path in Peru, the Baader-Meinhof group in Germany and the Red Brigades in Italy were ideological, typically some form of Marxism. One of the most shocking terrorist attacks was the taking hostage and then murder of 11 Israeli athletes competing at the 1972 Munich Olympics by the Palestinian group Black September.

Such activity led to a variety of political, diplomatic and military responses by individual governments and provided a background to domestic and international policy. However, we argue that there has been a significant sea-change in global politics as a result of George W. Bush's declaration on 20 September 2001 of a 'War on Terror' following the attack on mainland America conducted by Al-Qaeda on 9/11. It is essentially a struggle against organisations deemed as terrorists or regimes that support them. And it is this last part which is significant, transforming what had been primarily a state versus terrorist operation into one which is also sometimes state versus state.

Although the Obama administration uses the less emotive term 'overseas contingency operation', this is essentially a conflict between the world's superpower and its allies and identified non-state and state actors. Its impact on democratic politics has been broad, covering international relations, national security, technological developments and individual freedoms.

There are two strategic approaches to dealing with the War on Terror, and they are not mutually exclusive. The first involves the application of force, which America has been willing to use, for example in Iraq and Afghanistan. The second is to apply the rule of law – what the French philosopher Jacques Derrida referred to as the 'force of law'. De Goeda (2008) suggests that this is the approach of the EU, and notes that they have been willing to use pre-emptive security practice such as criminalising terrorist support, data retention and asset freezing.

The War on Terror raises serious questions for democracy. Youngs and Widdows (2009) are concerned that the rhetoric of fear has reframed global relationships along religious, cultural and social lines which challenge the core values of liberal democracy. There is also a suggestion that the War on Terror has had an effect on the political values of individuals, especially in the US. Hetherington and Suhay (2011) found that the average American has become more susceptible to 'authoritarian thinking'. It is for this reason that Kellner (2007) believed that Bush used fear to push through a right-wing agenda. Thus Brown (2003) from a left-wing perspective suggests that the War on Terror was the justification for dismantling the welfare state and the deregulation of corporations. The perceived threat on democracy of the War on Terror depends in large part on the ideological viewpoint of the commentator: for some it is terrorism and for others the response to that terrorism.

There is a concern that the greater surveillance required by security threats might be undermining individual rights. For example, James Brokenshire, the UK's Crime and Security minister, announced in 2013 that he intended to look at introducing measures to require Internet service providers and search engines to censor extremist content online. However, a counterweight argument is presented by Paliwala (2013), who believes that the Internet is based on an open culture, and attempts to introduce state regulation in the name of the War on Terror have been resisted. It is possible that the impact can at the same time be to enable governments to keep a closer watch on some citizens and encourage the promulgation of new ideas and information which enhance freedoms.

The War on Terror has raised issues of national sovereignty. For instance, the US military has used unmanned drones to monitor and attack key individuals and in so doing sometimes appearing to fly without permission over national airspace. When Osama Bin Laden was killed by US Special Forces in 2011 in Pakistan, this raised the question of whether or not they had permission for the incursion. This is a complex issue: it is quite possible that for internal audiences the Pakistan government have to deny giving such permission, yet plausibly they had a secret deal with the US.

We do not know, but the War on Terror does raise uncomfortable questions for democratic theory.

The War on Terror can also be used by other governments as a cloak for dealing with internal dissent. It gives them the possibility of curtailing individual freedoms on the basis that they also have a War on Terror: what is sauce for the goose is sauce for the gander.

TECHNOLOGY

Key issues are how politics influences the introduction and use of technology and how technology shapes politics. Technology serves political interests which drive the relationship between technology and politics. It may help maintain or change existing power structures, and we can identify two approaches for explaining this. The first is technological determinism and the second the orthodox contextual view.

Technological determinism, usually associated with Daniel Bell (1973) and Alvin Toffler (1980), implies that there is little that can be done to resist the impact of new technologies. They suggest it is the nature of the technology itself which is vital for understanding change. As part of the post-industrial world, politicians will have no option but to embrace new technology. Opposing determinism is the orthodoxy that the outcome of technological change for different individuals, societies and countries is not a given – rather, society, the economy and politics all shape the technology (Castells, 2002). For example, Everett Rogers (1995) tried to explain why innovations, be they ideas or technologies, were diffused at different rates in different countries. His conclusion was that political institutions and actors had an effect, either by encouraging technological development or acting as a brake. Thus, in most countries access to the Internet is open, but some governments place significant restrictions on its use. One of the more extreme examples is North Korea, where only a small elite have access to the Internet and it is highly controlled. For example, when Kim Jong-un's name is used it is in a slightly larger font size (Lee, 2012).

Bramley (2002) has identified in a very general sense seven technological revolutions over the past five centuries which have had an impact on societies and the quality of human life. Of these 'revolutions', two are nascent and likely to be ones governments will have to tackle, namely the biotechnology revolution of the 1990s and nanometrics (the precise measurement and manufacture of a variety of tools).

Although we have looked at them individually, these potential challenges are not autonomous; there exist linkages between them. As we see in Table 9.1, population shifts and racial and religious

Table 9.1 The challenges facing democracies

Issue	Nature of problem	Potential impact on democracy
Environmental issues	Natural or man-made changes to planet earth have raised serious questions which require national and international decisions.	Solutions may require compromises by democracies of the South. Reduction in economic performance for some democracies. Solutions may restrict individual and state freedoms.
Population change	Greater competition for scarce resources. Questions over what number of people the planet can sustain.	Population shifts to some democracies are putting huge strains on existing public services. How can democracies assimilate new immigrants without fundamentally changing political structures? How to 'manage' population growth without curtailing individual freedom?
Religious and ethnic conflict	Many countries of the South have to manage the continuing fallout from their colonial past. Often linked to access to economic resources.	Raises issues of equality and freedom within the rule of law. How to maintain an equitable access to economic resources?
War on Terror	The fear of indiscriminate non-state violence leading to political instability. Can be presented as essentially a North versus South conflict.	May require illiberal responses that may in the long term introduce changes which limit individual freedoms. May enhance the role of the state in commercial and private life.
Technology	Technology is neutral, what matters is how individuals, corporations and governments use it. Has created new economic and political elites.	Could lead to enhanced state surveillance of corporations and individuals. Will influence economic power.

conflict may result from essentially the same demographic changes. The response to the War on Terror is heavily dependent upon technological developments. Similarly, the ability to address environmental issues relies heavily on technological change. When we look at what the potential impact on democracies might be there are two common and related themes: changes in the access to economic resources; and possible restrictions to individual freedoms. If we simplify the concept of liberal democracy to a system based on the twin pillars of freedom and a capitalist economy, then potentially the impact is fundamental. Collectively, these challenges could affect democracy in individual countries and the concept of democracy worldwide. However, the authors suggest that while addressing these problems will have an effect on democracy, we do not expect the consequences to be terminal for the concept.

LOCALISM, NATIONALISM, RELIGION AND ETHNICITY

We have identified some of the challenges; there are as you might imagine a number of possible solutions. One sort of division which seems to be almost universal in larger political systems is what Allardt and Littunen (1964) have termed vertical lines of division – those between localities, regions, and, in some cases, national areas within states. It can be argued that, *ceteris paribus* (other things being equal), the closer people live together, and hence the more communication and, probably, economic and social interdependence there is between them, the more they are likely to perceive themselves as having interests in common. Hence, people in the village of Haworth may see themselves first as Haworth residents, then perhaps as people from the Bradford area or West Riding, almost certainly as Yorkshire folk, as English, as British, and possibly as Europeans too. Similarly, residents of Harlem may also feel themselves to be citizens of New York City and New York State, as well as of the United States. The influence of geographical nearness will be influenced by a host of other factors which may affect the strength of local or regional loyalties, such as how mobile the population is. If a resident of Haworth is commuting daily to Bradford and was born in nearby Keighley, then the West Riding identity may be more important than it is to someone born in

Lancashire. How socially and linguistically divided or united a geographical community is also important. A Welsh speaker may feel a greater separation from England than a Welsh person who only speaks English. The nature of the economy may also be an important factor: a self-sufficient peasant agricultural community encouraging much stronger local ties than a university-based one.

The Scottish/English dimension also suggests that the influence of historical conquests and of migration is a major factor in these sorts of divisions. Scots have, of course, historically moved (many would say been driven) both southwards into England and across the sea to Northern Ireland and North America. Here they and their descendants may retain, to a larger or smaller extent, a Scottish identity that can cut across their 'residential' identity. In New York almost everyone has such a secondary identity, being for example Puerto-Rican, Jewish, Irish or Afro-American. Such secondary or 'ethnic' identities are often related to former nationality (e.g. Irish-American), current religion (Jewish) or colour (Afro-American). Ethnicity may also relate to tribal affiliation, way of life and descent (e.g. Roma) or to a hereditary social status (caste in the traditional Indian social system). The term covers a variety of 'horizontal' lines of division dividing geographical communities into recognised sub-groups with, to some extent, different ways of life and prestige.

DOMINANCE, ASSIMILATION AND SOCIAL PLURALISM

As far as both ethnic and racial relations are concerned, three main alternative social and political patterns seem possible. First, a relationship of (usually racial) social and political dominance – the South African term of 'apartheid' being appropriate. An extreme expression of this pattern being where one group is enslaved by the other. In more recent years, however, such a frank state of affairs has seemed unacceptably bad public relations in a world in which the rhetoric, at least, of democracy predominates. Therefore, the language of equality and nationalism usually prevails. In America the official doctrine of 'separate but equal' prevailed between the landmark Supreme Court rulings of Plessey v. Ferguson (1896) and Brown v. the Board of Education of Topeka (1954), until it was conceded that such a doctrine was a contradiction in terms. In

Africa, white dominance in South Africa was justified by the creation of 'homelands' in which blacks were accorded the trappings of
sovereignty – millions of blacks being declared aliens in the land of
their birth. Similarly, in Malaysia, 'Malays' (those who speak Malay,
practise Islam and conform to Malay customs) have a special status
in citizenship and land law as opposed to others – in effect, those of
Chinese and Indian origin (Suffian *et al.*, 1978).

The most extreme expression of the attitudes towards racial and
ethnic difference implicit in a pattern of dominance is where state
machinery is employed in attempts to eliminate an ethnic, national
or racial group from a particular geographical area (or indeed
totally). This is known in international law as genocide. The best-
known example is the Holocaust, in which the Nazi state attempted
to eliminate European Jewry. Unfortunately, more recent examples of
'ethnic cleansing' can be cited in the former Yugoslavia, the Democratic
Republic of Congo and Rwanda. It is usually accompanied by
attempts to stereotype the victim group as subhuman and inferior.

An alternative approach to the management of ethnic and racial
differences is an assimilationist one in which members of 'minority'
communities are granted equality and rights to the extent to which
they adopt the way of life of the 'dominant' group. Thus French
colonial policy was based on the doctrine of the equality of all civilised
men – civilisation being equated largely with French education,
language and loyalty. In effect US and British citizenship policy has
had some elements of this, with requirements for fluency in English,
knowledge of the constitution and the swearing of allegiance.

Another model for achieving the integration of different ethnic
or racial groups in one society is the pluralist one – which, to a
large extent, has predominated in the US. In European terms one
might call it the Swiss model – in which separate groups respect
each other's linguistic, religious and cultural inheritances. While a
degree of convergence may take place in terms of values and political habits, there is no requirement that one group's values be seen
as the orthodoxy for society as a whole. Tolerance and negotiated
compromises must mark such a society if it is to endure.

From the point of view of political change and stability, the
domination of one ethnic or racial group over others may appear to
be a quite stable situation. In some cases such stability may be pur-
chased at the price of a certain element of stagnation since

intellectual and social change may be seen as threatening the ideology of the dominant group. It may well be accompanied by violent repression of dissent either by the state (as in apartheid South Africa and under colonial regimes) or by the dominant group (as with the Ku Klux Klan in the southern US). However, repression of a majority population is a dangerous strategy and carries with it the possibility of revolutionary upheaval.

Where policies of assimilation or pluralism are adopted then the possibilities for improvement for the less favoured groups reduce the likelihood of full-scale violent confrontation. Piecemeal adjustment of conflicts between groups is possible and long-term changes resulting from immigration or industrialisation may be more easily accommodated. Paradoxically, there may be more day-to-day overt expressions of ethnic and racial conflict than in situations of dominance, where frequently such conflicts are officially denied any existence.

A distinction should be drawn between social and political pluralism. What we have been describing is a model of social pluralism in an ethnically or racially mixed society. Politically this may be accompanied by explicit provision for the participation of different social groups in government. For example, in Switzerland the linguistically and religiously distinct cantons are traditionally guaranteed participation in the Federal Council (a similar arrangement has been attempted less happily in the Lebanon). In the Netherlands separate religious and political traditions are accommodated by having separate radio stations and schools. In the United States ethnic representation is accomplished through a flexible party and interest group system with a decentralised constitution.

Political pluralism, however, is a broader concept, which fits well with social pluralism in the sense we have used it, but is broader in that it suggests any group is free to pursue its interests in the political system and stands a realistic chance of exercising influence. A more sophisticated treatment of this concept requires us to consider additional kinds of social and political division.

THE FUTURE OF DEMOCRACY

In ancient Athens, because the majority of citizens had to be convinced before the community could act, it seems a very high standard of information and debate often existed, alongside great commitment and loyalty to the state. In such a system, individual citizens are encouraged to inform themselves, they are treated as moral beings with self-determination and are likely to identify with the community and its political life.

The idea of involving as many citizens as possible in the governmental process remains an important element in the concept of democracy, helping to support the maintenance of the local government system and the jury in Anglo-American democracies. The former USSR attempted to support its 'democratic' credentials by the election of large numbers of citizens to Soviets (councils), electoral commissions, factory and collective farm councils and the like.

We noted in Chapter 5 that there appears to be a growth in the number of democracies worldwide, which George (1999) suggests should lead to more peace in the world. This is predicated on the belief that democracies are inherently more peaceful than other regimes. Thus the more democracies there are, the fewer violent disturbances between nations there will be. A related idea is that of democratic peace – that democracies do not declare war on each other (Doyle, 1986). Democratic peace theory assumes that there is some link between domestic policy, especially public opinion, and international policy. Combined, these two ideas suggest we should have a more peaceful world.

A number of commentators have tried to predict how they believe democracies will or should evolve in the near future. Huntington (1991) identified three waves of democracy. The first was in the nineteenth century in Western Europe and North America. The second was in former axis powers and ex-colonial powers after World War Two. The last, still ongoing, started in 1974 with Portugal and includes Latin America and the former Soviet Bloc.

Berggruen and Gardels (2011) have created a normative vision of the direction that democracy should be taking which they refer to as 'intelligent governance'. They argue that the current democratic political systems were created in the nineteenth century and are not suitable to the population growth, leisure habits and consumerism of the twenty-first century. Thus, new democratic structures are required, and they suggest that there are likely to be differences between the traditional democracies and those of more recent adopters. In the North they argue that 'intelligent democracy' is based on a completely different representation system. They call for a community-based democracy which requires a hybrid structure, so that each level elects the level of representatives above it. It is therefore what they refer to as a base-to-top political system. Looking at China they suggest a different approach, one which combines Confucianism with democracy. Thus, a Chinese democracy would adopt traditional approaches and combine them with democratic principles. A second assembly might be selected by examination rather than election, but they also argue that the political system needs to create more accountability. We suggest that such an ambitious and radical vision of the desired future of democracy is unlikely to be achieved in the near future. However, there are current technological developments which we believe offer a more realistic future for democracy.

DIRECT DEMOCRACY AND E-REPRESENTATION

A major impact of new technologies is to create new elites, which reflects the pluralist and flexible nature of democracy. This indicates how the body politic can respond and incorporate new interests. Two very different research projects have highlighted the role of an engineering elite. Thomas Hughes (1983) looked at how electricity networks developed in North America and Western Europe. He found that a coalition of entrepreneurs, politicians and engineers was created and a technological network thus gained political influence. Medina (2011) told the story of how in the 1970s the Chilean government sought to create a socialist utopia and construct in Project Cybersyn, a means of using technology to manage the economy. The political elite set the wider goals, but it was the engineering elite that managed the detail of the programme.

We noted earlier that technology may be creating challenges for democracy, but it is also forming opportunities. Weare (2002) has identified three causal links between technology and democratic government:

1   the effects of technological innovation on different communication activities;

2 the role communications and information play in democratic governance;
3 political mechanisms by which technology transforms democratic processes and institutions.

It is this last link which has been the focus of much consideration of one technology, the Internet. Aristotle suggested that democracy was based on a geographic area that a man could walk across in one day, allowing him to journey in and have his say direct. This was possible with the city state, but once political entities became larger and more complex such direct democracy was no longer practical (if it actually ever existed). As a result liberal democracy (and the ideas we addressed in Chapter 5) is predicated on representative democracy. Thus, an essential part of political participation is to elect those who will represent citizens. However, the creation of the Internet has excited interest among some commentators, who see that technology has provided a means of transcending size of population and making direct democracy possible again.

The initial focus of political actors was their websites, and in particular how they might help win elections. In fact, although websites may be the public face of many politicians, parties and government, we argue that the more private face of email and e-newsletters makes them the more powerful campaigning tools. Jackson (2008) found that for some pioneering UK MPs, effective use of their e-newsletters as a representative tool had positive campaigning benefits. Since our last edition there have been two key related changes in the political use of the Internet. Political actors have increasingly adopted new web technologies such as Facebook, Twitter and YouTube, and this has been accompanied by a suggestion that the enhanced dialogue capabilities will change representation. However, this positive viewpoint of the impact of technology is not inevitable; we note that Jackson and Lilleker (2011) found that in the UK MPs were more likely to use Twitter for impression management rather than to enhance their constituency service.

The introduction of the Internet has accelerated interest in the idea of e-democracy. Since the early 1990s, a number of optimists have suggested that this new technology may transform the way in which citizens and governments communicate (Rheingold, 1993).

Posner (2003) has suggested that deliberative democracy, based on the Athenian model, is achievable. The logic of Posner's position is that if modern citizens can achieve the level of direct communication possible within the city state, then direct democracy is a practical alternative. More explicitly, Arblaster (2002) has suggested that direct democracy is achievable through modern technology. Thus, how far a man can walk in a day is replaced by how often a person can click in a day.

Another critique of traditional democracy is offered by Snallen (2001), who argues that the time of political representation is over and that it will be replaced by referenda, co-production of policies and continuous opinion polling. He argues that not only can it happen technologically, it is what people want. There have certainly been attempts at more referenda in Switzerland and California, but this does not automatically suggest that a groundswell of opinion exists. Nor are we convinced that the technology will work as a decision-making tool in the way Snellen suggests. Rather we argue that a more fruitful route than e-democracy is e-representation.

E-representation may offer a middle way between the Athenian model and representative democracy. The existence of the Internet has added to the debate regarding direct or representative democracy. On one side is the belief that the Internet will enhance representative democracy (Ward and Lusoli, 2005), on the other that it will transform it into direct e-democracy (Posner, 2003).

Direct democracy and traditional representation are based on an assumption of geographical representation, but both Warren and Castiglione (2004) and Rehfeld (2005) challenge this. If constituency does not automatically have to have a territorial aspect, then alternative forms of representation can be constructed. Lusoli's (2007) exploratory research identified theoretically that e-representation was based on three dimensions, namely *direct participation* versus *mediated representation*; *sending* versus *receiving*; *information* versus *debate*. Building on this framework, Jackson and Lilleker (2009b) suggest that there are effectively two types of e-representation. First, a parallel e-constituency where representatives use the Internet to add value to the service they provide their constituents. The second is a separate e-constituency based on a shared interest in issues and not geography. Jackson and Lilleker (2012) presented a model for e-representation based on data on how UK MPs used the Internet.

Table 9.2 The representative impact of the Internet

Type of democracy	Communication to decision-makers	Role of citizen	Architecture of representation
Representative democracy	Indirect via representatives	Essentially passive, with occasional involvement, e.g. during elections.	Primarily territory-based.
E-democracy	Direct	Active in that consulted on some issues.	Primarily issue-based.
E-representation	Both direct and indirect	Active both as constituent and beyond.	Both geography and issue-based.

They argued that the Internet is creating a new architecture of representation with both a *territorial* axis and an *issue* axis. It allows citizens to enhance their communication with their elected representatives and identify and talk with political actors who have shared interests and so find an online advocate. This is not a trait unique to the Internet, but the nature of the technology encourages the sort of dialogue that may be changing representation.

Jackson and Lilleker's data suggest that no model of e-representation is uniform across Internet modalities, probably reflecting inherent differences in each. The creation of a parallel e-representation is more likely to be encouraged by websites and e-newsletters, whereas a separate e-representation is more likely with social networking sites and weblogs. The future of democracy may well be a hybrid which applies both the geographic and interest forms of e-representation to add value to traditional representative democracy. As Table 9.2 shows, this combination may make democracy stronger and be key to how it defends itself in the face of current challenges.

TAKING POLITICAL ACTION

Every reader of this book about politics will, after reading it, go on to practise politics in the all-encompassing sense we defined it in Chapter 1. The most private of individuals will, none the less, inevitably need to work with, and on occasion come into conflict with, others in social situations. At every point on the globe some state will claim jurisdiction over your actions. It is hoped that this book will have given, at a minimum, some sense of the processes at work and suggested some sources of further information when they are required. It is hoped that some readers not already enrolled on politics courses may have been inspired to do so.

Politics is not only a spare-time or academic activity, however. There is truth in the feminist slogan 'The personal is the political'. It is worth reviewing your personal relationships, professional activities and plans to see if they are in accord with political principles you profess (although this can be rather sobering).

No sensible author would urge all their readers to go out and become professional politicians, but the authors share Aristotle's conviction that it is a mark of civilisation to wish to join in the public life of the community. There is great satisfaction to be had in not only discussing political issues in the abstract but also helping to build a better world through membership of voluntary organisations which attempt to influence events – from Greenpeace through to Unidentified Flying Object enthusiasts. Almost everywhere local party organisations tend to fall over themselves with eagerness to welcome new members. Independently readers may actually exercise real influence through writing to newspapers and their elected representatives.

If politics is thought of only in terms of the activities of the nation state, then the scope for ordinary citizens is necessarily a limited one. But the argument of this book has been that important political decisions can be made at the level of work, educational and leisure organisations, by local and regional authorities, voluntary interest groups and international co-operation. The scope for individual action is already large and should, in the authors' view, be made larger. Good luck on your journey of political activity.

CONCLUSION

Democracy has a long tradition but its success is not inevitable, and we have assessed some of the challenges facing democratic governments. However, one size does not necessarily fit all: the challenges facing first-, second- and third-wave democracies may be slightly different, and the literature is particularly concerned with how established democracies will respond and evolve. Some of these challenges are internal, others are external, and some could be both. Thus, declining civic engagement might be viewed as an internal issue, but it could arguably be a response to technological changes. However, as we might expect, democracy has developed strategies for responding to these challenges. We suggest that democracy has a future, but one which requires continual care and attention: it cannot be taken for granted.

FURTHER READING

Bradley, R. (2011) *Global Warming and Political Intimidation: how politicians cracked down on scientists as the earth heated up,* Amherst: University of Massachusetts Press.

MacLeavy, J. and People, C. (2010) 'War on Terror, work in progress: security, surveillance and configuration of the US workfare state', *GeoJournal,* 75 (4): 339–346.

Renshon, S. and Suedfeld, P. (eds) (2007) *Understanding the Bush Doctrine: Psychology and Strategy in an Age of Terrorism,* London: Routledge.

Saward, M. (1993) 'Direct democracy revisited', *Politics,* 13 (2): 18–24.

Scott, P. (2007) *The Road to 9/11: Wealth, Empire and the Future of America,* London: University of California Press.

Silke, A. (ed.) (2004) *Research on Terrorism: Trends, Achievements and Failures,* London: Frank Cass.

Sociological Forum (2013), 28 (3) – a special edition on security and surveillance.

REFERENCES

Abbott, W. (1918) 'The origin of the English political parties', *The American Historical Review*, 24 (4): 578–602.

Acemoglu, D. and Robinson, J. (2001) 'A theory of political transitions', *The American Economic Review*, 91 (4): 938–963.

Acharya, A. and Buzan, B. (2007) 'Why is there no non-western international relations theory? An introduction', *International Relations of the Asia-Pacific*, 7 (3): 287–312.

Acton, Lord (1887) Letter to Bishop Mandell Creighton, in A. Jay (ed.) (1996) *Oxford Dictionary of Political Quotations*, Oxford: Oxford University Press.

Adam, A. (2005) *Gender, Ethics and Information Technology*, Basingstoke: Palgrave Macmillan.

Agnew, J. (1999) 'Mapping Political Power Beyond State Boundaries: territory, identity and movement in world politics', *Journal of International Studies*, 28 (3): 499–521.

Aidt, T. and Albornoz, F. (2011) 'Political regimes and foreign intervention', *Journal of Development Economics*, 44 (2): 192–201.

Aitken-Turff, F. and Jackson, N. (2006) 'A mixed motive approach to lobbying', *Journal of Public Affairs*, 6 (2): 84–101.

Aldrich, J. (1993) 'Rational choice and turnout', *Journal of Political Science*, 37 (1): 246–278.

Alford, J., Funk, C. and Hibbing, J. (2005) 'Are political orientations genetically transmitted?', *The American Political Science Review*, 99 (2): 153–167.

Allardt, E. and Littunen, Y. (eds) (1964) *Cleavages, Ideologies and Party Systems*, Helsinki: The Westermarck Society.

Allison, G. (1987) *The Essence of Decision: Explaining the Cuban Missile Crisis*, New York: Harper College.

Almond, G. (1956) 'Comparative political systems', *Journal of Politics*, 18 (3): 391–409.

Almond, G. and Coleman, J. (eds) (1960) *The Politics of Developing Areas*, Princeton, NJ: Princeton University Press.

Andreski, S. (1968) *The African Predicament: A Study in the Pathology of Modernisation*, London: Michael Joseph.

Arblaster, A. (2002) *Democracy*, Buckingham: Open University Press.

Arendt, H. (1959) *The Human Condition*, Chicago: Chicago University Press.

——(1967) *The Origins of Totalitarianism*, 2nd edn, London: Allen & Unwin.

Aristotle (1946) *The Politics of Aristotle* (ed. by Ernest Barker), Oxford: Clarendon Press.

Armijo, L. (2007) 'The Brics countries as analytical category: mirage or insight', *Asian Perspective*, 31 (4): 7–42.

Axtmann, R. (2003) *Understanding Democratic Politics*, London: Sage.

Bachrach, P. and Baratz, M. (1970) *Power and Poverty*, New York: Oxford University Press.

Banfield, E. and Banfield, L. (1967) *The Moral Basis of a Backward Society*, Glencoe, IL: Free Press.

Barnett, S. (2002) 'Will a crisis in journalism provoke a crisis in democracy?', *The Political Quarterly*, 73 (4): 400–408.

Barreto, M., Cooper, B., Gonzalez, B., Parker, C. and Towler, C. (2012) 'The Tea Party in the age of Obama: mainstream conservatism or out-group anxiety?', *Political Power and Social Theory*, 22 (1): 105–137.

Barrett, S. and Fudge, C. (1981) *Policy and Action*, London: Methuen.

Barry, J. (1999) *Rethinking Green Politics*, London: Sage.

Baylis, J. and Smith, S. (eds) (2005) *The Globalization of World Politics*, 2nd edn, Oxford: Oxford University Press.

Behr, H. (2008) 'Deterritorialisation and the transformation of statehood: the paradox of globalisation', *Geopolitics*, 13 (2): 359–382.

Bell, D. (1960) *The End of Ideology*, New York: Basic Books.

——(1973) *The Coming of Post Industrial Society*, New York: Basic Books.

Ben-Eliezer, U. (1993) 'The meaning of political participation in a non-liberal democracy: the Israeli experience', *Comparative Politics*, 25 (4): 397–412.

Bennett, L., Wells, C. and Freelon, D. (2011) 'Communicating Civic Engagement: contrasting models of citizenship in the youth web sphere', *Journal of Communication*, 61 (5): 835–856.

Berggruen, N. and Gardels, N. (2011) 'The Future of Democracy', *Thinkery*, Winter: 55–69.

Bernstein, C. and Woodward, B. (1974) *All the President's Men*, New York: Simon & Schuster.

Beveridge, W. (1942) *Social Insurance and Allied Services*, London: HMSO.

Blair, T. (1994) *Socialism*, London: Fabian Society.

Blattberg, C. (2009) 'Political philosophies and political ideologies', in C. Blattberg, *Patriotic Elaborations: essays in practical philosophy*, Montreal and Kingston: McGill-Queen's University Press.

Bloch, M. (1961) *Feudal Society*, London: Routledge & Kegan Paul.

Blumenthal, S. (1980) *The Permanent Campaign: Inside the World of Elite Political Operatives*, Boston: Beacon.

Bohannan, P. (1965) 'Social and political organisation of the Tiv', in J. Gibbs (ed.), *The Peoples of Africa*, New York: Holt, Rinehart and Winston.

Bramley, D. (2002) 'Science, technology and politics', *Technology in Society*, 24 (1/2): 9–26.

Branch, J. (2011) 'Mapping the sovereign state: technology, authority and systemic change', *International Organisation*, 65 (1): 1–36.

Brandt, W. (1980) *North-South: A Programme for Survival*, London: Pan.

Braun, M. (2009) 'The evolution of emissions trading in the European Union: the role of policy networks, knowledge and policy entrepreneurs', *Accounting, Organisations and Society*, 34 (3/4): 469–487.

Brinton, C. (1965) *The Anatomy of Revolution*, London: Jonathan Cape.

Brown, W. (2003) 'Neoliberalism and the end of liberal democracy', *Theory and Event*, 7 (1). Available online at: http://muse.jhu.edu/journals/theory_and_event/v007/7.1brown.html (accessed 12 December 2013).

Bryson, M., Duclos, P. and Jolly, A. (2010) 'Global immunisation policy making processes', *Health Policy*, 96 (2): 154–159.

Bryson, V. (2003) *Feminist Political Theory: an introduction*, 2nd edn, Basingstoke: Palgrave Macmillan.

Buechler, S. (2000) *Social Movements in Advanced Capitalism*, Oxford: Oxford University Press.

Burnham, P. (2001) 'New Labour and the politics of depoliticisation', *British Journal of Politics and International Relations*, 3 (2): 127–149.

Butler, A. (2000) 'The Third Way project in Britain: the role of the prime minister's policy unit', *Politics*, 20 (3): 153–160.

Cairney, P. (2011) 'The new British policy style: from a British to a Scottish political tradition?', *Political Studies Review*, 9 (2): 208–220.

Campbell, P. (1965) *French Electoral Systems and Elections Since 1789*, rev. edn, London: Faber & Faber.

Castells, M. (2002) *The Internet Galaxy*, Oxford: Oxford University Press.

——(2009) *Communication Power*, Oxford: Oxford University Press.

Castilho, M., Mendendez, M. and Sztulman, A. (2011) 'Trade liberalisation, inequality and poverty in Brazilian states', *World Development*, 40 (4): 821–835.

Castles, F. and McKinlay, D. (1979) 'Does politics matter? An analysis of the public welfare commitment in advanced democratic states', *European Journal of Political Research*, 7 (2); 169–186.

Castles, S. and Miller, M. (2003) *The Age of Migration: international population movements in the modern world*, 3rd edn, Basingstoke: Palgrave Macmillan.

Cato, M. (2012) 'Green economics: putting the planet and politics back into economics', *Cambridge Journal of Economics*, 36 (5): 1033–1049.

Charney, D. and English, W. (2012) 'Candidate genes and political behaviour', *American Political Science Review*, 106 (1): 1–34.

Chen, C.-C. (2011) 'The absence of non-western IR theory in Asia reconsidered', *International Relations of the Asia-Pacific*, 11 (1): 1–23.

Christopher, M., Payne, A. and Ballantyne, D. (2002) *Relationship Marketing: Creating Stakeholder Value*, Oxford: Butterworth-Heinemann.

Cohen, B. (1963) *The Press and Foreign Policy*, Princeton, NJ: Princeton University Press.

Colas, A. (2002) *International Civil Society*, Cambridge: Polity.

Coleman, S. (2005) 'New mediation and direct representation: reconceptualising representation in the digital age', *New Media and Society*, 7 (2): 177–198.

Conaghan, C. and de la Torre, C. (2008) 'The permanent campaign of Rafael Correa: making Ecuador's plebiscitary presidency', *The International Journal of Press/Politics*, 17 (3): 262–284.

Crick, B. (2000) *In Defence of Politics*, 5th edn, London: Continuum International.

Dahl, R. (1961) *Who Governs?* New Haven, CT: Yale University Press.

——(2000) 'A democratic paradox? *Scandinavian Political Science*, 23 (3): 246–251.

Dal Bo, E., Dal Bo, P. and Snyder, J. (2009) 'Political dynasties', *Review of Economic Studies*, 76 (1): 115–142.

Dalton, R. (1988) *Citizen Politics in Western Democracies*, Chatham, NJ: Chatham House.

Deacon, D. and Golding, P. (1994) *Taxation and Representation*, London: John Libbey.

De Goeda, M. (2008) 'The politics of pre-emption and the war on terror in Europe', *European Journal of International Relations*, 14 (1): 161–185.

De Jouvenal, B. (1963) *The Pure Theory of Politics*, Cambridge: Cambridge University Press.

Derbyshire, J. and Derbyshire, I. (1991) *World Political Systems: An Introduction to Comparative Government*, Edinburgh: Chambers Political Spotlights.

——(1996) *Political Systems of the World*, New York: St Martin's Press.

Deutsch, K. (1963) *Nerves of Government*, Glencoe, IL: Free Press.

Devine, F. (2002) 'Qualitative methods', in D. Marsh and G. Stoker (eds), *Theory and Methods in Political Science*, Basingstoke: Palgrave: 197–215.

Diamant, A. (1959) 'Is there a non-western political process? Comments on Lucian Pye's "The non-western political process"', *Journal of Politics*, 21 (1): 123–127.

Diamond, L. (2008) 'The democratic rollback: the resurgence of the predatory state', *Foreign Affairs*, 4 March.

——(2012) 'The coming wave', *Journal of Democracy*, 23 (1): 5–13.

Dicey, A. (1959) *Law of the Constitution*, 10th edn, with introduction by E. C. S. Wade, London: Macmillan.

Diez, J. (2013) 'Explaining policy outcomes: the adoption of same-sex unions in Buenos Aires and Mexico City', *Comparative Political Studies*, 46 (2): 212–235.

Dilly, C. (1991) 'Changing forms of revolution', in E. Rice (ed.), *Revolution and Counter Revolution*, Oxford: Blackwell: 1–15.

Djilas, M. (1966), *The New Class*, London, Allen & Unwin.

Downs, A. (1957) *An Economic Theory of Democracy*, New York: Harper & Row.

Dowse, R. (1969) *Modernization in Ghana and the USSR*, London: Routledge & Kegan Paul.

——(1972) 'Functionalism in political science', *World Politics,* 18 (4): 607–622.

Doyle, M. (1986) 'Liberalism and World Politics', *The American Political Science Review*, 80 (4): 1151–69.

Drezner, D. and Farrell, H. (2004) 'The Power and Politics of Blogs', paper presented to the Annual Meeting of the American Political Science Association, September 2–5, Chicago.

Dryzek, J. (2006) 'Revolutions without enemies: key transformations in political science', *American Political Science Review*, 100 (4):487–492.

Duff, A. (ed.) (1993) *Subsidiarity within the European Community*, London: Federal Trust for Education and Research.

Duffy, C. (2009) *Politics, The Guardian*, 13 June. Available online at: www.guardian.co.uk/books/2009/jun/12/politics-carol-ann-duffy-poem (accessed 30 November 2012).

Duverger, M. (1972) *The Study of Politics*, London: Nelson.

Easton, D. (1979) *A Framework for Political Analysis*, Chicago: University of Chicago Press.

Eberhard, W. (1977) *A History of China*, 4th edn, London: Routledge.

Edelman, M. (1977) *Political Language*, London: Academic Press.

Edmundson, W. (2010) 'Political authority, moral purposes and the intrinsic value of obedience', *Oxford Journal of Legal Studies*, 30 (1): 179–191.

Edwards, L. (1927) *The Natural History of Revolution*, Chicago: University of Chicago (reprinted 1970).

Elazer, D. (1972) *American Federalism: a view from the states*, New York: Crowell.

Etzioni, A. (1995) *The Spirit of Community*, London: Fontana.

Eysenck, H. and Kamin, L. (1981) *Intelligence: The Battle for the Mind*, London: Pan Books.

Ferguson, J. (1990) *The Anti-Politics Machine: Development, Depoliticisation and Bureaucratic Power in Lesotho*, Cambridge: Cambridge University Press.

Finer, S. (1970) *Comparative Government*, London: Allen Lane/The Penguin Press.

——(1976) *The Man on Horseback*, 2nd edn, London: Pall Mall Press.

Firestone, S. (1971) *The Dialectic of Sex*, New York: Bantam Books.

Fischer, J. (2005) *Die Ruckkehr der Geschichte/Die Welt nach dem 11. September die Erneuerung des Westens*, Koln: Verlag Kiepenheuer & Witsch.

Fischer, M. (1980) *Iran: From Religious Dispute to Revolution*, Cambridge, MA: Harvard University Press.

Fisher, P. (2010) 'State political culture and support for Obama in the 2008 Democratic presidential primaries', *The Social Science Journal*, 47 (3): 699–709.

Flitcroft, K., Gillespie, J., Salkeld, G., Carter, S. and Trevena, L. (2011) 'Getting evidence into policy: the need for deliberative strategies', *Social Sciences and Medicine*, 72 (7): 1039–1046.

Fogarty, M. (1957) *Christian Democracy in Western Europe*, London: Routledge & Kegan Paul.

Foucault, M. (1980) *Power/Knowledge*, Brighton: Harvester.

——(1982) 'The subject and power', *Critical Inquiry*, 8 (4): 777–795.

Fowler, J. and Dawes, T. (2008) 'Two genes predict voter turnout', *Journal of Politics*, 70 (3): 579–594.

Friedman, M. (1962) *Capitalism and Freedom*, Chicago: University of Chicago Press.

Friedman, M. and Friedman, R. (1980) *Free to Choose*, Harmondsworth, Middlesex: Penguin.

Friedrich, C. (ed.) (1964) *Totalitarianism*, New York: Grosset & Dunlop.

Frienda, S., Knowles, E., Saletan, W. and Loftus, E. (2013) 'False memories of fabricated political events', *Journal of Experimental Social Psychology*, 49 (2): 280–286.

Frissen, P. (1994) 'The virtual reality of informatization in public administration', Conference on ICTs in Public Administration, London, 30 September.

Fuchs, C. and Dyer-Witheford, N. (2012) 'Karl Marx @ internet studies', *New Media & Society*, November 26. Available online at: http://nms.sagepub.com/content/early/2012/11/22/1461444812462854 (accessed 1 December 2013).

Fukuyama, F. (1992) *The End of History and the Last Man*, Free Press.

Gbadamosi, T. (1978) *The Growth of Islam Among the Yoruba, 1841–1908*, London: Longman.

George, A. (1999) 'Democracy and peace', *Scandinavian Political Studies*, 23 (2): 273–280.

Gerth, H. and Mills, C. Wright (eds) (1948) *From Max Weber: Essays in Sociology*, London: Routledge & Kegan Paul.

Gibbins, J. and Reiner, B. (1999) *The Politics of Postmodernity*, London: Sage.

Gluckman, M. (1965) *Custom and Conflict in Africa*, Oxford: Blackwell.

Golder, M. (2005) 'Democratic electoral systems around the world, 1946–2000', *Electoral Studies*, 24 (1): 103–121.

Goldman, E. (1915) *Anarchism and Other Essays*, New York: Mother Earth Publishing Association.

Gore, C. (2000) 'The rise and fall of the Washington consensus as a paradigm for developing countries', *World Development*, 28 (5): 789–804.

Gorovitz, S. (1976) 'John Rawls: a theory of justice', in A. de Crespigny, and K. Minogue (eds), *Contemporary Political Philosophers*, London: Methuen: 272–289.

Gramsci, A. (1969) *Selections from the Prison Notebooks*, New York: International.

Grant, W. (2000) *Pressure Groups and British Politics*, Basingstoke: Palgrave.

Green, T. (1941) 'Lectures on the principles of political obligation', cited in A. Milne (1962), *The Social Philosophy of English Idealism*, London: George Allen & Unwin.

Greenleaf, W. (1983) *The British Political Tradition*, London: Methuen.

Gregg, B. (2012) 'Politics disembodied and deterritorised: the Internet as human rights resource', in H. Dahms and L. Hazelrigg (eds), *Theorising Modern Society as a Dynamic Process* (*Current Perspectives in Social Theory*, 30, Bingley: Emerald): 209–233.

Grimmer, J. and Stewart, B. (2013) 'Text as data: the promise and pitfalls of automatic content analysis methods for political texts', *Political Analysis*, 21 (3): 267–297.

Guttal, S. (2007) 'Globalisation', *Development in Practice*, 17 (4/5): 523–531.

Hamilton, A., Jay, J. and Madison, J. (1961) *The Federalist Papers* (ed. by Jacob E Cooke), Middletown, Connecticut: Wesleyan University Press.

Hardt, M. and Negri, A. (2000) *Empire*, Cambridge, MA: Harvard University Press.

Hart, A. (2010) 'Death of the partisan? Globalisation and taxation in South America 1990–2006', *Comparative Political Studies*, 43 (3): 304–328.

Hayek, F. (1979) *Law, Legislation and Liberty*, London: Routledge & Kegan Paul.

Heclo, H. (2000) 'Campaigns and Governing: a conspectus', in N. Ornstein and T. Mann, *The Permanent Campaign and its Future*, Washington, DC: American Enterprise Institute and The Brookings Institution: 1–37.

Held, D. (1991) (ed.) *Political Theory Today*, Cambridge: Polity Press.

——(2011), '9/11 and the end of the American century, 9 September 2011'. Available online at: www.opendemocracy.net/david-held/911-and-end-of-american-century (accessed 6 June 2011).

Held, D., McGrew, A., Goldblatt, D. and Perraton, J. (1999) *Global Transformations*, Cambridge: Polity Press.

Henry, A. (2011) 'Ideology, power and the structure of policy networks', *Policy Studies Journal*, 39 (3): 361–383.

Hetherington, M. and Suhay, E. (2011) 'Authoritarianism, threat and Americans' support for the war on terror', *American Journal of Political Science*, 55 (3): 546–560.

Heywood, J. (1991) 'Political Science in Britain', *European Journal of Political Science*, 20 (3–4): 301–322.

Himmelweit, H., Humphrey, P. and Jaeger, M. (1985) *How Voters Decide*, Milton Keynes: Open University Press.

Hobhouse, L. (1964) *Liberalism*, New York: Oxford University Press (reprint of 1911 edn).

Hogwood, B. and Gunn, L. (1984) *Policy Analysis for the Real World*, Oxford: Oxford University Press.

Holland, T. (2005) *Persian Fire: The First World Empire, Battle for the West*, London: Little, Brown.

Holliday, I. (2000) 'Is the British state hollowing out?' *The Political Quarterly*, 71 (2): 167–176.

Hood, C. (1976) *The Limits of Administration*, London: Wiley.

Hope, C. (2012) 'A quarter of senior civil servants quit Whitehall under coalition', *The Daily Telegraph*, 13 April. Available online at: www.telegraph. co.uk/news/politics/9203416/A-quarter-of-senior-civil-servants-quit-White hall-under-Coalition.html (accessed 16 December 2013).

Horowitz, D. (1989) 'Is there a third-world policy process?', *Policy Sciences*, 22 (3/4): 197–212.

Horowitz, I. (1964) *The Anarchists*, New York: Dell Publishing.

Hughes, T. (1983) *Networks of Power: Electrification in Western Society 1890–1930*, Baltimore: Johns Hopkins University Press.

Huntington, S. (1957) *The Soldier and the State*, Cambridge, MA: Harvard University Press.

——(1988) 'One soul at a time: political science and political reform', *The American Political Science Review*, 82 (1): 3–10.

——(1991) *The Third Wave: Democratization in the Late Twentieth Century*, Norman: University of Oklahoma Press.

Irving, R. (1979) *The Christian Democratic Parties of Western Europe*, London: George Allen & Unwin.

Jackson, N. (2006) 'Dipping their big toe into the blogosphere: the use of weblogs by the political parties in the 2005 general election', *Aslib Proceedings: New Information Perspectives,* 58 (4): 292–303.

——(2008) 'MPs and their e-newsletters: winning votes by promoting constituency service', *Journal of Legislative Studies*, 14 (4): 488–499.

——(2009) 'All the fun of the seaside: the British party conference season', *E.Pol*, 2 (1): 8–10.

Jackson, N. and Lilleker, D. (2009a) 'Building an Architecture of Participation? political parties and Web 2.0 in Britain', *Journal of Information Technology and Politics* 6 (3/4): 232–250.

——(2009b) 'MPs and e-representation: me, myspace and I', *British Politics,* 4 (2): 236–264.

——(2011) 'Tweeting, constituency service and impression management – UK MPs and the use of Twitter', *Journal of Legislative Studies*, 17 (2): 86–105.

——(2012) 'The Member for Cyberspace: e-representation and MPs in the UK', in M. Sobaci (ed.), *E-Parliament and ICT-based Legislation: Concept, Experiences and Lessons*, Hershey; PA: IGI Global: 64–79.

Jacobsen, K. (2005) 'Perestroika in American political science', *Post-Autistic Economics Review*, 32 (5), article 6.

Jacques, M. (ed.) (1998) *Marxism Today*, Special Issue, London.

James, S. (2010) 'The rise and fall of euro preparations: strategic networking and the depoliticisation of Labour's National Changeover plan', *British Journal of Politics and International Relations*, 12 (3): 368–386.

Jamison, A. (2001) *The Making of Green Knowledge: Environmental Politics and Cultural Transformation*, Cambridge: Cambridge University Press.

Jansen, G., Evans, G. and Dirk de Graaf, N. (2013) 'Class voting and left–right party positions: a comparative study of 15 Western democracies, 1960–2005', *Social Science Research*, 42 (2): 376–400.

Jayasuriya, K. (2002) 'Post-Washington Consensus and the new Anti-Politics', in T. Lindsey and D. Howard (eds), *Corruption in Asia: Rethinking the Governance Paradigm*, NSW: Federation Press.

Johns, P. (2002) 'Quantitative methods', in D. Marsh and G. Stoker (eds), *Theory and Methods in Political Science*, Basingstoke: Palgrave: 184–211.

Johnson, N. (1987) *The Welfare State in Transition*, Brighton: Wheatsheaf.

Jones, M. (1960) *American Immigration*, Chicago: University of Chicago Press.

Karpik, L. (1978), *Organisation and Environment*, London, Sage.

Katzman, K. (2013) 'Bahrain: reform, security and US policy', Congressional Research Service. Available online at: www.fas.org/sgp/crs/mideast/95-1013.pdf (accessed 12 June 2013).

Keating, M. (2009) 'Putting European political science back together again', *European Political Science Review*, 1 (2): 297–316.

Keating, M., Cairney, P. and Hepburn, E. (2009) 'Territorial policy communities and devolution in the UK', *Cambridge Journal of Regions, Economy and Society*, 2 (1): 51–66.

Kellner, D. (2007) 'Bushspeak and the politics of lying: presidential rhetoric in the "war on terror"', *Presidential Studies Quarterly*, 37 (4): 622–645.

Keman, H. (ed.) (2002) *Comparative Democratic Politics*, London: Sage.

Keohane, R. and Nye, J. (1989) *Power and Interdependence: World Politics in Transition*, Boston: Little, Brown and Company.

Kettell, S. (2008) 'Does depoliticisation work? Evidence from Britain's membership of the Exchange Rate Mechanism 1990–1992', *British Journal of Politics and International Relations*, 10 (4): 630–648.

Kirshner, J. (2003) 'Money is politics', *Review of International Political Economy*, 10 (4): 645–660.

Kirton, J. and Bracht, C. (2013) 'Prospects for the 2013 BRICS Durban summit'. Available online at: www.brics.utoronto.ca/commentary/130322-kirton-bracht-prospects.html (accessed 22 October 2013).

Kogan, M. and Hawkesworth, M. (eds) (1992) *Encyclopaedia of Government and Politics*, London: Routledge.

Kotler, P. (1975) 'Overview of political candidate marketing', *Advances in Consumer Research*, 2: 761–776.

Kuhn, T. (1970) *The Structure of Scientific Revolutions*, Chicago: University of Chicago Press.

Lai, W. (2010) 'Political authority: the two wheels of the Dharma', *Buddhist-Christian Studies*, 30: 171–186.

Lane, D. (2009) '"Coloured revolution" as a political phenomenon', *Journal of Communist Studies and Transition Politics*, 25 (2/3): 113–135.

Lasswell, H. (1936) *Politics Who Gets What, When, How?* London: Peter Smith (reprinted).

——(1963) *The Future of Political Science*, New York: Atherton Press.

Lax, J. and Phillips, J. (2012) 'The democratic deficit in the states', *The American Journal of Political Science*, 56 (1): 148–166.

Lazarsfeld, P., Berelson, L. and Gaudet, H. (1944) *The People's Election*, New York: Columbia University Press.

LeDuc, L., Niemi, R. and Norris, P. (eds) (2002) *Comparing Democracies 2: New Challenges in the Study of Elections and Voting*, London: Sage.

Lee, M. (2012) 'North Korea: on the net in world's most secretive nation', BBC News. Available online at: www.bbc.co.uk/news/technology-20445632 (accessed 5 December 2013).

Lees-Marshment, J. (2001) *Political Marketing and British Political Parties*, Manchester: Manchester University Press.

LeGrand, J. (1982) *The Strategy of Equality: Redistribution and the Social Services*, London: Allen & Unwin.

Lemarchand, R. (ed.) (1977) *African Kingdoms in Perspective*, London: Frank Cass.

Lenin, N. (1917) 'The state and the revolution: Marxist teaching on the state', in K. Marx, F. Engels and V. Lenin (1960), *The Essential Left: Four Classic Texts on the Principles of Socialism*, London: Unwin.

Lieb, D. (2004) 'The limits of neo-liberalism: marginal states and international relations theory', *Harvard International Review*, 26 (1): 26–29.

Lilleker, D. and Jackson, N. (2011) *Campaigning, Elections and the Internet: US, UK, Germany and France*, Abingdon: Routledge.

——(2014) 'Brand management and relationship marketing in online environments', in J. Lees-Marshment, B. Conley and K. Cosgrove (eds), *Political Marketing in the United States*, London: Routledge.

Lin, K. and Rantalaiho, M. (2003) 'Family policy and social order – comparing the dynamics of family policy-making in Scandinavia and Confucian Asia', *International Journal of Social Welfare*, 12 (2): 2–13.

Lindblom, C. (1959) 'The science of muddling through', *Administrative Review*, 19 (Spring): 79–88.

Lipset, S. (1979) *The First New Nation: The USA in Comparative and Historical Perspective*, New York: Norton.

Liu, A. (2011) 'Linguistic effects of political institutions', *Journal of Politics*, 73 (1): 125–139.

Lovelock, J. (1979) *Gaia*, Oxford: Oxford University Press.

Luard, E. (1990) *The Globalization of Politics: the Changed Focus of Political Action in the Modern World*, New York: New York University Press.

Lukes, S. (2005) *Power: a Radical View*, 2nd edn, Basingstoke: Palgrave Macmillan.

Lusoli, W. (2007) 'E-citizens and representation: beyond the bleeding obvious', paper presented to OII workshop, Oxford, 14–15 June.

Mackintosh, J. (1966) *Nigerian Government and Politics*, London: George Allen & Unwin.

Madison, J. (1788) 'The structure of the government must furnish the proper checks and balances between the different departments', *Independent Journal*, Wednesday, February 6 (The Federalist Papers, No. 51).

Makumbe, J. (2003) *The Politics of Zimbabwe's 1995 General Elections*, Harare: University of Zimbabwe Publications.

Mangham, I. (1979) *The Politics of Organisational Change*, London: Associated Business Press.

Marcuse, H. (1964) *One Dimensional Man*, London: Routledge & Kegan Paul.

Margolis, M., Resnick, D. and Levy, J. (2003) 'Major parties dominate, minor parties struggle: US elections and the Internet' in R. Gibson, P. Nixon and S. Ward (eds), *Political Parties and the Internet: Net Gain?* London: Routledge: 53–69.

Marsh, D. and Savigny, H. (2004) 'Political science as a broad church: the search for a pluralist discipline', *Politics,* 24 (3):1 55–168.

Marshall, L. (1961) *Sharing Talking and Giving: Relief of Social Tensions among the !Kung Bushmen*, Africa, March.

Marx, K. and Engels, F. (1962) *Selected Works, 2 vols*, Moscow: Foreign Languages Publishing House.

Mazzoleni, G. (2000) 'A return to civic and political engagement: prompted by personalised political leadership?', *Political Communication*, 17 (4): 325–328.

McClellan, D. (1986) *Ideology*, Milton Keynes: Open University Press.

McDonald, P. (2011) 'Maoism versus Confucianism: ideological influences on Chinese business leaders', *Journal of Management Development*, 30 (7/8): 632–646.

McGrew, T. and Lewis, P. (1992) *Global Politics*, Cambridge: Cambridge University Press.

McKenzie, W. (1958) *Free Elections*, London: Allen & Unwin.

McKibbin, R. (1983) *The Evolution of the Labour Party 1910–1924*, Oxford: Oxford University Press.

McLaughlin, L. and Pickard, V. (2005) 'What is bottom-up about global internet governance?', *Global Media and Communication*, 1 (3): 357–373.

McLuhan, M. (1964) *Understanding the Media: the extension of man*, London: Routledge & Kegan Paul.

McNair, B. (2003) *An Introduction to Political Communication*, London: Routledge.

Mead, W. (2011) 'The Tea Party and American foreign policy', *Foreign Affairs*, 90 (2): 28–44.

Medina, E. (2011) *Cybernetic Revolutionaries: Technology and Politics in Allende's Chile*, Cambridge, MA: MIT Press.

Mehta, V. (2012) *The Sanjay Story*, HarperCollins.

Mellor, N. (1990) 'The Micronesian executive: the federated states of Micronesia, Kiribati and the Marshall Islands', *Pacific Studies*, 14 (1): 55–72.

Michels, R. (1915) *Political Parties*, New York: Constable (1959 reprint).

Milgram, S. (1965) 'Some conditions for obedience and disobedience to authority', *Human Relations*, 18 (1): 57–74.

Miliband, R. (1969) *The State in Capitalist Society*, London: Weidenfeld & Nicolson.

——(1983) 'State power and class interests', *New Left Review*, 138 (March/April).

——(1984) *Capitalist Democracy in Britain*, Oxford: Oxford University Press.

Mills, C. Wright (1956) *The Power Elite*, New York: Oxford University Press.

Milne, A. (1962) *The Social Philosophy of English Idealism*, London: Allen & Unwin.

Mitchell, D. (1959) *Sociology: the Study of Social Systems*, London: University Tutorial Press.

Moloney, K. (2006) *Rethinking Public Relations*, London: Routledge.

Morgan, R. (1981) 'Madison's analysis of the sources of political authority', *The American Political Science Review,* 75 (3): 613–625.

Morison, S. and Commager, H. (1962) *The Growth of the American Republic*, 5th edn, 2 vols, New York: Oxford University Press.

Mosca, G. (1939) *The Ruling Class* (ed. and rev. by A. Livingston), New York: McGraw-Hill.

Mozaffari, M. (2007) 'What is Islamism? History and definition of a concept', *Totalitarianism Movements and Political Religions,* 8 (1): 17–33.

Muller, J.-W. (2013) 'Towards a new history of Christian democracy', *Journal of Political Ideologies*, 18 (2): 243–255.

Naim, M. (2012) 'Mafia States', *Foreign Affairs*, 91 (3): 100–111.

Nettl, P. (1966) 'The concept of system in political science', *Political Studies*, 14 (3): 305–338.

Neustadt, R. (1960) *Presidential Power: the politics of leadership*, New York: Wiley.

Newman, D. (1998) 'Geopolitics renaissant: territory, sovereignty and the political world map', *Geopolitics*, 3 (1): 1–16.

Ngcobo, N. and Cameron, N. (2012) 'The decision-making process on new vaccines introduction in South Africa', *Vaccine*, 30 (1): C9–C13.

Norris, P. and Curtice, J. (2004) 'If you build a political website, will they come? The supply and demand model of new technology, social capital and civic engagement in Britain', paper delivered to the Annual Meeting of the American Political Science Association, Chicago, September.

Norton, P. (2005) *Parliament in British Politics*, Basingstoke: Palgrave Macmillan.

——(2008) 'A 20-point Tory lead: despite or because of David Cameron?', paper prepared for the symposium on David Cameron and the Conservatives, Centre for British Politics, University of Hull, 24/25 September.

Norton-Griffiths, M. (2010) 'The growing involvement of foreign NGOs in setting policy agenda and political decision making in Africa', *IEA Economic Affairs*, October: 29–34.

Nove, A. (1980) *The Soviet Economic System*, London Allen & Unwin.

Nozick, R. (1974) *Anarchy, State and Utopia*, London: Blackwell.

Oakeshott, M. (1962) *Rationalism in Politics and Other Essays*, London: Methuen.

Ochieng, C. (2007) 'Development through positive deviance and its implications for economic policy making and public administration in Africa: the case for Kenyan agriculture 1930–2005', *World Development*, 35 (3): 454–479.

Office for National Statistics (2012) National Statistics website. Available at: www.statistics.gov.uk.

Ornstein, N. and Mann, T. (2000) *The Permanent Campaign and its Future*, Washington, DC: American Enterprise Institute and The Brookings Institution.

Osborne, D. and Gaebler, T. (1992) *Reinventing Government: How the Entrepreneurial Spirit is Transforming the Public Sector*, Harmondsworth: Middlesex: Penguin.

Ostrom, E. (2000) 'The Future of Democracy', *Scandinavian Political Studies*, 23 (2): 280–283.

Paliwala, A. (2013) 'Netizenship, security and freedom', *International Review of Law, Computers and Technology*, 27 (1-2): 104–123.

Pareto, V. (1976) *Sociological Writings* (ed. by S. E. Finer), Oxford: Blackwell.

Parkinson, D. (2003) 'The Message Not the Medium', *VoxPolitics Bulletin*, reproduced in Netpulse 7(15): October 16 (www.PoliticsOnline.com).

Parsons, T. (1957) 'The distribution of power in American society', *World Politics*, 10: 123–143.

——(1963) 'On the concept of political power', *Proceedings of the American Philosophical Society*, 107 (3): 232–262.

Pateman, C. (1971): 'Political culture, political structure and change', *British Journal of Political Science*, 1 (3): 291–305.

Peach, L. (1987) 'Corporate responsibility', in N. Hart (ed.) *Effective Corporate Relations*, London: McGraw-Hill: 191–204.

Pennock, J. and Chapman, J. (eds) (1978) *Anarchism: Nomos XIX*, New York: New York: University Press.

Perloff, R. (2008) *The Dynamics of Persuasion: Communication and Attitudes in the 21st Century*, New York: Lawrence Erlbaum Associates.

Perrin, A., Tepper, S., Caren, N. and Morris, S. (2011) 'Cultures of the Tea Party', *Contexts*, 10 (Spring): 74–75.

Peters, G. (1999) *Institutional Theory in Political Science: the 'New Institutionalism'*, London: Pitman.

Phalen, P., Kim, J. and Osellame, J. (2012) 'Imagined presidencies: the representation of political power in television fiction', *The Journal of Popular Culture*, 45 (3): 532–550.

Pierre, J. and Stoker, G. (2002) 'Towards multi-level governance', in P. Dunleavy, A. Gamble, I. Holliday and G. Peele (eds), *Developments in British Politics 6*, Basingstoke: Palgrave: 29–46.

Plasser, F. (2002) *Global Political Campaigning: a Worldwide Analysis of Campaign Professionals and their Practices*, London: Praeger.

Polity IV Project (2013) *Political Regime Characteristics and Transitions, 1800–2012*. Available online at: www.systemicpeace.org/inscr/inscr.htm (accessed 23 July 2013).

Popper, K. (1960) *The Poverty of Historicism*, 2nd edn, London: Routledge & Kegan Paul.

——(1962) *The Open Society and its Enemies*, London: Routledge & Kegan Paul.

Posner, R. (2003) *Law, Pragmatism and Democracy*, Cambridge, Mass: Harvard University Press.

Poulantzas, N. (1973) *Political Power and Social Classes*, London: New Left Review Books.

Prawer, J. and Eisenstadt, S. (1968) 'Feudalism', in D. Sills (ed.), *International Encyclopaedia of Social Sciences*, vol. 5, New York: Macmillan: 393–403.

Pressman, J. and Wildavsky, A. (1973) *Implementation: How Great Expectations in Washington are Dashed in Oakland or Why it's Amazing that Federal Programs Work at All*, Berkeley and Los Angeles: University of California Press.

Puchala, D. (1997) 'Some non-western perspectives on International Relations', *Journal of Peace Research*, 24 (2): 129–134.

Pye, L. (1958) 'The non-western political process', *Journal of Politics*, 20 (3): 468–486.

Putnam, R. (2000) *Bowling Alone: The Collapse and Revival of American Community*, New York: Simon & Schuster.

Qureshi, M. and Wen, G. (2008) 'Distributed consequences of globalisation: empirical evidence from panel data', *Journal of Development Studies*, 44 (10): 1424–1449.

Rae, D. (1967) *The Political Consequences of Electoral Laws*, New Haven, CT: Yale University Press.

Raustiala, K. (1997) 'States, NGOs and international environmental organisations', *International Studies Quarterly*, 41 (4): 719–740.

Rawls, J. (1971) *The Theory of Justice*, London: Oxford University Press.

Rehfeld, A. (2005) *The Concept of Constituency: Political Representation, Democratic Legitimacy and Institutional Design*, Cambridge: Cambridge University Press.

Reischaur, E. (1956) 'Japanese feudalism', in R. Coulborne (ed.), *Feudalism in History*, Princeton, NJ: Princeton University Press.

Rheingold, H. (1993) *The Virtual Community: Homesteading on the Electronic Frontier*, Reading, MA: Addison-Wesley.

Rhodes, R. (1994) 'The hollowing out of the state: the changing nature of the public service in Britain', *The Political Quarterly*, 65 (2): 138–151.

——(1996) 'The New Governance: governing without government', *Political Studies*, 44 (4): 652–667

——(1997) *Understanding Governance*, Buckingham: Open University Press.

Richardson, J. and Jordan, A. (1979) *Governing Under Pressure: the policy process in a post-parliamentary system*, Oxford: Robertson.

Ridley, F. (1991) 'Theory and methods in British public administration: the view from political science', *Political Studies*, 39 (3): 533–544.

Risse-Kappen, T. (1995) *Bringing Transnational Relations Back In: non-state actors, domestic structures and international institutions*, Cambridge: Cambridge University Press.

Robinson, J. (1976) 'Interpersonal influence in election campaigns: two step-flow hypotheses', *Public Opinion Quarterly*, 40 (3): 304–319.

Rogers, E. (1995) *Diffusion of Innovation*, 4th edn, New York: Free Press.

Roscigno, V. (2011) 'Power revisited', *Social Forces*, 90 (2): 349–374.

Rose, J. (2011) 'Kingship and counsel in Early Modern England', *The Historical Journal*, 54 (1): 47–71.

Rose, N. and Miller, P. (2010) 'Political power beyond the state: problematics of government', *British Journal of Sociology*, 61 (1): 271–303.

Rose, R. (ed.) (1969) *Policy Making in Britain*, London: Macmillan.

Rothkopf, D. (2009) 'The BRICs and what the BRICs would be without China', *Foreign Policy*, 16 June. Available online at: http://rothkopf.foreign policy.com/posts/2009/06/15/the_brics_and_what_the_brics_would_be_ without_china (accessed 22 October 2013).

Rowbotham, S. (1972) *Women Resistance and Revolution: a History of Women in the Modern World*, New York: Random House.

Runciman, W. (1969) *Social Science and Political Theory*, Cambridge: Cambridge University Press.

Rush, M. (2001) *The Role of Member of Parliament since 1868: Gentlemen and Players*, Oxford: Oxford University Press.

Sabetti, F. (1984) *Political Authority in a Sicilian Village*, New Brunswick, NJ: Rutgers University Press.

Sabine, G. (1951) *A History of Political Theory*, 3rd edn, London: G. Harrap.

Saeidi, A. (2001) 'Charismatic political authority and populist economics in post-revolutionary Iran', *Third World Quarterly*, 22 (2): 219–236.

Said, E. (1987) *Orientalism*, Harmondsworth: Penguin.

Sampson, A. (2004) *Who Runs This Place? The Anatomy of Britain in the 21st Century*, London: John Murray.

Sandel, M. (1996) *Democracy's Discontent: America in Search of a Public Philosophy*, Cambridge, MA: Belknap Press.

Sartori, G. (1970) 'Concept misinformation in comparative politics', *The American Political Science Review*, 64 (4): 1033–1053.

——(1973) 'What is "politics"?', *Political Theory*, 1 (1): 5–26.

Saunders, P. (1995) *Capitalism: a Social Audit*, Buckingham: Open University Press.

Saward, M. (1997) 'In Search of the Hollow Crown', in P. Weller, H. Bakvis and R. Rhodes (eds), *The Hollow Crown: Countervailing Trends in Core Executives*, Basingstoke: Macmillan: 1–36.

Scammell, M. (2001) 'The Internet and civic engagement in the age of the citizen-consumer', *Political Communication*, 17 (4): 351–355.

Schapiro, L. (1965) *The Government and Politics of the Soviet Union*, London: Hutchinson.

Schattschneider, E. (1960) *The Semisovereign People*, New York: Holt, Rinehart & Winston.

Schier, S. (2011) 'The presidential authority problem and the political power trap', *Presidential Studies Quarterly*, 41 (4): 793–808.

Schmidt, M. (1989) 'Social policy in rich and poor countries: socio-economic trends and political-institutional determinants', *European Journal of Political Research*, 17 (6): 641–659.

Scholte, J. (2000) *Globalization: a Critical Introduction*, Basingstoke: Palgrave.

Schram, S. (2003) 'Return to politics: perestroika and post-paradigmatic political science', *Political Theory*, 31 (6): 835–851.

Schultz, R. (1980) *Responding to the Terrorist Threat: Security and Crisis Management*, New York: Pergamon.

Schumacher, E. (1973) *Small is Beautiful: a Study of Economics as if People Mattered*, London: Blond & Briggs.

Scott, J. (2009) *The Art of Not Being Governed: an Anarchist History of Upland Southeast Asia*, New Haven, CT: Yale University Press.

Seale, P. and McConville, M. (1968) *French Revolution*, Harmondsworth, Middlesex: Penguin.

Seckinelgin, H. (2007) *The International Politics of HIV/AIDS*, London, Routledge.

Sekhon, J. and Titiunik, R. (2012) 'When natural experiments are neither natural nor experiments', *American Political Science Review*, 106 (1): 35–57.

Sell, S. (2003) *Private Power, Public Law: the Globalization of Intellectual Property Rights*, Cambridge: Cambridge University Press.

Shaoul, J. (2011) 'Sharing political authority with finance capital: the case of Britain's public private partnerships', *Policy and Society*, 30 (2): 209–220.

Sharma, R. (2012) 'Broken Brics: why the rest stopped rising', *Foreign Affairs*, November/December. Available online at: www.foreignaffairs.com/articles/138219/ruchiv-sharma/broken/brics (accessed 20 September 2013).

Simon, H. (1953) 'Notes on the observation and measurement of political power', *Journal of Politics*, 25 (4): 500–516.

——(1959) 'Theories of Decision Making in Economics and Behavioural Science', *American Economic Review*, 49 (3): 253–283

——(1977) *The New Science of Management*, Englewood Cliffs, NJ: Prentice Hall.

Singh, N. (2003) 'Cold War redux: on the "new totalitarianism"', *Radical History Review*, 85 (Winter): 171–181.

Sklar, R. (1963) *Nigerian Political Parties: Power in an Emergent Nation*, Princeton, NJ: Princeton University Press.

Skogstad, G. (2003) 'Who governs? Who should govern? Political authority and legitimacy in Canada in the twenty-first century', *Canadian Journal of Political Science*, 36 (5): 955–973.

Slowe, P. (1990) *Geography and Political Power*, London: Routledge.

Smith, G. (1989) *Politics in Western Europe: a Comparative Analysis*, Aldershot: Gower.

Smith, R. (2002) 'Should we make political science more of a science or more about politics?', *PS: Political Science and Politics*, 35 (2): 199–201.

Snallen, J. (2001) 'ICTs, bureaucracies and the future of democracy', *Communication of the ACM*, 44 (1): 45–48.

Southern Electric (1994) *Caring for Customers*, Maidenhead: Southern Electric.

Spar, D. and La Mure, L. (2003) 'The power of activism: assessing the impact of NGOs on global business', *California Management Review*, 45 (3): 78–101.

Spence, M. (2011) 'The impact of globalisation on income and employment', *Foreign Affairs*, 90 (4): 28–41.

Stiglitz, J. (2002) *Globalization and its Discontents:* London: Allen Lane.

Stoker, G. (2006) *Why Politics Matters: Making Democracy Work*, Basingstoke: Palgrave.

Stokman, F. and Zeggelink, E. (1996) 'Is politics power or policy oriented? A comparative analysis of dynamic access models in policy networks', *Journal of Mathematical Sociology,* 21 (1/2): 77–111.

Stone, D. (2008) 'Global public policy, transnational policy communities and their networks', *Policy Studies Journal*, 36 (1): 19–38.

Suffian, T., Lee, H. and Trinidade, F. (1978) *The Constitution of Malaysia: Its Development 1957–1977*, Kuala Lumpur: Oxford University Press.

Sunstein, C. (2004) 'Democracy and filtering', *Communications of ACM*, 47 (12): 57–59.

Tajfel, H. and Turner, J. (1979) 'An integrative theory of inter-group conflict', in G. Austin and S. Worsche (eds), *The Social Psychology of Inter-group Relations*, Montery, CA: Brooks/Cole: 33–47.

Tansey, S. (1973) *Political Analysis: A report on a project of syllabus development*, MSc report, Birkbeck College, London.

——(1989) *Employers' Reactions to the Youth Training Scheme*, MPhil thesis, University of Bath.

——(2002) *Business, Information Technology and Society*, London: Routledge.

——(2010) 'Politics, political theory, political philosophy', *Thinking Philosophy (U3A Philosophy Network)*, Summer: 11–14.

Tawney, R. (1938) *Religion and the Rise of Capitalism*, Harmondsworth, Middlesex: Penguin.

Taylor, C. and Jodice, D. (1983) *World Handbook of Political and Social Indicators*, 3rd edn, New Haven, CT: Yale University Press.

Teegan, J., Doh, J. and Vachari, S. (2004) 'The importance of nongovernmental organisations in global governance and value creation: an international business research agenda', *Journal of International Business Studies*, 35 (6): 463–483.

Thaler, R. and Sunstein, C. (2008) *Nudge: improving decisions about health, wealth and happiness*, London: Penguin.

Themistocleous, M., Azab, N., Kamal, M., Ali, M. and Morabito, V. (2012) 'Location-based services for public policy making: the direct and indirect way to e-participation', *Information Systems Management*, 29 (4): 269–283.

Tilly, C. (1994) 'The time of states', *Social Research*, 61 (2): 269–5.

Toal, G. (1998) 'Borderless worlds? Problematic discourse of deterritorialisation', *Geopolitics*, 4 (2): 139–154.

Toffler, A. (1980) *The Third Wave*, London: Collins.

Torelli, C. and Shavitt, S. (2010) 'Culture and concepts and power', *Journal of Personality and Social Psychology,* 99 (4): 703–723.

Torgerson, D. (1999) *The Promise of Green Politics: Environmentalism and the Public Sphere*, London: Duke University Press.

Trotsky, L. (1945) *The Revolution Betrayed*, New York: Pioneer.

Tullock, G. (1965) *The Politics of Bureaucracy*, Washington, DC: Public Affairs Press.

Vander Broek, A. (2009) 'Ivy leaders', 4 February. Available online at: www.forbes.com/2009/04/02/politician-education-elite-leadership-ivy.html (accessed 10 December 2013).

Verney, D. (1959) *The Analysis of Political Systems*, Glencoe, IL: Free Press.

Vincent, A. (1992) *Modern Political Ideologies*, Oxford: Blackwell.

Voltaire (1756) *Essai sur l'histoire generale et sur les moeurs et l'esprit des nations*, Paris.

von Brück, M. (2010) 'Political authority: a Christian perspective', *Buddhist Christian Studies,* 30: 159–170.

Ward, S. and Lusoli, W. (2005) 'From weird to wired: MPs, the Internet and representative politics in the UK', *Journal of Legislative Studies,* 11 (1): 57–81.

Warren, M. and Castiglione, D. (2004) 'The transformation of democratic representation', *Democracy and Society,* 2 (1): 5–22.

Weare, C. (2002) 'The Internet and democracy: the causal links between technology and politics', *International Journal of Public Administration,* 25 (5): 659–691.

Weber, M. (1978) *Economy and Society: an outline of interpretive sociology* (ed. by G. Roth and C. Wittich), London: University of California Press (originally published 1922).

Weldon, T. (1953) *The Vocabulary of Politics*, Harmondsworth, Middlesex: Penguin.

Wheare, K. (1951) *Modern Constitutions*, Oxford: Oxford University Press.

——(1963) *Federal Government*, 4th edn, London: Oxford University Press.

White, R. and Hooke, W. (2004) 'Climate science, technology and politics: a tangled web', *Technology in Society,* 26 (2): 375–384.

Williams, G. (ed.) (1976) *Nigeria: Economy and Society*, London: Rex Collings.

Williams, P. (1964) *Crisis and Compromise*, Harlow: Longmans.

Wittfogel, K. (1957) *Oriental Despotism*, New Haven, CT: Yale University Press.

Wittman, D. (1991) 'Nations and states: mergers and acquisitions; dissolution and divorce', *American Economic Review,* 81 (2): 126–129.

Woodcock, G. (1975) *Anarchism*, Harmondsworth, Middlesex: Penguin.

Wray, M. (2009) 'Policy communities, networks and issue cycles in tourism destination systems', *Journal of Sustainable Tourism,* 17 (6): 673–690.

Wring, D. (2007) 'Focus Group Follies? Qualitative research and British Labour Party strategy', *Journal of Political Marketing,* 5 (4): 71–97.

Yazdani, S. and Dola, K. (2013) 'Sustainable city priorities in Global North versus Global South', *Journal of Sustainable Development*, 6 (7): 38–47.

Youngs, G. and Widdows, H. (2009) 'Globalisation, ethics and the "War on Terror"', *Globalisation*, 6 (1): 1–6.

Zakaria, F. (1997) 'The rise of illiberal democracy', *Foreign Affairs*, 76 (6): 22–43.

Zhu, Y. (2012) 'Policy entrepreneur, civic engagement and local policy innovation in China: housing monetarisation reform in Guizhou province', *Australian Journal of Public Administration*, 71 (2): 191–200.

INDEX

Lightning Source UK Ltd.
Milton Keynes UK
UKOW06f1057111116
287323UK00013B/268/P